WHEN SHOULD STATE SECRETS STAY SECRET?

Contrary to popular assumption, the development of stronger oversight mechanisms actually leads to greater secrecy rather than the reverse. *When Should State Secrets Stay Secret?* examines modern trends in intelligence oversight development by focusing on how American oversight mechanisms combine to bolster an internal security system and thus increase the secrecy of the intelligence enterprise.

Genevieve Lester uniquely examines how these oversight mechanisms have developed within all three branches of government, how they interact, and what types of historical pivot points have driven change among them. She disaggregates the concept of accountability into a series of specified criteria in order to grapple with these pivot points. This book concludes with a discussion of a series of normative questions, suggesting ways to improve oversight mechanisms based on the analytical criteria laid out in the analysis. It also includes a chapter on the workings of the CIA to which a number of CIA officers contributed.

Genevieve Lester is a research Fellow and lecturer at the University of California, Washington Center, and a nonresident Fellow at the Center for Strategic and International Studies in Washington, DC. She was a visiting assistant professor and coordinator of intelligence studies in the School of Foreign Service, Georgetown University, and a senior Fellow at the Center for Security Studies, also at Georgetown. Her areas of interest are international relations and security with an emphasis on intelligence and accountability.

When Should State Secrets Stay Secret?

ACCOUNTABILITY, DEMOCRATIC GOVERNANCE, AND INTELLIGENCE

Genevieve Lester

CAMBRIDGE
UNIVERSITY PRESS

CAMBRIDGE
UNIVERSITY PRESS

32 Avenue of the Americas, New York, NY 10013-2473, USA

Cambridge University Press is part of the University of Cambridge.

It furthers the University's mission by disseminating knowledge in the pursuit of education, learning, and research at the highest international levels of excellence.

www.cambridge.org
Information on this title: www.cambridge.org/9781107616530

© Genevieve Lester 2015

First published 2015

Printed in the United States of America

A catalog record for this publication is available from the British Library.

Library of Congress Cataloging in Publication Data
Lester, Genevieve, 1973–
When should state secrets stay secret? : accountability, democratic governance, and intelligence / Genevieve Lester.
    pages   cm
Includes bibliographical references and index.
ISBN 978-1-107-04247-6 (hardback) – ISBN 978-1-107-61653-0 (paperback)
1. Intelligence service – United States.   2. Legislative oversight – United States.   3. Disclosure of information – United States.   4. Official secrets – United States.   I. Title.
JK468.I6L46   2015
327.1273–dc23   2014038369

ISBN 978-1-107-04247-6 Hardback
ISBN 978-1-107-61653-0 Paperback

For Carole and Omar
and
In memory of Robert M. Hooven

CONTENTS

ACKNOWLEDGMENTS

This book is the creation of countless individuals, who dedicated their time, patience, and knowledge to its completion. Over the course of developing this book, I have been truly humbled by the generosity of the intelligence community. Some of my early interview subjects have become friends, providing insight and guidance as I investigated their world. I still cannot believe my luck in having had the opportunity to get to experience at least a small piece of the world I find so fascinating, and I owe many, many thanks to array of individuals who contributed to this work with their life experiences, opinions and wisdom. In particular, I would like to thank Charles E. Allen, Director James Clapper, Robert L. Deitz, Burton Gerber, General Michael Hayden, and Stephen R. Kappes, who all gave generously of their knowledge and time. I am also grateful to the many others whose names cannot be listed here.

This book stems from my doctoral dissertation at the University of California, Berkeley, where my committee was exemplary in its support of a rather unique topic. Thanks to Bruce E. Cain, Joel Aberbach, Ron Hassner, and Neil Fligstein for encouraging the project. Thanks also to John Berger, who believed in this book and had wonderful patience with a first time author.

Enormous thanks to Alissa Pelkola, Katie Poole-Jones, and Allison Theodore Low, who helped see this through, from the very beginning to the end. Michael Allen, Robert L. Deitz, Ed Doyle, Beth Green, Ben Oppenheim, Mark Schlegel, and Douglas Waller all read drafts of the early text and I am grateful for their kind but firm revisions and comments. Claudia Hofmann, Nina Kelsey, and Elizabeth M. Prescott were patient and encouraging, even when the book started to make me a little crazy.

At Georgetown, Bruce Hoffman provided invaluable support, guidance, and friendship. Elizabeth Stanley was a kind and persuasive proponent of completion. Laura Soerensson and Lauren Covert-Weber supported me, helped smooth over the edges in the final stages of the book, and were great happy hour friends. Ellen Noble and Shane Quinlan helped me pull this project together in innumerable ways.

In long projects such as this there are people one turns to over and over again for guidance, advice, or just to scream with frustration. For me, those individuals were Bruce E. Cain and Daniel L. Byman. I thank them for their patience over the years!

Finally, deepest thanks to Carole, Omar, and Dad.

ABBREVIATIONS

CI	counterintelligence
CIA	Central Intelligence Agency
COINTELPRO	Counterintelligence Program (FBI)
DCI	Director of Central Intelligence
D/CIA	Director, CIA (post–advent of Director of National Intelligence)
DHS	Department of Homeland Security
DI	Directorate of Intelligence
DNI	Director of National Intelligence
DO	Directorate of Operations
FBI	Federal Bureau of Investigation
FISA	Foreign Intelligence Surveillance Act
FISC	Foreign Intelligence Surveillance Court
FISCR	Foreign Intelligence Surveillance Court of Review
HPSCI	House Permanent Select Committee on Intelligence
HUMINT	human intelligence
IC	intelligence community
IG	Inspector General
IRTPA	Intelligence Reform and Terrorism Prevention Act
JTTF	Joint Terrorism Task Force
NCS	National Clandestine Service
NSA	National Security Agency

NSC	National Security Council
OGC	Office of the General Counsel
OIG	Office of the Inspector General
OSINT	Open Source intelligence
PFIAB/PIAB	President's Foreign Intelligence Advisory Board/ President's Intelligence Advisory Board
SSCI	Senate Select Committee on Intelligence
TECHINT	technical intelligence
TIARA	tactical intelligence and related activities
TSP	Terrorist Surveillance Program
WMD	weapons of mass destruction

1 AN ANALYTICAL APPROACH: INTELLIGENCE, ACCOUNTABILITY, AND OVERSIGHT

> For decades Congress and the courts as well as the press and the public have accepted the notion that the control of intelligence activities was the exclusive prerogative of the Chief Executive and his surrogates. The exercise of this power was not questioned or even inquired into by outsiders. Indeed, at times the power was seen as flowing not from the law, but as inherent in the Presidency. Whatever the theory, the fact was that intelligence activities were essentially exempted from the normal system of checks and balances.[1]

This quotation from the final report of the Church Committee – the Senate committee created in 1975 to investigate intelligence abuses – is indicative of the complex position that intelligence continues to hold in the American democracy. Intelligence comes laden with fiction, myths, and mysteries, as befits its unique status in the government and in the public mind. Intelligence activities exacerbate the information asymmetry issues inherent in representative government. The nature of the secret and technical work creates a unique culture distant from the regulatory mechanisms of conventional democratic governance. The problem of overcoming this information asymmetry is the core of accountability and oversight. Mechanisms have developed over several decades to rebalance this relationship and have had varying degrees of success. Total equilibrium, of course, between intelligence

---

[1] *Intelligence Activities and the Rights of Americans*, Book II, Final Report of the Select Committee to Study Governmental Operations with Respect to Intelligence Activities (Church Committee) United States Senate, Section IV. Conclusions and Recommendations, April 26, 1976, section (a).

actors and overseers will never be achieved due to the nature of the work, its inherent secrecy, and the traditional executive ownership and control of it.

In June 2013, Edward Snowden, a contractor working for the National Security Agency (NSA), leaked a trove of classified documents to which his position gave him access. The leaked documents outlined a range of programs in which the NSA had been engaged that were aimed at the domestic public. The stories first published in the British newspaper *The Guardian* told readers about massive programs that collected bulk metadata and Internet communications within the United States. Further reports described how the NSA was wiretapping the phones of foreign leaders and that gag orders were placed on companies ordered to provide the information. The response among both the public and, outwardly at least, policy makers was deep shock. Even many who had been aware of the nature of the programs were surprised at the breadth and depth of the NSA's activities. One of the outcomes of Snowden's leaks was a demand for the NSA to be reined in and for increased oversight to be put in place to monitor its activities. Legislators argued over new proposals to change legislation governing the NSA's activities, and the director of National Intelligence (DNI) was pressured to release court decisions regarding domestic intelligence collection. Subsequently, heavily redacted decisions issued by the Foreign Intelligence Surveillance Court were released to the public. While a good faith – and unprecedented – effort on the part of the administration was made to increase transparency, the results were inconclusive for outsiders trying to understand the extent of domestic surveillance for the first time.

To take another example of recent events regarding intelligence that have captured the public eye, in March 2014 Senator Dianne Feinstein, chair of the Senate's Select Committee on Intelligence, con-fronted Director of the CIA John Brennan about several incidents related to the committee's report on enhanced interrogation techniques (EITs). At root, the controversy surrounded the CIA Detention and Interrogation Program, a program that emerged quickly in the after-math of the attacks on 9/11 and used techniques such as waterboard-ing, shackling, stress positions, and culture-based humiliation in order to extract information from suspects. The program itself pressed the boundaries of prior post-Watergate CIA responsibilities, including detention in "black sites," or unacknowledged sites located in foreign countries, and interrogation methods that – it has been argued – can be considered torture. Reacting to CIA briefings on the program, the Senate Select Committee on Intelligence commissioned a report investigating the program. Taking three years to complete and ending up at about 6,300 pages, the report remains classified as of this writing. In the words of Senator Feinstein, the report "uncovers startling details about the CIA detention and interrogation program and raises critical questions about intelligence operations and oversight .... [T]he creation of long-term, clandestine 'black sites' and the use of so-called 'enhanced-interrogation techniques' were terrible mistakes."[2]

Why is the issue of this report so fraught? To begin, opinions vary on the use of these methods on alleged terrorism suspects. Some, such as former acting general counsel of the CIA John Rizzo argue that any tool should be used to defend the country.[3] Mr. Rizzo was acting counsel when the earliest decisions regarding the program were being taken and has let it be known that he could have stopped the program altogether. Along these lines, it is argued that is acceptable to treat an individual harshly to protect the greater number – the ticking bomb argument. Some suggested that the methods were not that extreme, as they are regularly used to train U.S. soldiers to resist their captors should they be taken prisoner. U.S. military Survival, Evasion, Resistance, and Escape (SERE) training includes extreme measures, such as waterboarding, to prepare soldiers to resist potential captors by acclimating them to the stress of the methods.[4] Former CIA director General Michael Hayden argues that the measures used against detainees were not as extreme as some have depicted them and had only been done a limited number of times against select individuals.[5]

---

[2] Feinstein Statement on CIA Detention, Interrogation Report, December 13, 2012, available at www.feinstein.senate.gov/.

[3] See John Rizzo, *Company Man: Thirty Years of Controversy and Crisis in the CIA* (New York: Scribner, 2014), for a discussion of these issues.

[4] Interview with Charles E. Allen, February 4, 2010.

[5] Interview with General Michael Hayden, April 7, 2010. General Hayden demonstrated one technique – walling – on himself to convince me that the methods were not egregious.

On the other side of the debate, critics argue that torture "degrades a society."[6] Some assert that it is operationally ineffective, although this again is a controversial claim, with senior CIA officials arguing that the program was an "irreplaceable tool" for the purposes of counter-terrorism.[7] This is, of course, a line of argument that is impossible to verify one way or the other. Others have more recently defended the program by stating that information elicited from detainees led to the eventual killing of Osama bin Laden. The methods used, as described by former detainees in journalistic accounts, break international law, violate human rights, and previously would have been considered war crimes.[8] Internally, CIA officers were concerned about the legality of the program and were anxious lest they be held personally liable for actions conducted according to its mandates. This extended to tapes recording the procedures, all of which were destroyed to protect the identities of the CIA officers involved in the interrogations.[9]

First, while there are ranging opinions on the value of the information gathered from the detainees, it is certain that these activities not only stretched the mission of the CIA but were also conducted with minimal accountability. Few within the intelligence community knew about the program or the locations of the sites, and even fewer still know exactly what occurred in these locations. In terms of mandated reporting to oversight mechanisms, there are many questions regarding how the program was reported to Congress. For example, there remains ambiguity as to whether the interrogation techniques were included in the original finding; second, there are concerns that the program was briefed to a limited number of individuals; and third,

---

[6] Richard A. Posner, "Torture, Terrorism, and Interrogation," in *Torture: A Collection*, ed. Sanford Levinson (Oxford: Oxford University Press, 2004), 292.

[7] Jane Mayer, "The Black Sites: A Rare Look Inside the CIA's Secret Interrogation Program," available at http://www.newyorker.com/reporting/2007/08/13/070813fa_fact_mayer?currentPage=all (as of January 24, 2012).

[8] According to Mayer, soldiers were court-martialed for waterboarding until as recently as the Vietnam War.

[9] See Rizzo, *Company Man,* for a discussion of the inception of the programs as well as the furor surrounding the destruction of the tapes. See Jose Rodriguez, Jr., and Bill Harlow, *Hard Measures: How Aggressive CIA Actions after 9/11 Saved American Lives* (New York: Threshold, 2013) for a self-exculpatory explanation of the use of the techniques as well as the destruction of the tapes cataloging their use.

the timing of the briefing was also ambiguous, with legislators stating that they were not sure whether the activities had already commenced when they were briefed, or whether the briefings occurred before the program started. There is also variation among individuals on how they were briefed and how detailed the information provided them was.

Beyond these arguments, public support for more extreme techniques tends to wane as the immediacy and uncertainty of the threat recede. As the United States assesses what security in a "post-post-9/11" threat environment should look like, the appropriateness of the more extreme methods chosen directly after the attacks is necessarily being scrutinized, even though the program was closed down by the Obama administration. The enhanced interrogation issue highlights both the weakness of current oversight mechanisms and the limitations on oversight practice. This issue of timeliness and its relationship to oversight impact will be a theme that runs throughout this book. When did the oversight committees know about the program? Did the members briefed have any recourse to change the program if they objected to it? How? Finally, the issue of the use of torture in this country is of monumental importance. It tests national values and ethics and challenges American adherence to international conventions. How can it occur without public accountability, and how can those charged with the oversight of all intelligence activities deny responsibility for the programs they are charged to supervise?

While conflict between the branches is built into the structure of the governmental separation of powers, conflict with regard to intelligence oversight is unique. It is one area where government goals are *seen* to be diametrically opposed, with the executive wanting – and *needing* – to maintain secrecy, while the legislative branch demands information, transparency, and relative openness. I explore whether this apparent mismatch – at least regarding transparency – is in fact the case. To understand this issue, I pose and explore a series of questions. How do the interbranch dynamics involved in oppositional oversight contribute to the incremental development of congressional oversight? How does internal executive control over intelligence operations interact with congressional oversight? Given that the major impetus for oversight change has been competition between the branches, how and

why do congressional overseers weaken their own efficacy and authority? Above all, do oversight mechanisms serve to expand public access
to intelligence information or, rather, do they increase the control over
intelligence activities through the development of a closed system?
The core argument of this book is how the entire mosaic of oversight
mechanisms works together to create an environment in which secrets
are actually easier to keep rather than, as one would assume, more
difficult.

Prior to these recent events regarding intelligence, the Obama
administration's targeted killing program using unmanned aerial vehi-
cles (UAVs), popularly known as drones, to target suspected terrorists
and terrorist affiliates brought issues of accountability and control to
the forefront of debate. In terms of the targeted killing program, the
administration has semiacknowledged the program to the public – that
is, although it is widely known to be a major pillar of the administration's counterterrorism platform, it was not acknowledged openly.
Government officials (John Brennan and others) spoke to various
aspects of the program in a series of speeches, but the rationale behind
the program was divulged only haltingly.

The complexities of modern governance require that mechanisms serve as proxies for the public at least partially because of
the inherent asymmetry of information on intelligence and security
matters, but also because of operational and classification impera-
tives that limit the transparency of intelligence activities and the
agencies that conduct them. The conundrum in terms of intelligence
and accountability is how to meet the transparency and governance
responsibilities of democratic government to the public when the
domain is secret, highly technical, and heavily defended. This is also
not just an academic matter. Operational requirements mandate that
the services support the entire range of government activities at all
times. Aside from academic concern over the balance of transparency and security, concrete security – in terms of understanding
emergent plans, terrorist groups, threats to infrastructure, threats to
overseas citizens and assets, and threats to the economy and public
health – must be maintained constantly. Oversight mechanisms in
the judiciary and legislative branches of government serve as proxies

for the role of the public in controlling and supervising intelligence activities, while control mechanisms in the executive maintain internal control of the programs according to the requirements of internal accountability.

Very few interest groups or private citizens have access to the intelligence agencies, leaving the agencies relatively opaque, apart from the apertures created by oversight mechanisms and, every now and then, a media break.[10] Because of the complexity and variety of intelligence tasks and the composite nature of legal guidance on intelligence matters, a range of mechanisms are charged with the duty of investigating and supervising how these activities are conducted. It is through these mechanisms that the intelligence services are integrated into a chain of accountability that connects the three branches of government horizontally to each other and vertically to individual agency leadership and to the public. Over the course of time, we discover that while internal accountability remains relatively strong and stable, external accountability is challenged at particular inflection points.

The development and process of the mechanisms that have been created to maintain accountability support broader expectations of governance. By thinking of accountability as the end objective of government activity, we can define it, observe the causal mechanisms that lead to it, and evaluate its efficacy. Further, without understanding how the branches engage with each other on these matters, and without considering the distinct limitations placed on both the judiciary and legislative branches by law, custom, and executive process, it is impossible to get a grasp on why intelligence oversight operates the way it does. The components of intelligence, oversight mechanisms, government agencies, the media, and the public are all linked together in chains of accountability. Taking an artificially narrow perspective that does not engage with the relational dynamics of accountability limits the explanatory power of any theory advanced on the issue. Finally, an understanding of the internal culture and process of the

---

[10] Loch Johnson, "The U.S. Congress and the CIA: Monitoring the Dark Side of Government," *Legislative Studies Quarterly* 5 (1980): 489, 495.

agency being assessed by external oversight mechanisms provides valuable insight into where and why these external mechanisms may face challenges.

The three examples that introduced this chapter will be discussed in much greater detail later in the book. They serve to illustrate the complexity of the problems that intelligence agencies and their overseers face when trying to balance necessary operational secrecy with the openness and transparency expected in a democracy. They all also raise questions core to the theme of this book – intelligence and accountability. There are many assumptions embedded within the concept of accountability, and this book explores as many as possible. Among them is the assumption that accountability results in greater transparency to the outside world. A second one is that forcing accountability on agencies slows down their work and hinders operational efficacy. A further assumption found in most of the conventional literature views oversight and accountability as punitive and driven by sanction and an eagerness to find fault. It also views the intelligence agencies as eager to avoid this supervision.[11] This perspective is built into the old trope about the intelligence agencies being "rogue" and also ignores the other side of the equation – that intelligence agencies may view external mechanisms as legitimizing forces that corroborate the appropriateness of decisions and programs. Oversight in this case could be *fault sharing* rather than fault finding. Intelligence officers assert, fairly in many cases, that overseers simply did not want the information or refused to take responsibility for having been briefed once a story about a program broke publicly.

This positive view of the credibility that can stem from active external involvement is supported by a series of theoretical points regarding institutional isomorphism made by scholars of organization theory, who assert that: "(a) [organizations] incorporate elements which are legitimated externally, rather than in terms of efficiency; (b) they

---

[11] For some examples of this approach, see John Diamond, *The CIA and the Culture of Failure: US Intelligence from the End of the Cold War to the Invasion of Iraq* (Stanford, CA: Stanford University Press, 2008); Tim Weiner, *Legacy of Ashes: The History of the CIA* (New York: Doubleday, 2007); and Amy B. Zegart, *Flawed by Design: The Evolution of the CIA, JCS, and NSC* (Stanford, CA: Stanford University Press, 1999).

employ external or ceremonial assessment criteria to define the value of structural elements; and (c) dependence on externally fixed institutions reduces turbulence and maintains stability."[12] These authors conclude in a comment that should be kept in mind as the reader peruses the empirical chapters here: "... [T]he use of external assessment criteria – that is, moving toward the status in society of a subunit rather than an independent system – can enable an organization to remain successful by social definition, buffering it from failure."[13] A final assumption is driven by competing arguments: on the one hand, that demands for accountability and oversight mechanisms themselves are too meddlesome and demanding; and on the other, that the mechanisms are weak and overseers too disengaged to be effective.

The core argument driving this book derives particularly from one of these assumptions – the expectation of transparency. I argue that contrary to popular assumption, oversight accountability through the development of stronger oversight mechanisms actually leads to greater secrecy rather than less.[14] This is by no means to argue that those involved in intelligence oversight are malevolent or intending to hide information unnecessarily from the public, but merely that the mechanisms themselves provide an inside system that, when joined with intelligence activities, can limit the apertures available to outside observers. This will be demonstrated through an examination of how the oversight mechanisms developed within each separate branch, how they interact with each other, and what types of historical pivot points have driven change among them. I disaggregate the concept of accountability into a series of specified criteria in order to grapple with these pivot points. I finish the book with a discussion of a series of normative questions followed by suggestions to improve oversight mechanisms based on the analytical criteria laid out in the analysis.

---

[12] John W. Meyer and Brian Rowan, "Institutionalized Organizations: Formal Structure as Myth and Ceremony," in *The New Institutionalism in Organizational Analysis*, eds. Walter W. Powell and Paul J. DiMaggio (Chicago: University of Chicago Press, 1991), 49.

[13] Meyer and Rowan, "Formal Structure," 49.

[14] I owe sincere thanks to Timothy Naftali for helping me tighten my argument around this core point. In addition to his helpful comments on my work, his book, *Blind Spot: The Secret History of American Counterterrorism*, was an excellent resource both in terms of its detail and powerful historical narrative.

AN ANALYTICAL APPROACH TO ACCOUNTABILITY

Accountability requires complex government activities to be subject to review, monitoring, and correction by mechanisms charged with the responsibility of supervision. By convention, accountability is taken to assume an external control over an agent – that is, accountability is maintained through external means, through a calling to account by an external supervisory body invested with authority. This external body is empowered with the ability to control the behavior of the supervised through consequences and sanction.

While most scholars point to the vagueness, abstractness, or all-inclusiveness of the term *accountability*, I would argue that the breadth of the term itself reflects the manifold understandings and uses to which accountability is regularly put.[15] I also argue that the concept can be salvaged and analytical promise restored. The core of the concept that transcends all applications is that it is *relational.* Accountability links one organization to another either through formal organized institutions, such as oversight mechanisms, governing bodies, or trustee groups, or through institutionalized processes, such as reporting requirements and regular review. The key characteristic of this relationship, wherever it occurs, and however its process is defined, is that it involves inequality; the supervisor has authority and the right of sanction over the supervised.

Two scholars define accountability as implying:

> ... [T]hat some actors have the right to hold other actors to
> a set of standards, to judge whether they have fulfilled their
> responsibilities in light of these standards, and to impose sanc-
> tions if they determine that these responsibilities have not

---

[15] See Mark Bovens, "Analysing and Assessing Accountability: A Conceptual Framework," *European Law Journal* 13 (2007); Ruth W. Grant and Robert O. Keohane, "Accountability and Abuses of Power in World Politics," *American Political Science Review* 99 (2005); Richard Mulgan, "'Accountability': An Ever-Expanding Concept?," *Public Administration* 78 (2000); and Richard Mulgan, *Holding Power to Account: Accountability in Modern Democracies* (Palgrave, 2003), for wide-ranging discussions of the definition and complexity of the term "accountability."

been met. Accountability presupposes a relationship between power-wielders and those holding them accountable where there is a general recognition of the legitimacy of 1) the operative standards for accountability and 2) the authority of the parties to the relationship (one to exercise particular powers and the other to hold them to account).[16]

The complexity of the apparently straightforward subordinate relationship in this context is that outside of the bounds of the accountability chain, the subordinate in almost every circumstance has the upper hand in terms of expertise; access to information; and freedom of decision making over process, tasks, and resources. In essence, accountability is an external check on explicit and specific power. The process of accountability acts to recalibrate this relationship into one where the titular authority, the overseer, can supersede the operational authority of the overseen.

Accountability has always been seen as a broad, vague, but nice virtue. In the words of scholar Mark Bovens:

> Accountability is one of those golden concepts that no one can be against. It is increasingly used in political discourse and policy documents because it conveys an image of transparency and trustworthiness. However, its evocative powers make it also a very elusive concept because it can mean many different things to different people....[17]

Oversight as a technical mechanism, on the other hand, has been viewed as something that operates poorly and often fails. Literature on the former engages with definition and philosophical direction; literature on the latter considers what goes wrong in Congress to create a situation in which legislators choose *not* to engage with their responsibility to oversee. In terms of accountability, few scholars of intelligence grapple with the complexities of the theoretical concept of accountability and focus instead on describing the empirical issues of the oversight mechanisms themselves, when they do address

---

[16] Grant and Keohane, "Accountability and Abuses of Power in World Politics," 29.
[17] Bovens, "Analysing and Assessing Accountability," 448.

accountability at all.[18] Rather than dealing with accountability, most literature on intelligence discusses how the agencies operate, asserts and describes how they function suboptimally, and recommends how they should change. This was the trend even prior to the 9/11, but intensified greatly after the attacks.[19] In the limited number of cases where scholars address issues of intelligence and oversight, they seldom address mechanisms in more than one branch of government, focusing solely on the practices within one branch. Very few focus on the mechanisms within the executive branch or within the CIA itself.[20] The limited work on the executive branch is due both to problems of access and an ostensible bias against including executive control under the rubric of accountability.

---

[18] The core works that demonstrate this approach are David M. Barrett, *The CIA and Congress: The Untold Story from Truman to Kennedy* (Lawrence, KS: University Press of Kansas, 2005); Frank J. Smist, Jr., *Congress Oversees the United States Intelligence Community: 1947–1994*, 2nd edition (Knoxville: University of Tennessee Press, 1994); and L. Britt Snider, *The Agency and the Hill: CIA's Relationship with Congress, 1946–2004* (Washington, DC: Center for the Study of Intelligence, 2008).

[19] There was a flood of work on the failure of the intelligence community, replete with extensive recommendations on how it should change to work with the changed security environment. Among the most solid of the book-length treatments are Richard K. Betts, *Enemies of Intelligence: Knowledge and Power in the American National Security* (New York: Columbia University Press, 2007); Richard A. Posner, *Preventing Surprise Attacks: Intelligence Reform in the Wake of 9/11* (Stanford, CA: Hoover Institution Press, 2005); and Amy B. Zegart, *Spying Blind: The CIA, the FBI, and the Origins of 9/11* (Princeton, NJ: Princeton University Press, 2007). Tim Weiner contributed a controversial and biased account of CIA failure in *Legacy of Ashes*. An excellent critical approach to the common arguments about blame for 9/11 is Paul R. Pillar, *Intelligence and U.S. Foreign Policy: Iraq, 9/11, and Misguided Reform* (New York: Columbia University Press, 2011).

[20] The most commonly cited work on executive control is William J. Daugherty, *Executive Secrets: Covert Action and the Presidency* (Lexington: University of Kentucky Press, 2008), but this work has numerous flaws of fact and is journalistic rather than scholarly. A second, dated work that includes executive decision making regarding intelligence is John M. Oseth, *Regulating U.S. Intelligence Operations: A Study in the Definition of the National Interest* (Lexington: University of Kentucky, 1985). Other works address executive decision making in terms of covert action, but rarely describe the details of internal control in any depth. The limited nature of external contact with internal executive process was demonstrated by the behavior of a former senior CIA official who became incredibly anxious that he had given me confidential information on internal practice. He pointed out that these matters were never discussed by CIA officials outside of their community.

According to conventional wisdom, Congress has played a single-handedly pivotal role in the development of intelligence oversight. This development has occurred in a quirky, stepwise manner, constrained but also guided by the opaque activities of intelligence agencies, the custom of executive privilege, the political dynamics of specific time periods, and varied interest on the part of would-be congressional supervisors. This complex relationship between the intelligence community and Congress is very important, but it provides only one stream of information on intelligence activities. The term *oversight* calls up images of imperious congressional committees demanding an accounting for the activities of the intelligence agencies, usually the CIA, and usually after a particularly scandalous operation was made public by accident. While congressional oversight is core to maintaining the accountability of intelligence in the American democracy, it does not capture the entire range of activities that must occur to ensure that intelligence activities are both conducted within the expected bounds of an advanced democracy and are also effective in helping maintain the security of that democracy.

These additional oversight activities include judicial review by a secret court, the Foreign Intelligence Surveillance Court, and the multiple mechanisms that control intelligence activities within the executive branch. Conventional conceptions of intelligence also do not often engage with the post-9/11 explosion of intelligence units, some of which straddle multiple lines between the government and private sector, foreign and domestic intelligence, and agencies from the federal down to the local level.[21] Further, due to the exponential growth of intelligence information production and consumption, traditional concepts of oversight do not grasp the complexities of the layered, interwoven, but still atomized intelligence community. This network involves all branches of the government, the media, the public, and internal accountability mechanisms within the agencies

---

[21] See Henry Willis, Genevieve Lester, and Gregory F. Treverton, "Information Sharing for Infrastructure Risk Management: Barriers and Solutions," *Intelligence and National Security* 24 (2009): 339–65, for a discussion of the complexities of the relationship between public and private sectors in terms of intelligence information sharing in the more integrated post-9/11 security environment.

themselves. These relationships are constantly in dynamic, iterative motion, responding to political activity, the vagaries of partisan politics and ideology, and the changing threat environment.

In order to grasp the complexities of the range of players in the world of accountability and their multifarious preferences, roles, cultures, and processes, I use two separate sets of criteria – one for external accountability, and one for internal – as analytical building blocks for my framework. The categories that comprise external accountability are knowledge conditions, that is, awareness of activities as well as appropriate expertise to understand them; external autonomy, which is independence of the overseer from the overseen and available recourse to change behavior; organizational complexity, that is, the impact of the institutional structure of the overseen on the mechanism; and temporality, which is the moment in the process of intelligence activity that the mechanism is made aware of the program prior to, during, or after the activity. A final category is transparency – the level of transparency of the activities of the mechanism both to other members of government and to the public. Internal accountability relies on a different set of criteria: hierarchical authority, organizational complexity, bureaucratic process, legality, recourse, and internal autonomy. The last two of these criteria require further explanation. Recourse entails the ability to deliver consequences to correct behavior, while internal autonomy requires that the internal culture and rules of the organization not inhibit the activities of the mechanism. I describe the characteristics and some implications of these categories in the following sections to provide the contours of the framework. The empirical chapters of this book will provide the bulk of the relevant detail.

CHARACTERISTICS OF EXTERNAL ACCOUNTABILITY

- Knowledge Conditions
- Autonomy
- Organizational Complexity
- Temporality
- Transparency

Knowledge Conditions

Central to accountability is the need to rectify the information asymmetry among agencies that conduct secret activities, the rest of government, and the public. Information runs the entire intelligence enterprise, and thus access to this flow is key to the efficacy of any external oversight mechanism. A break in the smooth delivery of intelligence information can cause external oversight mechanisms to break down completely. Access to information, breadth and depth of information provided, the timeliness of delivery, and the openness of the intelligence community regarding the details of intelligence programs are all clearly of core importance to the efficacy, validity, and legitimacy of accountability. Further, there are other aspects of knowledge that are key to the success of the mechanisms. Beyond the crucial access to intelligence information, competencies on the part of the staff of the oversight mechanisms are also important. These include enough expertise on technical matters of intelligence to be able to interpret the programs that are presented; appropriate staffing support, particularly for the congressional committees; and appropriate infrastructure for reading and analyzing intelligence information. Compared to the major core issues, information asymmetry and access to intelligence information, these last issues seem minor, but in fact, the practical details of process – engaging with and understanding intelligence – have been a sticking point both for overseers, particularly congressional committees, and for the intelligence community.

First, it takes years to understand the technicalities of intelligence, and for many decades both intelligence oversight committees had term limits on the members' participation. This was intended to limit capture, but on the whole, it resulted in limited and superficial knowledge of the technicalities involved with intelligence oversight. Second, as is well known, Congress does not function without the support of staff. Legislators are spread too thin across too many issue areas to have time to delve deeply into the particular arcane details of an intelligence program. Thus, appropriate staffing levels as well as staff access to intelligence briefings are key to the efficacy of oversight. This, in practical terms and in order for oversight to be effective, means that staff must have appropriate clearances and that specialized subgroup briefings, such as to the Gang of Four or Eight, that exclude both staff and prohibit note taking should be limited. Limited briefings are discussed in greater detail later in this book, but they occur when the executive branch decides that a matter is too sensitive to be briefed to the full committee. The main anxiety here on the part of the intelligence community is, of course, a fear of the details of a program being leaked to the media.

In terms of the judiciary, knowledge conditions have a different cast. In some ways, the Foreign Intelligence Surveillance Court has more direct authority than the congressional committees, as the court can deny or require extensive revisions to order requests – how this process works is discussed in detail later in this book. On the other hand, the scope of the court's authority is narrow and its current or *post facto* recourse options are very limited. Thus, there are trade-offs when it comes to knowledge of intelligence activities and the processes of oversight that have developed to balance the information asymmetry with the executive branch and maintain accountability over intelligence.

Autonomy

Autonomy is key to the authority of accountability and to oversight mechanisms. Within the context of the present framework, this requires that the mechanisms have an independent and autonomous role from the overseen; that they have a separate statutory basis for their operations, and, thus, that their activities and decisions cannot be influenced by pressure from the overseen. Further, external independence means that mechanisms can provide information on intelligence activities to other branches of government and to the public – usually, of course, in redacted form. Most important in terms of the actual autonomy of the mechanism is recourse, that is, the ability of the supervisor to exact consequences and require change in behavior through these consequences. Within the world of intelligence oversight, external supervision has tended to be played down, a victim, perhaps, of gentlemen's agreements and an overall unwillingness to engage with secret and sometimes suspect matters.

External autonomy and authority over the supervised is different from the managerial control that a mechanism responsible for internal accountability might possess. Although external autonomy is quite a strong remedy against bureaucratic overstepping, it still occurs some distance away from actual bureaucratic managerial control over an agency activity. *Control*, as such, is discussed in further detail in the next section, which focuses on the categories that comprise internal accountability. An interesting boundary spanning amalgam of internal and external independence is presented by the role of the statutory inspector general in Chapter 2 of this book. While the role itself, as well as the activities of one of the inspectors general, have created considerable irritation within the CIA, the rationale behind why this is the case is explained by the analytical criteria I advance here.

Organizational Complexity

The complexity of the organizations that the mechanisms are charged with overseeing has a clear impact on the efficacy of accountability. This is the case on two levels: first, overall, the intelligence community is enormous and complicated; second, the intelligence entities themselves are composed not only of multiple components, but of components that vary in composition, tasks, workload, transparency, and objectives. Further, there is variation across the oversight mechanisms in terms of the breadth of the programs and agencies they are responsible for. Thus, while Congress oversees the full range of activities, the oversight mechanism in judiciary, the Foreign Intelligence Surveillance Court, is responsible for only a slim sector of foreign intelligence gathering. The depth and breadth of a mechanism's activities have an effect on the efficacy of oversight and thus the maintenance of accountability; the level of organizational complexity can confound both the depth and breadth of information gathered on that agency.

Temporality

Temporality is key to conceptualizing accountability. Within the context of this framework, it includes the time in the process of planning, conducting, and reviewing intelligence programs where the oversight mechanism is involved. It also includes the *frequency* of involvement per program. The common concept of accountability is an external *post facto* accounting of acts committed by public officials. I expand the use of this term in the book to include all aspects of temporality; that is, while accountability is generally defined as after the fact, the process of maintaining the chain of responsibility over intelligence activities occurs prior to, during, and after the conduct of the relevant programs. The space where oversight occurs varies across the mechanisms: for example, judicial oversight occurs before the activity; executive control occurs prior to, during, and after the fact; and legislative oversight occurs also along the spectrum of temporality – from the required notice of covert action to yearly reviews of programs as the committees go through the authorization and appropriations process. Frequency refers to the number of times the mechanism will deal with a particular program. This is quite important, because if a mechanism is charged with preview, in process review, and then *post facto* review, it has numerous occasions to change intelligence behavior through the consequences that it levies on the agencies responsible for the programs. The level of recourse is thus heightened by contact at multiple points. The linked issues of temporality, frequency, and strength of recourse clearly vary depending on whether we are discussing external or internal accountability. These categories form the basis of the stability of internal accountability in contrast to the incremental development and change of external mechanisms.

Transparency

Transparency has many facets. On the broadest level, governmental openness and transparency are key features of democratic governance. Demands by the public for greater information by the public have increased in recent decades, and procedures have been put into place to accede to these demands. Expectations have risen:

populations in advanced democracies expect to be informed about the decisions their governments are making on their behalf.[22] The "right to know" has increasingly been accepted as fundamental to democratic governance.[23] In the United States, this right to know, or the idea that the population should have access to government records, was codified in the Freedom of Information Act (FOIA). This "sunshine" concept and assumption of governmental transparency have, however, been challenged by the exceptional nature of national security issues. As Alasdair Roberts points out, "In many countries, disclosure laws have been carefully tailored to ensure that the security sector survives as an enclave of security."[24] The United States is one of the countries where this is the case, and in the post-9/11 threat environment, increasingly so.

Transparency is crucial to the efficacy of accountability in a democracy, but a key question is how much transparency is sufficient when it comes to matters of national security. Where should the balance between openness and security fall, and how can the appropriateness of this balance be gauged when the matter is subjective and opinion so widely varied? Finally, issues of national security have traditionally fallen outside the common expectations of openness required of "regular" government, including exceptions to Freedom of Information Laws and other laws intended to create a more open government. What level of openness, thus, should be expected of the national security agencies to their overseers and finally to the public? This question is particularly pertinent when it comes to secret activities done in the name of the country, as the history of intelligence abuses directed against the American population was actually the driving force behind establishing intelligence oversight mechanisms. These questions are all part of my analytical

---

[22] Bruce E. Cain, Patrick Egan, and Sergio Fabbrini, "Towards More Open Democracies: The Expansion of Freedom of Information Laws," in *Democracy Transformed? Expanding Political Opportunities in Advanced Industrial Democracies*, eds. Bruce E. Cain, Russell J. Dalton, and Susan E. Scarrow (Oxford: Oxford University Press, 2003), 115.

[23] Alasdair Roberts, *Blacked Out: Government Secrecy in the Information Age* (Cambridge, UK: Cambridge University Press, 2006), 9.

[24] Roberts, *Blacked Out*, 18.

approach to understanding the importance of transparency within the overall frame of accountability, as well as attempting to gauge the balance of its worth in relation to national security concerns. Finally, as I argue throughout this book, the oversight mechanisms that have developed over the years to supervise intelligence actually provide a system that facilitates the close hold of information and thus overall secrecy rather than unequivocally supporting greater openness to the public.

CHARACTERISTICS OF INTERNAL ACCOUNTABILITY

- Hierarchical Authority
- Organizational Complexity
- Bureaucratic Process
- Legality
- Recourse
- Internal Autonomy

Arguments about intelligence and accountability tend to focus on the idea that intelligence agencies must be overseen by external mechanisms because they are "rogue," uncontrolled, and conduct activities that are indiscriminately illegal. Misunderstandings about the goals and management of intelligence activities are active in the public imagination, and thus it is integral to an advanced study of the subject to grasp not only the internal institutions and constraints, but also to understand how activities are constrained by internal structures, cultures, and fail-safes. Intelligence agencies conduct activities that break foreign laws; this is the cornerstone of all intelligence information gathering. They organize the tasks and output of the organization as do regular bureaucracies, but they also provide a framework for conducting activities that are outside domestic legal constraints. The constituent characteristics of internal accountability also take for granted issues that are problematic for external accountability, such as knowledge conditions. The problem of acquiring intelligence information – *the* most penetrating issue for external accountability – is not a fraught issue in internal accountability. There are variations to this, of course, and I will describe where compartmentalization can hinder appropriate internal accountability due to organizational complexity, as well, but information is accessible internally in contrast to the massive asymmetry with regard to the flow of intelligence information to the rest of the government.

Another matter that bears some attention is the difference between external accountability and the rather limited spectrum of recourse channels available to it and the very direct management or *control* of internal activities. There is variation in how this works internally: for example, internal institutions within the CIA review very carefully the facets, including legality, of covert actions. Programs proceed through several layers of legal and operational review and can be altered or canceled at any stage. As will be discussed in further detail later in this book, the National Security Council conducts a similar review process that engages with programs prior to conduct, during the program, and after the program has concluded. This monitoring process is very much management – or control – in comparison with the rather looser structure that comprises external accountability, reliant as it is on the openness and actual generosity of the intelligence community for its information. The difference between the external maintenance of accountability and internal control over activities is demonstrated by the variables that cause change in the mechanisms. External mechanisms change because of political factors, scandal, changing threat environments, and executive *rule breaking.* This last category corresponds to several instances in which executive behavior crossed the boundaries of law and regulation, but was then later incorporated into changing institutional oversight mechanisms. Internally, change does not occur this way. Internal mechanisms change in response, variously, to presidential edict and policy directives, an administration's ideological standpoint on matters of security, changing agency leadership, changing interpretation of the law, and the changing threat environment. While rule breaking of external constraints is an acceptable form of executive behavior, internal rule breaking within an agency, particularly the CIA, is swiftly punished, using the full spectrum of sanctions, including professional shunning.

Hierarchical Authority

Authority and power are both fundamental issues in the study of political science and public administration. In terms of administration, one goal of authority serves to coordinate the individuals within that organization to serve specific goals. Authority, according to Herbert A. Simon, influences the decisions of the individual within an organization.[25] Authority gives an organization its formal structure and is a *relational* property – that is, it is order constructed upon a relationship between two individuals: one the superior and the other the subordinate. Further, it is important to highlight the distinction between authority – or control – and influence that Simon makes.[26] This is present in the difference between internal accountability and external: the former being the result of direct management; and the latter built increasingly on statute, but dependent on custom, normative expectations of transparency, and generosity of the overseen in terms of information sharing.

In terms of this work, authority incorporates several key factors: the importance of internal control and command for internal accountability; responsibility on the part of seniors for the behavior of their subordinates; and, finally, the integration of the entire organization into a chain of accountability. In terms of operational activity, the internal chain of accountability runs in both directions: from the superiors to subordinates through the use of authority, and from the subordinate to the superior in terms of having individual recourse to correct perceived malfeasance through reporting up the chain of command. The legitimacy of the accountability chain can be demonstrated by whether there is legitimate corrective response, such as sanctions delivered in response to reporting. As an interesting, relevant note, Simon states: "The notion of an administrative

[25] Herbert A. Simon, *Administrative Behavior*, 4th edition (New York: Free Press, 1997), 177.
[26] Simon, *Administrative Behavior*, 179–80.

hierarchy in a democratic state would be unthinkable without the corresponding notion of a mechanism whereby that hierarchy is held to account."[27]

Organizational Complexity

The institution's internal organizational structure has an effect on accountability. Information gathering about internal activities becomes increasingly time consuming with greater internal organizational complexity. With many cycles of tasks being conducted concurrently, it is also much more difficult to maintain internal supervision over daily activities. Further, as is pointed out in the boundary spanning literature, increased complexity of internal technology creates an environment in which that technical core is highly protected, making even internal access to this core through oversight increasingly difficult. There is also variation among agencies in terms of how well managed they are and whether their work is heavily compartmentalized and thus not transparent even to internal overseers.

Bureaucratic Process

Bureaucratic process entails an orderly, institutionalized, and just manner by which to sanction behavior that does not correspond to the demands of internal accountability, both internal regulations and the overall objectives of the organization. The credibility of process rests on the evenhandedness of the application of sanction. Beyond the theoretical, bureaucratic process, terms of accountability should include records taken of events, transparency of process, full knowledge of the charges leveled against one, and the right to respond to these charges. Some examples of bureaucratic process and the CIA that are novel and relate to the relationship of the CIA with the external world and the relationship between domestic and foreign law follow here. In some cases, CIA officers have been tried in court for the activities they performed at the behest of the Agency and the executive branch. This

---

[27] Simon, *Administrative Behavior*, 188.

mismatch between internal expectations and *changing* external expectations on the part of the executive branch is a challenge. The "look back" period tends to be seen as a time of incipient danger for intelligence officers. Bureaucratic process in terms of internal accountability should correct activities done within the requirements of the organization internally. In the case of the CIA, numerous senior officers have taken out personal liability insurance so that they can protect themselves should they face accusations related to acts performed while they were employed by the CIA.

Legality

Legality as a category of internal accountability requires that internal activities be constrained by a legal structure. This category should be very straightforward, and it is, generally, but once again, when activities that are on the border of legality are required of an organization, infringements can happen both by accident and by design. Intelligence agencies, after all, are expected to adhere strictly to domestic law while adhering to an operational mandate that requires breaking foreign law. This creates a complex incentive structure as well as a distinctive internal operational culture. The CIA is imbued with a layered and particularly dense culture of legality. Attorneys are involved at every stage of decision making regarding covert action and are embedded within individual units to make sure that a current legal check occurs at every decision point. There is also another dynamic inherent to the CIA legal framework, which is the internal paranoid – but legitimate – fear of being forced to take the blame by the political administration when operational events go awry. Additional legal checks within the agency as well as outside of the agency with attorneys in the Justice Department, on the Hill, and in the National Security Council are also intended to provide cover to operators, particularly in the case of covert action, where mistakes can have very real political, legal, and lethal consequences.

Recourse

Recourse internally is the same as external recourse, although the available sanctions are quite different. Recourse is the authority and ability to correct behavior through the application of such sanctions. Internally, there is a much wider range of sanctions of behavior available to the mechanism, including both formal and informal correction, whereas external accountability is limited to specific pathways to change behavior. The dynamics and limitations of both processes are discussed in detail in the empirical chapters later in this book.

Internal Autonomy

Internal autonomy, a rather unique category, involves the independence of an internal mechanism from the rest of its home organization. Statutory inspectors general (IG) perform this role in government agencies. The CIA was exempt for many years from the requirement due to national security concerns, but the position has become firmly entrenched – not without controversy – over three decades. The boundary-spanning position of the internal oversight mechanism is unique in terms of its dual role: internal and thus part of the internal hierarchy, but external in terms of its responsibility to the outside world and its freedom from internal sanction in terms of its professional activities.[28] The controversy surrounding the IG highlight the complexities of competing incentives between the executive and legislative branches that according to my argument have driven the incremental development of congressional intelligence oversight mechanisms. The controversy also demonstrates where the chains of internal and external accountability conflict and underscores what the various outcomes of the conflict mean for accountability overall.

Internal autonomy and the boundary spanning capability of the inspector general both illustrate a key point provided by the analytical framework: there are fundamental differences in the roles and responsibilities of those within an intelligence agency and those without. The external world views the activities of the agency with skepticism and possesses an inherent desire to acquire more information on internal

---

[28] Meyer and Rowan, "Formal Structure," 42. See also W. Richard Scott, *Organizations: Rational, Natural, and Open Systems*, 5th edition (New Jersey: Prentice Hall, 2003), for a more in depth discussion of the nature of organizations and how boundary spanning functions.

workings, while the agency protects itself from the external world through all information control avenues available to it: classification, compartmentalization, and, in some cases, obfuscation. This is not to claim especially malevolent intentions on the part of the agency. The *most* crucial task of an intelligence agency is to protect the information it gathers. This information must be kept secret, in some cases, to protect programs, intelligence personnel, sources, and methods. In other cases, the use of intelligence information has crossed the border into illegality and abuses; this line is fine when it comes to behavior that customarily breaks foreign laws but must adhere to domestic legal constraints.

Understanding where the dividing line is can be complex. Intelligence agencies are also sometimes pressed to push the boundary to perform tasks requested by the president or other members of the executive branch. The legality of intelligence activities will be discussed in detail in the chapters that follow. This issue of crossing lines, though, has relevance for the perception of the difference between *internal* and *external* functions with regard to intelligence. My analysis creates a strict divide between the two spheres, arguing that culture, information asymmetry, expectations, and internal control make the internal and external worlds clearly differentiated from one another. My framework for accountability relies on this separation for its validity and for its explanation of the tensions between the overseer and the overseen. Boundary-spanning behavior on the part of a small number of actors invades this space to a degree that has caused controversy on both sides of the divide.

These separate categories comprise the range of required elements in order for accountability to be effective. In the chapters that follow, I use the development of the oversight mechanism within each branch of government as a path to understanding how the set of categories either thrives or fails at a series of pivot points. The objective to breaking down the larger category of accountability into smaller constituent parts is to understand in greater nuance which particular aspects of accountability are lacking or are particularly strong. This analysis will then provide the foundations for a series of recommendations on policy decisions for the future regarding intelligence and accountability.

Analysis of the structure constraining intelligence activities in the United States is not purely an academic discussion, but rather has tremendous implications for both the active defense of civil liberties and the operational efficacy of intelligence. Change of these constraints tends to follow a pendulum-like pattern. In the face of political scandal, oversight mechanisms and legal structures intended to constrain and define what constitutes appropriate behavior on the part of intelligence operators are installed. Internal investigations and efforts to "reestablish propriety" are characteristic results of a political scandal.[29] Openness to the public and the importance of integrating intelligence agencies into regular government become dominant rhetorical themes directed at the population.[30] Conversely, when there is an operational intelligence failure – such as a successful attack that is perceived to be the result of a failure of intelligence information dissemination – the opposite cycle takes place. Restrictions on intelligence activities are loosened, structures intended to constrain are adapted to absorb the exigencies of the emergent threat, and citizens are exhorted to *trust* their government. In both sets of circumstances, public acquiescence to government decision making is key to sustainable security policy and thus indirectly to the continuity of intelligence activities.

In pursuing this line of argument, the first chapter of this book begins with a discussion of the CIA's institutional culture: understanding the organization and its incentives, mission, and mechanism of internal control. Chapter 2 expands the view by addressing the development of oversight mechanisms in the legislature. Congressional oversight is the core of external supervision of intelligence activities, and thus, to begin, I describe how the mechanisms have developed and how events have changed them. Chapter 3 looks more closely at

---

[29] Genevieve Lester, "Societal Acceptability of Domestic Intelligence," in *The Challenge of Domestic Intelligence in a Free Society: A Multidisciplinary Look at the Creation of U.S. Domestic Counterterrorism Intelligence Agency*, ed. Brian A. Jackson (Santa Monica, CA: RAND, 2009), 81. For a broader discussion of this trend, see also Peter Gill, *Democratic and Parliamentary Accountability of Intelligence services after September 11*, presented at Workshop on Democratic and Parliamentary Oversight of Intelligence Services, Geneva, October 2–5, 2002.

[30] Gregory F. Treverton, "Intelligence: Welcome to the American Government," in *A Question of Balance: The President, the Congress, Foreign Policy*, ed. Thomas E. Mann (Washington, DC: Brookings Institution, 1990), 70–108.

the process of legislative oversight within the context of an oppositional relationship with the executive branch, investigating in some
detail how the budget process – the "power of the purse" – works
and assessing its effectiveness, while also looking more deeply at key
political moments in the development of the legislative mechanisms.
This chapter also engages with the varieties and vicissitudes of covert
action, exploring how this particular tool of foreign policy works
and how it has had a clear impact on the development of oversight.
Following this investigation of congressional oversight mechanisms,
I explore the judicial branch and its intelligence-focused court, the
Foreign Intelligence Surveillance Court (FISC). This chapter points
out the specific complexities of judicial engagement in the oversight
of intelligence, describing legal development within this realm while
highlighting the unique characteristics and challenges of this court.
While historically very opaque, the court has been the focus of greater
attention and analysis in light of the Snowden leaks.

Included will be a discussion of the trends of oversight development, focusing on how the unique mosaic of American oversight
mechanisms combines to bolster an internal security system and thus
to increase the secrecy of the intelligence enterprise. The book ends
with a discussion of how the mechanisms can be transformed not only
to meet recent expectations of greater transparency, but also to grapple with the requirements of an eternally dynamic and emergent threat
along with changing technological and political demands, which continually beset the intelligence community and those who watch over it.

2 ORGANIZING SECRECY: THE CIA AND INSTITUTIONAL CONTROL

Remember, we go where others never go!

Charles E. Allen (CIA)[1]

Maintaining accountability of government agencies nestled within the executive branch has long been the concern of the two other branches of government. As will be discussed throughout this book, the accountability and control specifically of intelligence agencies have had a more intermittent trajectory, with the oversight mechanisms developing incrementally and with the public and decision makers both interested in intelligence matters only from time to time. The cycle of exposure of the intelligence agencies tends to be very public during national crises, with accusations requiring that deeply secretive individuals come forth at these moments of perceived failure.

Recent examples of this cycle include multiple testimonies by DNI James Clapper in front of the intelligence oversight committees; NSA Director General Keith B. Alexander called to testify on domestic surveillance on U.S. persons, as well as on European politicians and private citizens; and an angry speech by Senator Dianne Feinstein about the CIA's behavior regarding a lengthy report on the Agency's detention and interrogation program. Prior to this, there were ample other examples of top-level officials called into Congress to explain the use of drones, enhanced interrogation techniques, and black sites. The 9/11 Commission hearings brought heads of agencies, administration officials, and other experts forward to answer for their decisions that

[1] Personal communication, October 7, 2010.

apparently failed to stop the terrorist attacks. Beyond this, there are lasting television images of Oliver North testifying about Iran-Contra in the 1980s, as well as photos of Senator Frank Church holding a dart gun, allegedly used by the CIA during testimony provided to his Senate investigatory committee in 1975.

When there is not a public scandal or operational failure, intelligence agencies and their work tend to fade into the national background. This dynamic creates not only a complex and varied relationship between the intelligence agencies and overseers, but also contributes to an off-kilter sense of intelligence identity and culture among the public. Apertures that provide light to opacity only in moments of crisis skew public images of what the intelligence agencies actually do, how and when they are successful, and what internal and external forces constrain and guide them as they act in their roles as legitimate members of the government. This cycle introduces challenges for the consideration of secrecy in the open American democracy. It also raises the question of how this culture of institutional secrecy has developed and been maintained, even when it is challenged from time to time by exposure.

Theories of accountability focus on the relationships between the "overseen" – the agencies supervised by external bodies – and the overseers themselves. Most of this book does as well, defining efficacy in terms of external accountability and assessing the oversight mechanisms that provide accountability. This chapter, in contrast, builds on the disaggregated conception of accountability to include *internal accountability*, arguing that it is difficult to understand how external accountability can be effective when internal determinants dictate standards of appropriate performance and behavior. Internal accountability of the CIA is strong and breaches of it are noticeable and quickly punished; external mechanisms of accountability falter at the limits of asymmetric information regarding intelligence information, insufficient skill on the part of overseers to decipher the technical details of the programs, the complications of political preferences, and a limited desire to engage on the part of some legislators.

A large segment of the discourse about intelligence oversight has arguably missed the point, mainly by focusing most discussion of intelligence oversight complexity as a function of the "brokenness" of the system in Congress. This discussion has limited its focus not only to the legislative branch but also to a narrow, operational interpretation of oversight. In traditional terminology, as described in the introductory chapter of this book, oversight is a function that the legislative branch is seen to perform, but in actuality, *intelligence* oversight is unique – it occurs in all three branches of government, and a wider understanding of how the parts interact with each other provides insight into whether oversight is, indeed, "broken," or rather if the system of monitoring intelligence is entirely misunderstood by those external to its practice. This suggests that a different frame of reference may aid in understanding the unique requirements, not only of the intelligence services, but of the particular balance among the branches of government in an area fraught with contradiction, ambiguity, politicization, threat, and secrecy.

An internal assessment of the CIA highlights institutional structures that have contributed to the information asymmetry inherent to the nature of intelligence activities – that is, the core mechanisms that keep intelligence secret and contained. Institutional rules and organizational culture keep CIA operations secret. External accountability of the intelligence community attempts to recalibrate this information asymmetry vis-à-vis other government institutions and the public, while oversight mechanisms are the actual tools used to leverage the relationship. Each step of mechanism development in all three branches pivots around rebalancing an asymmetry that will never completely balance due to the specialized tasks, requirements, and characteristics of the intelligence services. Finally, these oversight mechanisms actually facilitate the maintenance of secrets. The institutions developed within the branches create a closed system within which information travels along deliberate pathways that close them off from outside intervention.

This chapter first describes CIA organizational structure and process, and institutional culture and control mechanisms. Beyond the structural and institutional characteristics of the CIA, this chapter aims to provide an internal context for the behavior of intelligence officers and an understanding of internal accountability processes within the Agency. It contributes to an understanding of how officers align their behavior with expected institutional behavioral norms in an environment where extralegal activities are core to the mission, and explains how deviations from these norms are corrected. In pursuit of this understanding, the main themes that this chapter introduces to the discussion of intelligence oversight are, first, the importance of internal agency organizational culture in both understanding internal mores and in understanding how implicit and explicit norms control the behavior of intelligence personnel; second, how this internal cultural control maintains internal standards that may deviate from external societal norms; and third, how those who challenge the dichotomized universe of the CIA – within the Agency and outside of it – are treated.

The crucial question that frames the discussion of internal accountability and control is as follows: how can an oversight structure be built which is resilient enough to engage with a differentiated view of legal constraints – that is, which conforms to domestic law but breaks foreign law purposefully? Throughout, I focus on how secrecy is managed within an organizational context. The core issue of the CIA is how to gather and control secret information. Beyond the security measures that have been created to carry out this task, the institutional culture around the mission and handling of information is unique, providing a distinct environment that can conflict with or complement external oversight activities.

The five characteristics used to explain both the change and efficacy of *external* mechanisms throughout this project are knowledge conditions; autonomy; organizational complexity; temporality; and transparency. In contrast, this chapter elaborates on internal accountability by focusing on six *internal* characteristics: hierarchical authority; organizational complexity; bureaucratic process; legality; recourse; and internal autonomy. The inflection point in terms of the CIA for these six characteristics is particularly salient in the position of the statutory inspector general, a position that crosses the boundary between internal and external accountability.

THE GENESIS OF THE CENTRAL INTELLIGENCE AGENCY: A CULTURE ROOTED IN WARTIME CAPABILITY

For an agency that is remarkably insulated, the Central Intelligence Agency's vulnerability to the exigencies of a changing political environment has had an inordinate impact on the development of its internal institutional culture. This is due, of course, to the inherent secrecy of the Agency's work, but also to other factors, such as the unique relationship the Agency has with the president, its sense of elitism and the sacrifices its officers are expected to make in terms of their own privacy and safety, and its complex relationship to the law, both foreign and domestic. The CIA is a creature of the executive, specifically, the tool of the president. This tight relationship changes over time, based on a range of variables, including the threat environment, the president's reliance on and trust of covert action, the personal relationship between the president and the director of Central Intelligence (now Director/CIA), and the political environment, which has an impact on the acceptability of secret operations. It is held within a network of expectations in terms of operational capability, legality, and political appropriateness. These expectations come from the president, from Congress, from the media, and, increasingly, the public.[2] They also come from within the Agency itself, naturally the most potent control mechanism over any CIA activity. These expectations affect how high-level operational goals are developed on a strategic level, but also how individual intelligence officers conduct their daily operations within the bureaucracy. These expectations also affect how individuals inside the institution exist in relationship with external oversight mechanisms.

The foundations of the CIA were established in the Office of Strategic Services (OSS), developed and run by William J. "Wild Bill" Donovan during World War II. Donovan, observing the piecemeal and disorganized intelligence components serving the departments of War, the Navy, and State and other smaller operations, recommended to President Roosevelt early in 1941 that information drawn from the various intelligence services be coordinated under a single organization.[3] He also suggested that the organization integrate collection, analysis, and operations.[4] Up to the point of the Pearl Harbor

---

[2] Interview with former Senator Chuck Hagel (R-NE), June 27, 2011.

[3] Amy B. Zegart, *Flawed by Design: The Evolution of the CIA, JSC, and NSC* (Stanford, CA: Stanford University Press, 1999), 166.

[4] Douglas Waller, *Wild Bill Donovan: The Spymaster Who Created the OSS and Modern American Espionage* (New York: Free Press, 2011), 70.

attacks in December 1941, seven intelligence agencies reported to President Roosevelt but there was very little coordination among them. Even the information drawn from Magic, a code-breaking capability, was not coordinated between the intelligence components of the Army and Navy. The services actually reported this intelligence information to the president on alternate days because they were unable to work together smoothly.[5] The attacks on Pearl Harbor reinforced the need for a more unified system with which to convey intelligence information to the executive branch in support of wartime decision making.[6] When it was established in June 1942, OSS tasks included espionage, covert action, counterintelligence, and intelligence analysis.[7]

Populated by highly educated, generally upper-class men – a "league of gentlemen," as Donovan called his rapidly growing team – the OSS was a small and extremely elite club whose experience and skill in tradecraft was usually outweighed by enthusiasm and a sense of entitlement.[8] The culture that went along with this slice of society carried over into the new organization, the CIA, and only began to dissipate after the investigations of the 1970s that occurred simultaneously with vast changes in American civil society. The CIA's organization also reflected the internal structure of Donovan's agency, which by mid-1942 was divided into four branches: Secret Intelligence, focused on espionage and collection; Special Operations, responsible for propaganda, guerrilla warfare, and other types of covert action; Foreign Nationalities, focused on gathering information and potential covert action recruits from ethnic groups present in the United States; and Research and Analysis, the analytic section.[9] Donovan even developed projects that have later analogues to controversial responsibilities of the CIA's Science and Technology Division, for example, investing in research on truth drugs and even conducting experiments

---

[5] Waller, *Wild Bill Donovan*, 78.

[6] See the classic by Roberta Wohlstetter, *Pearl Harbor: Warning and Decision* (Palo Alto, CA: Stanford University Press, 1962).

[7] Jeffrey T. Richelson, *The US Intelligence Community*, 5th edition (Boulder, CO: Westview Press, 2008), 17.

[8] Waller, *Wild Bill Donovan*, 93. This is not to discount the increasingly acknowledged role of women in the OSS. They numbered in the thousands.

[9] Waller, *Wild Bill Donovan*, 96.

on unsuspecting individuals – presaging programs such as the CIA's MKULTRA, which focused on psychological experimentation and control.[10]

Further, the office created a pattern of intelligence sharing, particularly with the British, that set the precedent for later liaison work between the CIA and foreign intelligence agencies. Overall, the office was imbued with a culture of adventure and irreverent experimentation. This was due to the nature of the work, but also to the elevated social position of the majority of the officers. Taking risks and breaking rules were part of a dynamic institutional culture, a culture much at odds with conventional government practice and, particularly, the military mores of the time. In the words of General John Magruder, Donovan's deputy at the end of the war, "Clandestine intelligence operations involve a constant breaking of all the rules. To put it baldly, such operations are necessarily extra-legal and sometimes illegal."[11] This sense that breaking the rules creatively is part of the job has continued, to some extent, in the present-day incarnation of the Special Activities Division of the OSS, the National Clandestine Service (more commonly known by its decades-long title Directorate of Operations). Some argue that the CIA's current emphasis on paramilitary activities is a return of the CIA to its OSS roots.[12]

Donovan argued strenuously after the war that it was critical for the United States to keep a central intelligence agency even in peacetime.[13] Donovan was sidelined from the intelligence business after the war, but after a two-year gap, during which a rather anemic Central Intelligence Group (CIG) struggled to find its way during postwar demobilization, the Central Intelligence Agency was created in 1947. The CIA was originally intended to focus on coordinating, analyzing, and disseminating intelligence information, but not to have as a primary mission the collection of intelligence or covert action.[14] The

---

[10] Waller, *Wild Bill Donovan*, 103. Its context is explored in Chapter 4 of this book.

[11] Tim Weiner, *Legacy of Ashes: The History of the CIA* (New York: Doubleday, 2007), 12. This book is biased and sensationalist; however, it engages interestingly with historical records, when viewed with the skepticism it is due.

[12] Interview with a former House Permanent Select Committee on Intelligence (HPSCI) staffer, March 13, 2011.

[13] Waller, *Wild Bill Donovan*, 333.

[14] Zegart, *Flawed by Design*, 163.

structure and mission of the CIA were the outcome of the bureaucratic infighting of a large number of government players, each of
whom had a vested interest in maintaining its section of intelligence
"turf." An example of this is the domination of the FBI over any
domestic intelligence gathering. It was not only due to a fear of an
"American Gestapo" that the CIA was not and is not permitted to
operate within the United States, but rather also to the ferocious hold
that J. Edgar Hoover and the FBI had on the domestic sphere of law
enforcement.

The statute that created the CIA – the National Security Act of
1947 – is notable for its vagueness regarding specifics of the CIA. The
main focus of the Act was the military; it created the Air Force and
established the National Security Council and the position of secretary of defense. Congress, intently focused on military unification, did
not pay much attention to the new "central" agency; however, those
involved in existing intelligence operations in the War, Navy, Justice,
and State departments opposed the new agency fiercely, setting the
stage for decades of future turf wars.[15] The sections of the Act on the
CIA were ambiguous, with no mention at all of covert operations.[16]
The authority that allowed the CIA to operate secretly all over the
world was extrapolated from a vague "Fifth Function" of the National
Security Act (1947), which ordered the CIA "to perform such other
functions and duties related to intelligence affecting the national security as the [NSC] may from time to time direct."[17] This Fifth Function
is the entire original basis for the authorization of CIA covert action.
The ambiguity of the Fifth Function continues to plague the practice
of the oversight of covert action to this day, not least because with
increasing Pentagon activity in this arena, it can be difficult to determine which oversight processes apply to a particular action.

The armed services had never supported a centralized intelligence
apparatus and were intent that the new agency would be weak. The
strenuous opposition of the armed services is noticeable in terms of
the fact that the services kept their individual intelligence components

[15] Amy Zegart, *Eyes on Spies: Congress and the United States Intelligence Community* (Stanford: Hoover Institution Press, 2011), 46.

[16] Weiner, *Legacy of Ashes*, 25.

[17] 50 U.S.C. § 403(d) (1988).

even after a "central" agency was established.[18] Disinterest in the creation of a new intelligence agency extended to other branches of government; Congress, for example, had a minimal role in the genesis of both the CIG and the CIA. Truman disbanded the OSS and created the interim CIG without any input from Congress.[19] Both the House and Senate passed the National Security Act (1947) with very little comment as well, deferring to the executive branch.

These early bureaucratic issues – fragmented intelligence responsibility, a heavy asymmetry toward the military intelligence apparatus, and an ambiguous and changing mission – remain to this day. Within the institution, the irreverence and expectations of rule breaking and risk taking that characterized the OSS are all embedded in the culture of the clandestine side of the CIA. While it could be argued that the "rogue" characteristics of the OSS fit the operations side of the CIA, the analytical side has always had a different culture, focused on logic, rationality, and analytical prowess. The two sides have evolved side by side but with different values and attitudes toward risk, success, and failure. They have also developed to incorporate the necessary norms, expectations, and rules of modern bureaucracy. Both sides constitute a closely held tool of the presidency, evolving in response to presidential need.[20]

ORGANIZATIONAL CULTURE AND INTERNAL CONTROL

The organizational culture of the CIA has been blamed for a calcifying and tedious bureaucratic process that, it has been argued, led to, among other things, the failure to prevent the attacks on 9/11. This criticism has been repeated often throughout official commission reports and briefings in the last decade, but it is not understood in any nuanced fashion. Critics of the intelligence community, particularly of the CIA, want it both ways: they want to argue that the culture leads to an institutional rigidity, risk aversion, and failure to achieve operational success, while simultaneously arguing that the CIA is rogue and uncontained by the rule of law.

---

[18] Zegart, *Flawed by Design*, 171.
[19] Zegart, *Flawed by Design*, 172.
[20] Zegart, *Flawed by Design*, 186.

While seen as an organization that operates remotely from "regular" government, the CIA is an institutionalized bureaucracy with cultural norms, tasks, and performance objectives. In terms of our model of internal accountability, there is a strict hierarchical authority, standard operating procedures, and a layered review system for every piece of analytical work, as well as for every operational program. In fact, perceived problems with rigid bureaucratic operating procedures and organizational culture have formed the core of criticism of the Agency in post-9/11 analysis, contrasting with earlier criticisms of rogue behavior. Over the past decades, in fact, the CIA has been blamed often for being risk averse and unwilling to take chances. Former case officers have pointed to a sclerotic structure that requires endless waits for approval on time-sensitive operations and a bureaucratic attitude of unwillingness to accept blame for an operation's failure.[21]

The perceptions of insiders highlight a unique and insular world, one that has found a way of making extralegal and dangerous activities part of a code of siblinghood that several officers described as a "family." This extreme level of closeness is rare within bureaucracies, and its importance was repeated over and over again in my interviews. This connectedness – or in military terms, cohesion – is very important in terms of creating trust within teams in order to enable them to complete risky missions, or even to sacrifice themselves to the objectives of their assigned missions.[22] Along with this cohesion, there is a strong sense of leadership and difference to authority. The culture fosters closeness first through rigorous self-selection; the CIA is not an organization one joins accidentally, with its extremely high barriers to entry, including a polygraph and full background check once the first phases of employment are achieved. Tradecraft is taught, either analytic or operational, and the Agency's message of sacrifice, focus

---

[21] Many memoirs are somewhat self-aggrandizing, but they do all point to similar criticisms of the CIA culture. See Ishmael Jones, *The Human Factor: Inside the CIA's Dysfunctional Intelligence Culture* (New York: Encounter, 2008); Tyler Drumheller, *On the Brink: An Insider's Account of How the White House Compromised American Intelligence* (New York: Carroll and Graf, 2006).

[22] The sentiment I heard repeated in almost every interview resembles Wilson's definition of mission: "When an organization has a culture that is widely shared and warmly endorsed by operators and managers alike ...." James Q. Wilson, *Bureaucracy* (New York: Basic Books, 1989), 95.

on mission, and patriotism is inculcated continually. Further, while most positions no longer require misleading one's family about one's employer, extreme secrecy about tasks and travel is still very much the operational norm, and open discussion about one's employer still usually off limits. Limits are also placed on public appearances, public statements, publications, travel, outside employment, and associations with foreign nationals.[23]

The image of the CIA is controlled in terms of information dissemination. The official "voice" of the CIA is carefully modulated, with specific spokespeople the only conduits for information outside of the Agency. Over the past decade, there have been attempts to create a more accessible image. These have included collaboration on films and television shows and an enhanced social media presence. Jennifer Garner, an actress who played a spy in the television show *Alias*, appeared on the Agency's Web site as a recruiting tool. More recently, the CIA joined Twitter, with its first tweet being the rather humorous, "We can neither confirm nor deny that this is our first tweet."[24] This tweet had been retweeted a quarter of a million times by the time of this writing and excited much media commentary. The Twitter feed includes factoids about the CIA, images of spy gadgets, and patriotic commentary. Other public events intended to portray a controlled and specific image of the CIA include efforts to reach out to academic institutions overtly and offer joint cooperation in conferences and other large events.

There has been an interesting repetition of the theme of "normalizing" the exceptionalism of the CIA, while at the same time highlighting the uniqueness of the Agency. One proponent of this perspective is General Michael Hayden, who made a concerted effort to make the Agency more transparent and more "normal" in the eyes of Americans.[25] Thus, he personally reiterates his modest, non–Ivy League beginnings, his military service, and his devout Catholic faith. He also is renowned for using sports metaphors to describe the exigencies of the service as well as to connect with his

---

[23] Interview with a former CIA analyst, August 15, 2013.

[24] Twitter, June 6, 2014.

[25] This focus on perception is a function of interviewer intervention – my being an outsider to the community, I believe.

audience. Finally, I would argue that his military persona and bearing contributed to the legitimacy of authority in leadership. This combination of tightly networked relationships and an intense mission focus also can introduce complications into the operational side. One former senior officer pointed to the case of Khost, Afghanistan as a demonstration of the risk taking inherent to internal operational culture. As he put it, the diligence and intent of the team led to extreme risk taking and disaster, as eager focus on the mission objectives combined with inexperience led to problematic security measures and the deaths of seven CIA officers.[26]

The obverse of this closeness, insularity and hierarchical authority is not as congenial: trespassers of institutional mores and norms, particularly those dealing with confidential information, are not only punished bureaucratically, but in some cases shunned and prosecuted. Those who cross the boundaries between the "inside" and "outside" worlds are met with a great deal of suspicion, even if the role, such as the inspector general, is instituted by statute. The CIA operates within a very Manichean universe, unsurprisingly, but organizationally this means that it operates within a series of very clearly demarcated spheres within spheres. These spheres do not just enclose and protect the activities of the CIA from the outside world; they also exist within the Agency, most obviously through the organization of work – in divisions with very disparate cultures and through the management of information – the compartmentalization of secret information into categories to which only select individuals have access (based on "their need to know").

Activities within the CIA are divided into two spheres: analysis and operations. Four directorates divide this work among them. Each of the directorates has a very distinct culture and incentive structure. The two most well-known divisions are the Directorate of Intelligence (DI), responsible for intelligence analysis, and the Directorate of Operations (DO), recently renamed the National Clandestine Service, responsible

---

[26] Interview with Charles E. Allen, September 22, 2011. The Khost incident was ruled a failure of security when a double-agent killed seven CIA officers in a suicide attack. The double-agent had not been properly vetted, standard security measures at the base had not been taken, and the physical security of the base was compromised. To add to the tragedy, a number of those killed were the Agency's best experts on Al-Qaeda.

for covert activity. The Directorate of Science and Technology focuses on technical development and has, in the past, engaged in a range of experiments as well as developed the technical mechanisms that support espionage. The Directorate of Support provides infrastructure and other logistical support at home and abroad. In terms of internal organizational structure, the divisions within the CIA each have different incentive structures, making internal oversight extremely complex. In the words of former DCIA Hayden: "CIA is not *the CIA*, it is several CIAs."[27] The cultural differences between CIA divisions are clear and have been discussed often. The sense of a strong division in terms of potential blame and liability for retroactive criminal acts is profound, resulting in resentment among DO operatives against not only the Office of the Inspector General (OIG) but also other divisions within CIA.[28] Anecdotally, the film *Rendition* (2007), which is about a CIA situation, differentiates between the "knuckle draggers" (DO) and the "pencil pushers" (DI). In more detail, General Hayden responded to the question of what had surprised him – a career intelligence officer – the most about the CIA. His response was as follows:

> Actually, I was pretty familiar with it [the CIA], but there was one thing that struck me. I kind of expected it but didn't understand how deeply important it was. And that was the fact that there were multiple cultures inside CIA. I frequently talk about when looking at the Agency from Route 123, you think it's a singular noun. But on most days, at best, it's a collective noun, and on some bad days it's a plural. Each of the four big directorates has its own culture. But I respected the cultures; they were there for a reason. And I didn't want to destroy them or threaten them, but I wanted to overlay them with a stronger Agency culture. You could have the kind of "fighter pilot" mystique in the National Clandestine Service (NCS), or the "tenured faculty" mystique in the Directorate of Intelligence (DI), but there were still some unifying themes that made you a CIA officer. And we set about to do that, fairly gently, but I thought it was important.[29]

[27] Interview with General Michael Hayden, March 9, 2011.
[28] Interview with a CIA case officer, March 1, 2011.
[29] Mark Mansfield, "A Discussion on Service with Former CIA Director Michael Hayden," *Studies in Intelligence* 54 (2010): n.p.

Strict adherence to the constraints of the spheres is required; deviation, even in a self-proclaimed innovative agency, is permitted much less than an outsider would expect. Methods to discover and correct questionable behavior – such as polygraphs, oaths of secrecy, required internal publication review, travel and interaction with foreigner constraints, security investigation, and even counterintelligence investigations – would be considered extreme in the outside world. With one mind, we are accustomed to considering the wild stories of counterintelligence operations, usually from the Soviet era, that sometimes occurred through the streets of Washington. It is quite different, however, to consider what such an investigation directed at an officer suspected of being a mole would look like in contemporary America. Counterintelligence will be discussed in greater depth later in this chapter; my main point here is to introduce the reader to the bifurcated mindset required to understand intelligence in this country, particularly as conducted by the CIA. On the one hand, this is an American bureaucracy organized to be efficient and effective in completing its various tasks; on the other, the exceptional nature of those tasks, as well as the secrecy and danger involved, creates a culture of control, order, and delimitation from the open democratic society that the officers are, according to their mantra, dedicated to protecting.

Burton Gerber, a senior CIA operations officer who was chief of station in Moscow and Belgrade during the Cold War, returning to Langley to run the Soviet Union and Eastern Europe Division, pointed out that, in his view, institutional mores required superlative professionalism and ethics.[30] Or put more directly, "As a case officer... a guy who goes out and recruits other spies abroad, I was lying and cheating and stealing," Gerber explained in a talk to undergraduate students. "All of you were taught as youngsters not to lie, or cheat or steal. But yet we expect the people who are going to be the case officers for our intelligence agency to do those things .... The question in the business of spying is, for what ends are you doing it? You are lying, cheating

---

[30] Interview with Burton Gerber, April 13, 2010. This dynamic is well described in the book by Milton Bearden and James Risen, *The Main Enemy: The Inside Story of the CIA's Final Showdown with the KGB* (New York: Random House, 2004), which also, incidentally, stars Burton Gerber as one of the main protagonists.

and stealing but it's your job and it's for the good of the country."[31] Gerber clarified his statements by adding:

> In pursuing intelligence information through espionage, the case officer is likely to find him/herself in a situation which I and others have called the need to lie/cheat/steal. What does this mean? In targeting an individual who may have information vital to American national security, the case officer often will approach the individual and pursue him/her in the developmental phase without revealing his/her real interest in the person. Cheating refers to the fact that in collecting intelligence in a target country, one is cheating by violating the laws of that country. Stealing has the same connotation. One obtains the secret information necessary to the United States in an illegal (under the foreign country's laws) act, which needs to be hidden from that country's authorities.[32]

As David Aaron, a Church Committee task force leader and the architect of the Church Committee recommendations, which led to the current intelligence oversight system, put it, "There is a lot of internal accountability because [the CIA was part of a] culture that suggested that if you're doing illegal things [abroad], you must keep meticulous records."[33] Former senior operations officer Stephen R. Kappes made a strenuous point about the importance of covert actors abiding by U.S. legal constraints.[34]

Former CIA Director Michael Hayden reinforced this point: "If you're doing 'illegal' activities, you need to be extra honest."[35] Hayden emphasized that "illegal" was not with respect to US law. Both General Hayden and long-time CIA officer Charles E. Allen have made the point that the CIA does what no other agency is asked to do or allowed to do. As they and others put it, using General Hayden's phrase, the CIA should have "chalk on the cleats."[36] General Hayden points to a moral

---

[31] Burton Gerber, "The Ethical Aspects of Intelligence Work: The Cold War and Beyond," DePauw University, March 22, 2001. Available online at http://www.depauw.edu/news-media/latest-news/details/11432/.

[32] Personal communication with Burton Gerber, September 2014.

[33] Interview with David Aaron, April 6, 2010.

[34] Interview with Stephen R. Kappes, September 22, 2011.

[35] Interview with General Michael Hayden, March 9, 2011.

[36] Interview with General Michael Hayden, April 7, 2010; presentation by Charles E. Allen, University of California Washington Center, Washington, DC, November 12, 2009. Interview with Charles E. Allen, February 4, 2010.

obligation or ethical responsibility to push to the edge of the boundaries of authority in order to keep the country safe. He has emphasized on multiple occasions that this is, in fact, a personal responsibility of Agency leadership and an overall aspect of the institutional culture. In multiple cases, officers pointed to the visceral reactions of officers to the attacks on 9/11 – not just the general shock and horror felt by many, but a feeling of shame at having let the country down.[37] Along these lines, then, it could be argued that the CIA has developed its own culture and internal incentive structures to support behavior that could be deemed insupportable externally – at least according to common American societal mores – but are considered necessary within the organization in order to complete the mission. In response to requirements of extremity – both of activity and legality – the internal structures and decision-making processes that contain these foreign law-breaking activities are rigorous, well defined, and hierarchical.

Much is made of the insularity of the CIA and its elitist attitude with respect to other agencies within the intelligence community. Some of the elite attitude has roots in the foundations of the Agency, when it was the bastion of the northeastern elite, with members recruited from the universities of the Ivy League. One former very senior CIA officer highlighted this attitude in a statement that CIA officers view themselves as the "chosen ones, with access to the deepest secrets, who write the best assessments."[38] This official also pointed out that the CIA views itself as something sui generis, with a mission-focused, innovative culture based on the view that the members of this elite group are a tightly knit family that serves the president and makes sacrifices to keep the country safe.[39] This view was extended by former senior operations official Kappes, who views the bond between officers as one created by the willingness to sacrifice actively in support of a greater good.[40] This operator pointed to a culture "Jesuitical in nature, with a focus on a greater mission and a clear understanding of good and evil."[41] General Hayden reinforced this point in a comment about CIA personnel: "They're just solid Americans who are very talented, doing things no one else is asked to do, and no one

[37] Interview with a senior CIA official, September 21, 2011.
[38] Interview with Charles E. Allen, September 22, 2011.
[39] Interview with Charles E. Allen, September 22, 2011.
[40] Interview with Stephen R. Kappes, September 22, 2011.
[41] Interview with Stephen R. Kappes, September 22, 2011.

else is allowed to do. That's a special vocation. And I mean that in the religious sense of the word. It's a vocation."[42]

As described in the preceding, a strong internal culture guides the behavior of CIA officers and tight links with other executive branch entities, such as the NSC, guide specific types of intelligence programs, such as covert action, through a multiplicative legal review process. The intelligence community is imbued with this reliance on legal opinion, and this holds true for the internal structure of the CIA. Legality is also a fundamental pillar of the internal accountability framework. As Michael Scheuer, the former head of the Bin Laden unit at the CIA, put it: "There is no operation at the CIA that is conducted without approval of lawyers. I can't go to the bathroom at CIA without a lawyer."[43] This reliance on internal legal structure once again differentiates the CIA from the outside world. The CIA's legal culture focuses on internal structure to maintain adherence to American law while, at times, breaking foreign laws. It is a unique arrangement, based on tight internal communication and attorneys present at all levels of CIA operations, as well as at every level of decision making.

As a case in point, the Office of the General Counsel provides the CIA internal legal advice regarding the legality and appropriateness of its operations.[44] As such, it performs an internal oversight role in terms of monitoring and guiding the operations of the CIA, particularly those of the National Clandestine Service. Internal mechanisms such as the OGC perform an interesting balancing act; they are charged with producing legal justification for Agency activities, yet they are reinforcing activities that are, in many cases, illegal. This office grew out of the Church Committee hearings, when it was expanded and empowered in order to control for any potential abuses such as those that catalyzed the hearings. The attorneys who joined the CIA during this period actually referred to themselves as "Church babies."[45]

[42] Mansfield, "A Discussion on Service with Former CIA Director Michael Hayden," n.p.

[43] Quoted in Jack Goldsmith, *The Terror Presidency: Law and Judgment inside the Bush Administration* (New York: W. W. Norton, 2007), 130.

[44] See John Rizzo, *Company Man: Thirty Years of Controversy and Crisis in the CIA* (New York: Scribner, 2014), for a discussion of the development of this office post–Church Committee investigations.

[45] Rizzo, *Company Man*, 45.

Most discussions on the internal legal capacity of the CIA focus on its role in creating a risk-averse culture among personnel. Too careful, too worried, the legal culture is deemed a hindrance to the effective conduct of necessary intelligence operations. On the other hand, the legal structure within the CIA is viewed as a fail-safe for officers who are operating at the far reaches of the law. This fear of crossing over into illegality is not just present at the institutional level. Individual officers often feel that while their activities may be authorized by one administration, they may be penalized under the next for activities once judged entirely legal. This view that the political framework within which intelligence operations function is slightly unsteady runs throughout virtually all of the interviews I conducted. Some take out personal liability insurance to hedge against potential lawsuits should the next administration engage in a "look back" period.[46]

The general counsel (GC) works with director of the CIA, the deputy director of the CIA, and the deputy director of Operations. The GC is nominated by the president and confirmed by the senate. Thus the GC is bound to the political cycle and chosen, at least to some extent, based on loyalty to the president and party.[47] Attorneys have a range of functions within the CIA, but the main purpose for all of them is to understand, decide, and explain exactly how far intelligence officers may go in their activities. It is often remarked that the role of the OGC (CIA) is to push legal constraints as far as possible in order to support the operations of the Agency. As a former assistant general counsel (CIA) points out: "Especially important are internal checks on officers who operate on the dark side. Lurking in the shadows, spymasters convince people from other countries – clerks, diplomats, soldiers, and hostile intelligence officers – to commit espionage. The challenge for U.S. clandestine operators is to induce and facilitate such lawbreaking despite the great risks that

---

[46] This feeling of potential risk runs throughout my interviews – not only with operators. Interestingly, the public relations officer under George Tenet felt the same way. Interview with Bill Harlow, March 28, 2011. General Hayden attempted to make a point to Congress by subsidizing liability insurance for his officers. Interview with General Michael Hayden, March 2, 2011. The point did not resonate among legislators.

[47] A. John Radsan, "*Sed Quis Custodiet Ipsos Custodes:* The CIA's Office of General Counsel?" *Journal of National Security Law and Policy* 2 (2006–8): 210.

it involves."[48] This requires a legal team to understand and dissect where that changing line of chalk is.

In addition to providing legal advice to senior CIA personnel, the GC is also a sounding board for whistleblowers. CIA regulations require CIA employees to report to the GC or IG if they believe a CIA rule, executive order, or the Constitution has been violated. "The General Counsel, along with the Inspector General, is supposed to provide a safe haven for employees with complaints."[49] If the GC receives a complaint from an internal CIA whistleblower, it goes to the inspector general, who will transmit the complaint to the D/CIA. The D/CIA then must send the complaint to the congressional oversight committees, or in some cases the employee will be allowed to appear before the committees directly.[50] Interestingly, a direct appearance before the committees must be coordinated with senior officers at CIA; a CIA employee cannot go straight to the Hill. The importance of whistleblowers and leaks in maintaining informal oversight over intelligence activities will be discussed in the next chapter, which is engaged with the role of the public in controlling intelligence activities.

While the OIG can be considered an adversary, the OGC is definitely an ally and guide. The OGC provides a legal context and culture of legality within the CIA, helping determine appropriate behavior but not providing a check that has any sense of distance from the activity to be monitored. This culture of legality highlights, once again, the dichotomy inherent to the organization of the Agency. On the one hand, legal constraints imbue the organization with a rigid framework and set of operating principles, a practice common to most bureaucracies. On the other hand, mechanisms such as the counterintelligence function of the Agency clearly point to the exceptionalism of the operations conducted there, as well as how internal control has a different role within the CIA in comparison with other agencies.

---

[48] Radsan, "*Sed Quis Custodiet Ispos Custodes,*" 204.
[49] Radsan, "*Sed Quis Custodiet Ispos Custodes,*" 210.
[50] Radsan, "*Sed Quis Custodiet Ispos Custodes,*" 211.

COUNTERINTELLIGENCE AND INTERNAL CONTROL

In order to understand internal control of the CIA's intelligence operations, it is important to understand what *counterintelligence* is, how it works, and how its practice interacts with and affects the organizational culture and accountability of the Agency. The popular conception of counterintelligence tends to stem from the Cold War, a *Spy vs Spy* operation conducted through the streets of Washington or Moscow as one superpower tries to hinder the penetration of its intelligence services by the other. This image is a tiny part of the larger mosaic that constitutes the counterintelligence task. Counterintelligence is present in all aspects of the intelligence enterprise. "Counterintelligence is not a separate step in the intelligence process. CI should pervade all aspects of intelligence, but is often pigeon-holed as a security issue. CI does not fit neatly with human intelligence, although CI is, in part, a collection issue. Nor does it fit with covert action. It is also more than security – that is, defending against or identifying breaches – because successful CI can also lead to analytical and operational opportunities. In sum, CI is one of the most difficult intelligence topics to discuss."[51] Former CIA analyst, Mark Lowenthal, categorizes CI into three main types: collection, involving gathering information on an adversary's attempt to collect on one's own service; defensive counterintelligence, involving defending and countering foreign attempts to penetrate one's service; and, offensive counterintelligence, involving direct attack on the adversary's efforts against one's own service. Attacks could include trying to "turn" an agent and convince that agent to spy for one's service or manipulating the information given to the adversary.[52]

The three aspects of counterintelligence overlap and cross the boundaries of external and internal activities. What concerns us most here is how the use of counterintelligence can be used to maintain internal control. As mentioned earlier in the chapter, barriers of entry are high at the CIA. The polygraph is used not only to weed out

---

[51] Mark Lowenthal, *Intelligence: From Secrets to Policy*, 5th edition (Washington, DC: CQ Press, 2012), 163.

[52] Mark Lowenthal, *Intelligence: From Secrets to Policy*, 4th edition (Washington, DC: CQ Press, 2009), 151.

undesirable potential employees, but also regularly to monitor current employees, as well as to follow up on allegations of wrongdoing among the staff. Personal behaviors are monitored carefully; these include changes in income or spending, increased debt, increased alcohol use, or deviant sexual behavior. While in earlier years sexual issues, particularly homosexuality, would be a particular target for counterintelligence, currently finances tend to be a specific focus for internal investigation – even more so than drug use. Excessive debt could be a vulnerability for an officer – one that could make the officer susceptible to being turned by a foreign service. The increased focus on finances has come in the wake of two cases of moles within the FBI (Hanssen) and the CIA (Ames). Both spent excessively beyond their means and maintained lifestyles not deemed in accordance with their pay grades. In order to monitor finances, officers are required to submit financial disclosure forms at regular intervals. While, according to one senior CIA officer, the forms are so convoluted as to not convey much meaning, the point is that there is a remarkable level of acceptability of invasive practices used to control the behavior of personnel already "inside."[53]

I mention the preceding as examples of what could be perceived of as personal infringements. There are, of course, numerous other methods by which personnel and information are controlled and tracked. The point here is that some methods of counterintelligence intended to ferret out those who are being disloyal to the U.S. government – or those who seem to be *at risk* of being disloyal – would be deemed transgressions of civil liberties outside of the CIA realm within which they are culturally accepted. They are accepted and, in some cases, extolled within that environment. Having said this, counterintelligence has a difficult history within the CIA and finding the appropriate balance of acceptable investigation and suspicion has proven difficult over the course of decades. This is partially due to the impact of specific personalities on the process.

James Jesus Angleton, the head of CIA's counterintelligence division from 1954 to 1974, is the core of complication and suspicion when it

---

[53] Personal communication with a senior CIA official, September 14, 2011.

comes to the issue of counterintelligence (CI). Methods used to check up on employees regularly seem relatively banal when one investigates the extent to which Angleton was willing to go to discover subterfuge within the Agency. His extreme suspicion about his fellow officers created such a level of distrust that the operations of the CIA during that period, and for a long period after, were deeply harmed. Morale in this atmosphere of distrust plummeted and operational effectiveness dropped. This is where the concept of counterintelligence and internal control becomes very complex. CI is extremely difficult to conduct well; officers are trained and adept at developing layer upon layer of deception if required, and extraordinarily sensitive in terms of how it impacts the internal balance and ongoing operations of an intelligence agency. In scholar Robert Jervis' words: "Since by definition it is very hard to detect a good spy and at least as hard to tell whether one of your spies has been 'turned' and is now feeding you false information and betraying secrets to the adversary, a heightened and indeed hypersensitive readiness to perceive deception comes with the territory."[54] He adds: "But the inevitable cost of this stance will sometimes be to see plots that do not exist, to discount accurate information, to disregard if not jail loyal informants, and to induce a great deal of paranoia within one's government if not country."[55] As he summarizes the problem, Jervis asks, "How can one maintain one's balance in an area where almost anything could be true, where appearances are designed to be deceiving, and in which familiar signposts may have been twisted to point in the wrong direction?"[56]

Regardless of whether these are officers from adversarial services attempting to outwit each other or an internal double agent attempting to outwit his employer, these are highly skilled professionals, adept at remaining undetected. Also, what does the Agency do to deal with a suspected mole? At a very basic level, a polygraph will be conducted, an investigation started, and the suspect questioned, leading perhaps to arrest. But what recourse does the Agency have if the case is

---

[54] Robert Jervis, "Intelligence, Counterintelligence, Perception, and Deception," in *Vaults, Mirrors and Masks*, ed. Jennifer E. Sims and Burton Gerber (Washington, DC: Georgetown University Press, 2009), 69–80, at 71.

[55] Jervis, "Intelligence, Counterintelligence, Perception, and Deception," 71.

[56] Jervis, "Intelligence, Counterintelligence, Perception, and Deception," 73.

inconclusive, as many of them are? It has been argued that one reason harsher punitive measures are not used is the wealth of knowledge the spy holds. This makes the issue of dealing with an alleged spy within the Agency a complicated and dangerous human resources problem. It also adds an interesting dimension to our accountability framework when the crux for external accountability is access to knowledge and information, and the internal analogue is the danger of the access to knowledge and information.

The role of CI within the context of this chapter is multifaceted. First, it includes some of the active measures taken directly at CIA personnel in order to control their behavior. Second, it once again demonstrates the ambiguity, secrecy, and deception inherent to intelligence activities. This is not to suggest that each intelligence officer is attempting to lie to his employers or obfuscate his or her real allegiance, but rather that the uncertainty in terms of understanding others' motivation is a key aspect of the intelligence lifestyle and culture. Third, it marks where a crossing of the boundaries between internal and external activities takes place. Most of the purpose of counterintelligence is to block the adversary's intelligence service from accessing information in this country or from our services. The critical piece, however, for the purposes of this argument, is the integration of this primary – external – aspect with a secondary aspect – internal – that of controlling our services from within.

Counterintelligence activities, organizational cultural expectations, and legal constraints are all components that keep CIA personnel within the expected norms of Agency behavior. When there is perceived failure to adhere, the bureaucratic process disciplines the individual, and, in extreme cases, the inspector general investigates any alleged deviation from the rules. The first three of these mechanisms occur in current time – they control behavior at all times, whereas the latter, the IG's investigations, occur retroactively. The IG's role – and the complexities of its dual nature – will be discussed in the next section. What is interesting for the current discussion is that given the characteristics of the very invasive internal mechanisms maintaining order within the CIA, what are catalysts to deviate from such rigid expectations? There are many ways to deviate – one could be spying for an adversary – but that is too extreme a case to be illustrative within the current context of the subtle pressures and mechanisms of internal control. More salient is the issue of whistleblowing on behavior that an individual deems unacceptable; behavior that others within the Agency may find necessary to the continued mission.

INDIVIDUAL DECISIONS: WHISTLEBLOWING, LEAKING, AND INTERNAL CONTROL

Internal individual initiatives to change behavior, such as whistleblowing through leaking to the media, provide a substantive challenge to both the cohesive organizational culture and the internal mechanisms described here. This issue has obviously been of major importance in light of the Edward Snowden disclosures of National Security Agency programs. This ties together with the investigatory mechanisms, such as the IG and the counterintelligence function. Arguably, there are two sides of accountability when it comes to the leaking of information. There is a dichotomy at the point when an officer leaks information about a particular operation or issue to the media – the officer is choosing an individual perception of accountability over cohesion to the organization culture. This refusal to be bound by internal constraints is immensely complicated within this secret, national security context. It also brings up ethical issues such as where the balance between loyalty to the organization or to one's own sense of moral responsibility should be struck.

Many intelligence officers speak of a personal sense of moral responsibility to push the boundaries of legality in order to protect; it could easily be the case that an officer feels that protection lies in a different direction than management's conception – this would hardly be unusual – or that the importance of transparency to the public transcends the need for secrecy. These issues, usually painted black and white in public discussions, are immensely complex and subjective. We see this over and over again in terms of the debate over Snowden: is he a hero or a traitor? Should he be feted or incarcerated? The issues are not clear-cut. Essentially, they introduce the question of what recourse an individual with secret information has when evidence of rule breaking is clear, and what this recourse – or lack thereof – means for both internal and external oversight of the CIA. Further, it introduces the question of why individuals feel the need to go to the media when, ostensibly, there are numerous other mechanisms – both within the CIA and external to it –they can use to voice their disapproval.

Leaking challenges the questions of accountability that were introduced at the beginning of this book. When asking whether oversight – the mechanism of accountability – is effective, how should efficacy be defined? On the one hand, those involved in the practices within the CIA observe that efficacy of oversight means appropriate internal *control* over intelligence activities, limiting outside intervention, while some view external oversight as providing transparency and external accountability to the other branches of government and to the public. Leaking and the statutory IG both provide a bridge across this definitional divide. I argue that leaking challenges both internal and external accountability. These two aspects of accountability are, however, divided by the obvious division: that of legality.

Prior to the Snowden leaks, the most famous example of leaking to the press based on disagreement with governmental policy position was, of course, Daniel Ellsberg, then of the RAND Corporation, who leaked what became known as the Pentagon Papers to the *New York Times*. His trial under the Espionage Act ended in acquittal due to prosecutorial misconduct. NSA employee Thomas A. Drake, who leaked information on an NSA program, was originally accused – also under the Espionage Act – of sneaking documents out of the NSA in order to leak them to *Baltimore Sun* journalist Siobhan Gorman.[57] The case was ultimately settled when a judge required that classified information to be used as evidence by the NSA be released to the public. Rather than expose the information, the NSA withdrew its exhibits, causing the prosecution to collapse. Drake eventually pled guilty to a misdemeanor of misusing a government computer to provide information to an unauthorized person.[58]

The Drake case brings up a host of issues bearing on the trade-off between transparent legal procedure and protected national security

[57] Jane Mayer, "The Secret Sharer: Is Thomas Drake an Enemy of the State?" *New Yorker*, May 23, 2011.
[58] Ellen Nakashima and Jerry Markon, "NSA Leak Trial Exposes Dilemma for Justice Department," *Washington Post*, June 10, 2011.

material, as well as the balance between an employee's required loyalty to the government and agency, and personal views of responsibility and rectitude that may deviate from this requirement. Further, there are different types of leaks – those that expose abuses and waste in government, and those that knowingly expose national security information. The problematic ethics of drawing all of these comparisons was highlighted during the WikiLeaks scandal, which did not release any material of strategic value, but succeeded in embarrassing many in the government. While DNI James Clapper stated that he did not think the releases were damaging to security, he did fear that a perceived lack of security of classified information could cause a chilling effect on the willingness of foreign services to share intelligence information with the United States.[59] Interestingly, the Obama administration, while professing support for whistleblowers, has prosecuted more leakers than all of the previous administrations combined.[60]

More currently, and more relevant to the issue of internal CIA control, senior CIA officer Mary O. McCarthy was alleged to have leaked information to *Washington Post* reporter Dana Priest regarding the secret CIA detention centers – or "black sites" – located in Eastern Europe.[61] The disclosures, which McCarthy ultimately admitted to providing Priest, were the basis for Priest's Pulitzer Prize–winning articles in the *Post*.[62] McCarthy was investigated and given a polygraph. Some, such as journalists David Johnson and Scott Shane, suggest that when the answers to the polygraph appeared questionable, she confessed to having leaked the material.[63] Others think that she decided to quit the security vetting process as it was under way. She was then fired, stripped of her clearances, and escorted from the building. Her case was then referred to the Department of Justice.[64] CIA spokesperson Paul Gimigliano explained the firing in a statement: "A CIA officer has been fired for unauthorized contact with the media and for the unauthorized disclosure of classified information. This is a violation of

[59] Interview with DNI James Clapper, January 25, 2011.
[60] Mayer, "The Secret Sharer."
[61] Interview with Charles E. Allen, September 22, 2011.
[62] See David Johnston and Scott Shane, "CIA Fires Senior Officer over Leaks," *New York Times*, April 22, 2006.
[63] Johnston and Shane, "CIA Fires Senior Officer over Leaks."
[64] Interview with Charles E. Allen, September 22, 2011.

the secrecy agreement that is the condition of employment with CIA. The officer has acknowledged the contact and the disclosures."[65]

Responses to the firing were varied, as would be expected. Some felt that McCarthy had a responsibility to report what she felt was wrong; others felt that individuals in sensitive positions should not take it upon themselves to choose what information should be published in the public media. An interesting fact that did *not* create a furor around those unfamiliar with internal CIA control mechanisms is that Ms. McCarthy was working for the inspector general, John Helgerson, at the time of the disclosure. The OIG is expected to be maintain a separate – and objective – stance from normal CIA operations. In addition, the discovery that McCarthy was a moderate supporter of the Democratic Party added a political dimension to the situation that was exploited widely in blogs, if not as overtly in the mainstream media.

Leaking of national security information to the public is clearly a fraught issue that focuses again on the disparity between the strength of internal control in contrast to external oversight measures. In two of the most publicized cases in recent history – Ellsberg and Drake – the prosecution erred or became hopelessly entangled in trying to balance national security constraints with process and individual rights. The McCarthy case did not lead to prosecution, but it did lead to immediate dismissal. I do not delve into a further analysis of the Snowden case within this context, as it remains to be seen whether he will be repatriated and if so what legal charges will be brought against him. If he does return to the United States to face censure, his case could provide an entirely new frontier to judicial decision making and national security leaks, not least because of the sheer magnitude of the documents Snowden took and his apparent willingness to disseminate them.

In all four of these cases, the information the leakers were trying to convey eventually made it into the public domain. In all four cases, the security agencies turned on those they felt had turned on them before evidence could be appropriately presented in court. Ellsberg's case has faded into storied history and the Watergate incident; Drake was hounded and discredited; McCarthy was fired and sidelined. Snowden could end up as a hero and martyr, or a prisoner of the federal government.

[65] Johnston and Shane, "CIA Fires Senior Officer over Leaks."

INTEGRATING CULTURE AND OVERSIGHT THROUGH
BOUNDARY SPANNING: INSPECTOR GENERAL OF CIA

The discussion of organizational culture throughout this chapter has highlighted the opacity, secrecy, and insider mentality of the CIA world. The Manichean worldview of the CIA is represented well by the story of the CIA inspector general. Because the IG is both insider and outsider, privy to secrets, meetings, and personnel off limits to the outside world, but simultaneously is responsible uniquely to the outside world, he or she holds a delicate position within the Agency. Further, in terms of the accountability framework, the statutory IG can contribute one aspect to internal accountability absent in the other realms of internal control mechanisms: internal autonomy.

With the Inspector General Act of 1978, statutory inspectors general were installed across federal agencies. Nominated by the president, confirmed by the Senate, and required to report to *both* the agency head and Congress, the holder of the position is unique in crossing the boundaries between the branches of government. Intended to be relatively independent, offices of inspectors general were established with the intention that they fight fraud, waste, and abuse.[66] The IGs' main responsibilities are grouped into four categories: conducting and supervising audits of agency programs and operations; providing leadership and coordination in support of improved economy, efficiency, and effectiveness of programs; preventing and detecting waste, fraud, and abuse in agency programs; and keeping the agency head and Congress fully informed and current about problems and recommended corrective action for these problems.[67] Section 5 of the original Inspector General Act, which governs reporting to agency heads and Congress, is key to this discussion. It requires that agency IGs submit semiannual reports to Congress that list agency audit details, problems, deficiencies, and

---

[66] Frederick M. Kaiser, "Statutory Offices of Inspector General: Past and Present," *CRS Report for Congress*, updated September 25, 2008, 1.

[67] Inspector General Act of 1978 (as amended), 5 USC APPENDIX – INSPECTOR GENERAL ACT OF 1978; Kaiser, "Statutory Offices of Inspector General," 1–2.

failures, in addition to proposed corrective action. The individual inspectors general are required to list what recommended corrective action had not been undertaken or completed, and also to report any matters referred to prosecutorial authorities and the results of any prosecutorial action.

Inspectors general are required to submit information on any "significant management decision" with which the inspector general disagrees.[68] This requirement is intensified when the IG discovers a serious problem and must report it to the agency head, who then has seven days in which to correct the problem and report to Congress.[69] The autonomy of the IGs' offices is guaranteed through a range of checks. In support of their responsibility to audit the agency and conduct investigations, for example, IGs have access to program records, information, and personnel. They can hire staff and issue subpoenas, and their activities are protected from outside interference. They report generally only to the heads of agencies, but the head may not prevent or hinder the activities of the office. Finally, to protect the independence of their roles, they are not allowed to take action in response to their own findings of malfeasance, but rather must pass recommendations on the agency heads.[70] Follow-up on the recommendations is guaranteed, or at least reinforced, by the reports to Congress regarding agency responses to criticism.

The Inspector General Act introduced several aspects of a new era in governance that stemmed at least partly from the political climate of that period. In the post-Watergate environment of a crisis in government legitimacy, independent authority was considered key to improved transparency. There was also a sense that had begun to develop throughout the 1960s that bureaucracies were cumbersome, wasteful, and opaque. These views contributed to the "government openness" legislation that began in the 1960s and continued into the 1970s, including the Freedom of Information Act (FOIA), the Government in the Sunshine Act, and a range of oversight measures.

---

[68] Inspector General Act of 1978 (as amended), 5 USC APPENDIX – INSPECTOR GENERAL ACT OF 1978 Sec. 5.

[69] Margaret J. Gates and Marjorie Fine Knowles, "The Inspector General Act in the Federal Government: A New Approach to Accountability," *Alabama Law Review* 36 (1985): 473.

[70] Kaiser, "Statutory Offices of Inspector General," 2.

Like most broad developments in intelligence governance, the creation of a strengthened IG CIA has roots in the 1970s investigations of intelligence abuses. With the argument that national security concerns made a statutory IG inappropriate, the CIA had been originally exempt from the requirement when the IG Act was passed. There had actually been a CIA IG since 1952, but the IG was chosen from upper-CIA management by the DCI and it reported directly to the DCI. The IG had limited freedom and certainly no requirement to report internal activities to any external body.[71] It is interesting to note that the CIA was exempted from this step toward accountability at exactly the same time that intelligence oversight mechanisms were being established in the legislative and judicial branches. The House and Senate intelligence committees were established in 1977 and 1976, and 1978 marks the year that the Foreign Intelligence Surveillance Act (FISA) was passed and instituted in the judiciary. Internal CIA intransigence on a statutory IG was apparently mirrored by congressional reluctance to press the CIA on this sensitive matter. This can be seen in the brief legislative history regarding the act.

One commission and two committees charged with investigating the intelligence abuses of the 1950s through the 1970s – the Rockefeller Commission, the Pike Committee, and the Church Committee – recommended strengthening the role of the inspector general with intelligence agencies in light of their findings, but this was not actually done in the CIA until after the Iran-Contra scandal of 1988. The congressional committee that investigated the Iran-Contra scandal concluded that the scandal could have been averted if the IG had had appropriate "authority and independence from the director and the administration to follow the trail where it led."[72] In its investigation of the IG of that period, the Rockefeller Commission pointed out that the IG had only five staffers and its purview as well as its access to internal information was limited.[73] The commission also remarked on the fact

---

[71] L. Britt Snider, *The Agency and the Hill: CIA's Relationship with Congress, 1946–2004* (Washington, DC: Center for the Study of Intelligence), 147.

[72] Frederick P. Hitz, *Why Spy? Espionage in an Age of Uncertainty* (New York: Thomas Dunne), 96.

[73] Rockefeller Commission Report, 88–9. See also L. Britt Snider, "Creating a Statutory Inspector General at the CIA," *Studies in Intelligence* 44 (2001): 88.

the role of the IG varied, depending on the wishes of the director, and the size of the IG's office was a reflection of the director's view on how much oversight power the office should be granted as well as how much faith he felt should be placed in the agency's chain of command.[74] At the time of the Rockefeller Commission's investigation – 1975 – the IG's office had, in fact, recently been reduced from fourteen to five staff members, forcing it to desist in conducting one of its primary tasks, that of component review. Even when the staff had had a larger complement, component reviews were conducted only every three to five years, and, the report points out, the staff was not always granted access to the appropriate information in order to conduct a complete review. The director, in fact, as the report pointed out, could grant waivers for specific materials he did not wish to be provided to the inspector general's office.

The Church Committee noted a similar but wider range of issues with regard to the efficacy of the CIA inspector general's office. The main contention according to its findings was that the IG had not been granted access to important information and had therefore been limited in its ability to conduct thorough investigations. In terms of recourse, its recommendations had been in ignored, and it in turn was not making regular reports to the attorney general regarding suspected illegal acts.[75] The Pike Committee, for its part, expanded on the Senate recommendations and suggested the creation of an inspector general with jurisdiction over the entire intelligence community.[76] The committee's recommendation was for an increase in size, as well as an increased reporting requirement, mandating that its reports be provided to other executive branch offices, such as the National Security Council.[77]

While pressure built in Congress for the installation of the new independent role, fundamental tension was exhibited by DCI William

---

[74] Rockefeller Commission Report, 88.

[75] Church Committee, Book I, 294–304, 394, 460–1; Book II, 333–5. Snider, "Creating a Statutory Inspector General at the CIA."

[76] U.S. Congress, House of Representatives, Select Committee on Intelligence, *Recommendations of the Final Report*, House Report No. 94–833, 94th Congress, 2nd Session (GP: Washington, DC, 1976), 6.

[77] Snider, "Creating a Statutory Inspector General at the CIA"; Rockefeller Commission Report, 88–9, 94.

H. Webster's arguments against the need for a statutory IG. Among them was the claim that the Agency *could* be trusted. He argued that the CIA could police itself and stated so vehemently in testimony before Congress. His argument was that Congress should trust the internal control already brought by a nonstatutory IG.[78] This strenuous argument in the wake of a bruising political scandal suggests several things: first, that there was anxiety about the increased power and transparency that a statutory IG would bring to the CIA; second, that there was still benefit to arguing that the Congress, and thus also the public, should trust the CIA categorically even though all branches of government were engaged in building institutions to oversee and constrain intelligence activities at that time; and finally, that there was still a firm belief that the organizational culture of the CIA was strong enough to maintain the appropriate level of discipline without external intervention.

Particular attention should be paid to the genesis of the position of statutory IG in the CIA and its emergent role in the network of oversight mechanisms. The political complexities that led to the creation of the role exhibit prescient dynamics in terms of the oppositional relationship that will be discussed in depth in the next chapter of the book, as well as in terms of the accountability framework that is core to the relationship. The controversy touches upon several separate themes that run throughout the history of intelligence oversight in the United States, such as executive privilege, executive information ownership, and independent oversight. Finally, and a raw vulnerability for the Agency, the role of statutory IG creates a scenario in which insider knowledge is required to be reported in full to an outside audience. This breaks down the secret system that has developed between the intelligence community and its overseers. The position spans the boundaries of the organization with the outside world.

The concept of boundary spanning is introduced in some depth in the organization theory literature, the contours of which are worth investigating briefly here. Internal control requires that the units of an organization be subordinate to that organization.[79] The boundary-spanning

---

[78] Interview with Charles E. Allen, October 5, 2010.

[79] James D. Thompson, *Organizations in Action: Social Science Bases of Administrative Theory*, 4th printing (New Jersey: Transaction, 2006), 66. This classic, originally published in 1967, laid the foundations for the assessment of boundary spanning activity.

position requires not only that the expectations of the internal universe be met, but also that external objectives be reached. "The crucial problem for boundary spanning units of an organization ... is not coordination (of variables under control) but *adjustment* to constraints and contingencies not controlled by the organization – to what the economist calls exogenous variables."[80] A traditional concept behind the boundary spanner is that the position functions to bridge the gap to the outside world. The boundary spanner represents the organization to the outside world, but also protects the key internal functions of the organization; in the term of art, the position protects the technical core. To protect internal operations, the boundary spanner filters information from the external environment to avoid destabilizing internal processes and, accordingly, distributes appropriate levels of information outward.[81] In some cases, boundary spanners are used to enhance the legitimacy of an organization. An example of such an organization might be a prestigious board of directors or a law enforcement community outreach program. In other instances, boundary spanners are responsible for more mundane tasks that support the organization's effort, such as purchasing or recruiting.[82]

Openness to boundary spanning, the number of personnel in the position, and the responsibilities of the position vary across types of organization, tasks, and organization size. A further cause of role differentiation is technology, with different types of technology being buffered to varying to degrees. Openness to the external world varies depending on the type of technology being used by the organization.[83] The classic three types of technology in an organization are *long-linked* – meaning sequential, such as an assembly line; *mediating*, the bringing together of different parties; and *intensive*, the complex engagement of multiple parts.[84] Why are these classifications meaningful for the current project? Intelligence is clearly an *intensive* technology. It requires the concurrent and full integration of a multiple moving

[80] Thompson, *Organizations in Action*, 667.
[81] Howard Aldrich and Diane Herker, "Boundary Spanning Roles and Organization Structure," *Academy of Management Review* 2 (April 1977): 218.
[82] Aldrich and Herker, "Boundary Spanning," 220.
[83] Aldrich and Herker, "Boundary Spanning," 222.
[84] Thompson, *Organizations in Action*, 16–17.

parts. According to the theory, intensive technology is the most avidly defended from external forces. This is certainly the case when it comes to the intelligence enterprise. Linking this back to the section on the framework criteria, internal autonomy creates an interesting analytical problem. The literature hypothesizes that organizations using intensive technology will separate those involved in boundary spanning from the technical core.[85] We see this occur with the position of inspector general, but we also see an entire network of complexity regarding that position, both in terms of the organization theory literature and the internal culture of the CIA. The reasoning behind introducing the concept drawn from the literature is to reinforce how strong the difference between internal and external worlds is within the intelligence community and thus to show how different a boundary spanner operates within that context in contrast to the "regular" organizational paradigm. The regular organization relies on the boundary spanner for mediation, prestige heightening, and other forms of internal bolstering; the boundary spanner in the CIA – the statutory IG – is reviled by many, considered untrustworthy by others, and in some cases seen as illegitimate.

Briefings to Congress on regular intelligence matters can be organized to control and limit information dissemination; the statutory IG is required by law to report any internal transgression. I must add here that I do not assert that the CIA lies or obfuscates intentionally in these cases. Rather, I think management tries hard to provide the information deemed appropriate for the oversight committees to receive so that they may engage in their supervisory responsibilities. The matter comes down to a question of a culture of control of information and the inherent asymmetry of information among the branches of government regarding intelligence. Naturally, then, drawing upon a deep cultural inheritance of intense secrecy, the Agency feels far more comfortable controlling any aperture that could allow information flow, and the position of statutory IG conflicts with every aspect of this desire for opacity. This is particularly the case because inspectors general, usually chosen from within the ranks of the Agency, are expected to report on the activities of their own.

---

[85] Aldrich and Herker, "Boundary Spanning," 223.

Ultimately it was the drive of two senators, John Boren (D-OK) and Arlen Specter (R-PA), in the wake of the Iran-Contra scandal, that proved decisive in the creation of a statutory IG in the CIA. When the scandal came to light in 1986, the IG joined the numerous other investigations of the malfeasance. While the office produced a report, it apparently paled in comparison to the other lengthy and detailed investigation reports of the time, leading Congress to assert that the IG was understaffed and otherwise ill equipped to conduct thorough investigations.[86] Thus began the debates to remove CIA's exception from the Inspector General Act, forcing the Agency to comply with this boundary spanning oversight mechanism. While far down on the list of the institutional changes recommended during that period, the statutory IG became somewhat of a pet project for Senator Specter. Senator Boren originally had some misgivings about this position, concerned that it could pose a hindrance to CIA operations, as well as disturb the balance of oversight mechanisms in *favor* of the internal mechanism and away from congressional control.[87] An unenthusiastic Boren, responding to a very stubbornly anti-IG DCI Webster, decided that rather than enforce a statutory IG immediately, he would take Webster's assertions of CIA cooperation at face value and allow him to self-monitor. He was ordered to produce reports to the committees on the activities of the IG's office, including when the DCI himself interfered in any way with the IG's activities.[88] Faced with entirely inadequate reports from the CIA and potential alternative legislation from Senator John Glenn (D-OH), Boren acted to introduce legislation to install a statutory IG and to make sure that the CIA IG reported to the intelligence committees. After some negotiation, the bill was signed on

---

[86] U.S. Congress, House Select Committee to Investigate Covert Arms Transactions with Iran and the Senate Select Committee on Secret Military Assistance to Iran and the Nicaraguan Opposition, *Report on the Iran-Contra Affair*, House Report No. 100–433; and Senate Report no. 100–216, 100th Congress, 1st Sess (Washington, DC: GPO, 1987), 425. Quoted in Snider, "Creating a Statutory Inspector General at the CIA"; Rockefeller Commission Report, 88–9, 94.

[87] Snider, "Creating a Statutory Inspector General at the CIA," 95. Interview with L. Britt Snider, July 28, 2010. It should be pointed out here that Snider not only served as general counsel on the Senate Select Committee on Intelligence (SSCI), but also was the second statutory inspector general (CIA).

[88] Interview with L. Britt Snider, July 28, 2010.

November 30, 1989. There was still congressional anxiety regarding an independent IG by virtue of the fact that the IG was not originally granted subpoena power under this legislation; this power was granted, to match the powers of other federal IGs, only in 1998.[89]

Installation by statute, confirmation by the Senate, and responsibility to both Congress and CIA management did not bring an end to complications surrounding the role of the CIA inspector general. The IG crosses every sacred cultural boundary established by the CIA, but is bestowed with methods of recourse and internal autonomy, two key factors in the maintenance of appropriate accountability. As an employee of the CIA, the IG has responsibility for monitoring the internal activities of the Agency. This includes supporting the D/CIA in facilitating good management, advising the D/CIA, attending high-level staff meetings, and sharing information and coordinating with other offices within the CIA. In terms of thorough oversight, the CIA IG has the main prerogatives of internal access to personnel, materials, and exigencies, while also bringing an awareness of internal culture and normative expectations in terms of performance.[90]

The responsibilities of the statutory inspector general are divided into three areas: audits, inspections, and investigations.[91] These correspond to those areas put forth in the original Inspector General Act. Audits and routine surveys are not a serious problem to most CIA officers; investigations are a different issue altogether.[92] Audits are, as the name suggests, regular checks to ascertain whether components are using funds appropriately. Surveys are slightly more complex, requiring that the OIG conduct in-depth investigations on performance levels of the various components, whether that is a division, another domestic unit, or an overseas station. The role of the survey is to review performance as well as assess local grievances among officers. According to senior CIA officials, the survey is a management

---

[89] House Report 105–350, Committee Reports, 105th Congress. Section 402, matched in both House and Senate, granting the IG (CIA) subpoena power.

[90] Interview with a former CIA official, September 17, 2010.

[91] Interview with former inspector general John L. Helgerson; interview with a former chief of station, March 1, 2011.

[92] Interview with General Michael Hayden, March 9, 2011; interview with a former chief of station, March 1, 2011. Interview with a former case officer, March 1, 2011.

tool intended to assess performance but also to understand morale and any other potential problem among personnel.[93]

The key point of friction, of course, is the fact that in addition to internal management responsibilities, the IG provides an additional stream of information to the congressional oversight committees, as the position also involves statutory requirements mandating that the IG report biannually to Congress. Thus, the IG introduces an interesting dynamic of "dual reporting" between the CIA and Congress. This additional stream of information is important; as one former CIA officer – who had served in both the OIG and OGC – commented, Congress has a very limited oversight capability.[94] Put another way, congressional oversight committees rely on the IG because the committees have responsibility for far too much and have short attention spans; it is impossible for them to conduct oversight in depth. From the perspective of the IG, this relationship is fundamental to the independence of the IG, as congressional committees help guide investigations and protect IG independence.[95]

Dual reporting has proven to be a major point of contention in the network of oversight responsibilities, because the IG actually transcends the demands of internal loyalty drawn from CIA culture. The director (formerly the DCI) has traditionally been the point person on dealings with Congress, but the IG contributes a secondary stream of information and a resource from which Congress can demand briefings and explanations. This dual-reporting requirement is extremely controversial. Former CIA director Michael Hayden argues that dual reporting, which requires that the IG report internal CIA matters to Congress biannually, is a violation of managerial control and he even questions how this might be consistent with the separation of powers.[96] He questions how one position can be responsible to two branches. On the other hand, many argue that the IG, having access

---

[93] Interview with a former chief of station, March 1, 2011. Interview with Peter Earnest, former National Clandestine Service officer, IG inspector, and currently director of International Spy Museum, March 8, 2011.

[94] Interview with a former CIA officer, September 17, 2010.

[95] Interview with former IG John L. Helgerson, September 29, 2010.

[96] Interviews with a senior CIA officer, October 27, 2010, November 8, 2010; interview with Michael Hayden, March 11, 2011; personal communication with Michael Hayden, November 22, 2014; interview with DNI James Clapper, January 25, 2011.

to internal information and sources as well as access to the Hill, holds an extremely important role with regard to intelligence oversight – perhaps somewhat more pertinent and penetrating than congressional oversight.[97] I would argue that the autonomy of the IG's office is key to its efficacy, and the dual-reporting requirement is symbolic of this independence, which is crucial to internal accountability. I would also suggest that although there is significant independence in the role, anyone determined to cross the boundaries of oppositional loyalty is likely to conflict with CIA's internal administration.

In reviewing how the CIA IG compares to other statutory IGs in most "regular agencies," the main point of control that the D/CIA exerts over the autonomy of the IG is the agency head's right to prevent the IG from conducting an audit or investigation for specified reasons, such as due to national security concerns or because the investigation could harm an ongoing criminal investigation. The director of the CIA is one of six agency heads to have this right, but he or she must notify the House and Senate intelligence committees within seven days of having halted an IG investigation.

While the aforementioned functions tend to be rather conventional and bureaucratic, it is the investigative responsibility of the OIG that tends to catalyze anxious responses among CIA officers.[98] This is a function of many variables, not least the institutional cultural differences among the other divisions, particularly between DI, responsible for analysis, and DO (now National Clandestine Service, or NCS), responsible for covert action and other activities, such as those involving paramilitary projects. Internally, there has continued to be resentment about the IG's role among the directorates. One former IG investigator argues that this is because the IG is viewed as both external and ineffective.[99] This same investigator pointed out that the Agency culture allowed for very little patience with activities that were perceived to distract from the mission at hand, and that taking time to participate in an IG investigation was distracting and a hindrance to effective intelligence work. Other case officers view the IG as having a

---

[97] Interview with a former CIA officer, October 8, 2010.

[98] A unifying factor among all of the operations subjects (DO, now NCS) I interviewed was the emotional and somewhat aggrieved response to OIG investigations.

[99] Interview with a former CIA officer, April 11, 2011.

particular vendetta against the National Clandestine Service. A former CIA attorney pointed out that the reality of the IG's office was lost careers and indictments.[100]

It is clear that the IG is still a source of controversy and friction when it comes to internal oversight of intelligence. In theory, the dual-track reporting and unique boundary spanning capability of the OIG should lend it a degree of independence and the necessary autonomy; in actuality, this has not proven to be the case. This was demonstrated by a series of clashes between former director Hayden and the IG during his tenure, John L. Helgerson. The relationship between Hayden and Helgerson highlights a range of issues that go beyond oversight but also are relevant to an understanding of the culture of the CIA. The original catalyst for the friction was the investigation by Helgerson's office into the shooting down of a U.S. missionary plane in Peru. The investigation lasted seven years and was considered by the National Clandestine Service a targeted attempt to discredit CIA operators. Helgerson was seen as having a vendetta against the NCS. Other complaints about Helgerson included his "prosecutorial mentality" and his second-guessing of legal decisions made by the Office of General Counsel, which led to uncertainty, a drop in institutional morale, and risk aversion.[101] In the words of a watchdog organization that researches inspectors general:

> ... The now-departing IG at CIA has managed to focus on sensitive and controversial issues – programs whose scrutiny did not win the IG any love from his agency – that go to the agency's fundamental mission and let the American people know what is being done in their name. For instance, the CIA IG investigated the Agency's interrogation methods for alleged terrorists; issued a blistering report on its failure to prevent or warn about the attacks of September 11, 2001; and issued a report on the circumstances surrounding the shoot-down of a U.S. missionary plane over Peru, based on CIA officers' mistaken identification of the aircraft, and the subsequent cover-up.[102]

---

[100] Interview with a former CIA attorney, April 21, 2010.

[101] Walter Pincus, "Lawmakers Criticize CIA Director's Review Order," *Washington Post*, October 13, 2007.

[102] POGO,. *Inspectors General: Accountability Is a Balancing Act* (Washington DC: POGO, 2008), 20. For the IG report on the 9/11 attacks, see Central Intelligence Agency, Inspector

The mistaken shoot-down was followed by Helgerson delving into even more controversial Agency operations, such as investigations into the CIA program on detention, interrogation, and rendition methods that continues to be a serious issue. For example, in one report Helgerson argued that interrogation procedures authorized by the CIA might violate some provisions of the International Convention against Torture. In addition to the concerns involved with potential violations of international law, Helgerson also pointed out that the techniques could expose CIA officers to legal liability.[103] While the issues themselves are still very sensitive, the major grievance directed toward Helgerson by Agency operatives was that his methods were viewed as unfair and particularly unfairly directed at the clandestine side of Agency operations.[104]

The friction between the OIG and other components of the CIA came to a head in 2007, when General Hayden launched an internal management review of the OIG. Conducted by a senior aide to Hayden, Robert L. Deitz, the review – all of the individuals involved in the proceedings took pains to remark that it was not an investigation or a probe, but rather a "management review" – was quite controversial. The investigation caused a minor uproar within Congress and among others familiar with the IG process. In the words of the first CIA statutory IG, Frederick P. Hitz, "I think it's a terrible idea. Under the statute, the inspector general has the right to investigate the director. How can you do that and have the director turn around and investigate the IG?"[105] Hitz also pointed out that friction between the OIG and other components within the CIA is quite natural, including friction between

General, *OIG Report on CIA Accountability with Respect to the 9/11 Attacks: Executive Summary*, June 2005, publicly released April 2007. Available online at https://www.cia.gov/library/reports/Executive%20Summary_OIG%20Report.pdf (downloaded March 18, 2009); Central Intelligence Agency, Inspector General, *Key Unclassified Conclusions from CIA Inspector General Report: "(U)Procedures Used in Narcotics Airbridge Denial Program in Peru, 1995–2001,"* August 25, 2008. Available online at http://hoekstra.house.gov/UploadedFiles/Peru__Release__Key_Unclassified_Conclusions_from_CIA_Inspector_General_Report.pdf (downloaded March 6, 2009).

[103] Douglas Jehl, "Report Warned CIA on Tactics in Interrogation," *New York Times*, November 9, 2005.

[104] Mark Mazzetti and Scott Shane, "Watchdog of CIA Is Subject of CIA Inquiry," *New York Times*, October 11, 2007.

[105] Mazzetti and Shane, "Watchdog of CIA Is Subject of CIA Inquiry," *New York Times*, October 11, 2007.

the OIG and Office of General Counsel when the OIG contests specific legal decisions after the fact.[106]

Criticism from both Republicans and Democrats on the Hill suggested that the investigation – or review – could have a "chilling effect on Mr. Helgerson's independence."[107] Further, in the words of Representative Silvestre Reyes (D–TX), then chair of the House intelligence Committee, the investigation into the IG was "'troubling' because of its possible impact on the official's independence, which Congress established and will very aggressively preserve."[108] Senator Kit Bond (R-MO) supported this opinion by stating that Congress depends heavily on the IG to help oversee CIA activities, and that by reinforcing the IG's role, Congress would help ensure that the IG would "be watching carefully to make sure that nothing is done to restrain or diminish that important office."[109]

The ultimate outcome of the review was the installation of a series of internal procedures to protect individual officers during IG investigations. Among these measures, the position of ombudsman was created to listen to CIA officers' concerns as well as to ensure the fairness of internal agency investigations. Interviews must now be recorded, and a quality control officer has been installed in the office to make sure all evidence in each investigation is appropriately considered.[110] In response to the procedural changes to the IG's office, Senator Ron Wyden (D-OR) stated: "I'm all for the inspector general taking steps that help CIA employees understand his processes, but that can be done without an approach that can threaten the inspector general's independence."[111] Helgerson retired from the Agency in

[106] Mazzetti and Shane, "Watchdog of CIA Is Subject of CIA Inquiry," *New York Times*, October 11, 2007.

[107] Mark Mazzetti, "CIA Chief Defends Review on Agency's Inspector General," *New York Times*, October 23, 2007.

[108] Walter Pincus, "Lawmakers Criticize CIA Director's Review Order," *Washington Post*, October 13, 2007.

[109] Pincus, "Lawmakers Criticize CIA Director's Review Order," *Washington Post*, October 13, 2007.

[110] Mark Mazzetti, "CIA Tells of Changes for Its Internal Inquiries," *New York Times*, February 2, 2008.

[111] Mazzetti, "CIA Tells of Changes for Its Internal Inquiries," *New York Times*, February 2, 2008.

2009, to be replaced eventually by David Buckley more than eighteen months after Helgerson's departure. Buckley has since resigned from the CIA.

CONCLUSIONS

This chapter set out to provide a deeper understanding of what makes the institutional culture of the Agency important to those within it and by extension to understand how this internal view has an impact on external accountability. Further, it is key to understand how internal accountability develops differently from external and thus where weaknesses lie in both structures, particularly when it comes to *when* intelligence oversight occurs. The timeliness of the conduct of oversight – when it occurs in the cycle of development and conduct of an intelligence operation – is crucial to understanding the effectiveness of it. The fact that the executive branch has continual control and perfect information throughout the process of developing intelligence activities means that internal accountability remains strong in contrast to external oversight, which is reliant on executive information sharing and can generally conduct its strongest oversight only after the fact.

In terms of the accountability framework, internal accountability is strong on all fronts except for transparency, which should come as no surprise. It faces crisis only when confronted with an actor who has allegiances to both the internal ecosystem and the external world, such as the inspector general. This role challenges the strength of the secrecy environment that oversight mechanisms have created in tandem with the intelligence community. The statutory inspector general creates a new dimension in accountability as differentiated between internal and external accountability. This role provides great analytical traction on the conceptual understanding of accountability, but ultimately very little in terms of active internal control. I would argue, substantiated by the majority of intelligence officers I interviewed, that the inspector general trades off internal authority and legitimacy for autonomy and external validity. The role does not match the circumstances of external accountability in the face of a strong internal culture and set of control mechanisms. The boundary spanning institution is broken down too easily by both the strength of internal control and the weakness of external accountability. Beyond the IG, transparency as a criterion clearly comes into play when there is a political scandal or an intelligence failure and thus the intelligence community is forced to expose its activities to the outside world. Part of the fear of transparency on the part of insiders during these moments of scandal is because of a legitimate apprehension of being forced to take the blame. Lack of transparency can be quite useful when risky activities must be undertaken; the opacity provides cover. When this cover is removed, however, there are very few proponents of the CIA who will defend its operations in public. Essentially, this is a trade-off – perhaps an unfair one – between a level of freedom provided by the secrecy system and the open support of outsiders when failure occurs. The CIA has no other interest groups or constituencies that can defend its interests openly.

Further, the CIA is enmeshed in a community of sixteen other agencies, all of which interact and impact each other's work. Thus, even in an assessment of the CIA's internal institutional culture, the critiques of other agencies should be considered, allowing the CIA's function as well as its oversight to be understood in context. Other criticisms beyond the CIA and inclusive of the intelligence community overall have included a weak culture of collegiality and consensus within the community; balkanized, atomized, and overlapping organizations and tasks; group-think; and cherry-picking. The latter two are the most common criticisms regarding the analytical components.[112] Further inspections reveal the complexities of analysis in a state of constant information overload and failures of agency coordination and integration.[113] Finally, other organizational critiques include stovepiped information – that is, information that proceeds through the

---

[112] Philip H. J. Davies, "Intelligence Culture and Intelligence Failure in Britain and the United States," *Cambridge Review of International Affairs* 17 (2004): 503. See also Paul R. Pillar, "Intelligence, Policy and the War in Iraq," *Foreign Affairs* (March/April 2006); Peter Gill, "The Politicization of Intelligence: Lessons from the Invasion of Iraq," in *Who's Watching the Spies*, eds. Hans Born, Loch K. Johnson, and Ian Leigh. (Washington, DC: Potomac, 2005), 12–33; Richard K. Betts, *Enemies of Intelligence: Knowledge and Power in American National Security* (New York: Columbia University Press, 2007), 104–23.

[113] Davies, "Intelligence Culture," 507.

intelligence cycle within a specific intelligence discipline, potentially leaving out alternative explanations.[114] Ownership and delivery of the information are thus very limited and tend to play out in a competitive relationship among the intelligence disciplines. As can be noted from some of the aforementioned examples, an inordinate amount of time was spent assessing information-sharing failures and developing new approaches to interagency communication, with the intention of the commentary being to identify where efforts toward reform must be made. Indeed, several commentators have pointed out that there was no call for personal responsibility among the community or from the investigators appointed to clarify how the intelligence community failed to stop the attacks.

While many of the investigations into recent failures, such as the 9/11 and WMD (Silbermann-Robb) commissions, have tried to pinpoint blame, they have generally ended up with systemic critiques of the intelligence community overall. This means that rather than focusing on individual failures, criticism has been focused on failed connections among agencies, organizational cultures so diverse from one another that entirely different lexica and even software are used to perform similar tasks. Criticism has also focused on the complications of communication within this framework that have made achieving mutual interests impossible. Further, even when analytical failures are discussed, failures that could be seen as individual, the *culture* of the agency has been blamed in these analyses. Hamilton Bean notes, rightly, that criticism during the post-9/11 phase of investigations focused on system- or agency-level problems, never on the failure of particular individuals.[115] Focus on individual "failure," such as by the CIA inspector general on DCI Tenet and twelve other CIA officers met with severe resistance from both DCIs Porter Goss and Hayden. The 9/11 Commission, it has been argued, strenuously avoided any mention of personal responsibility.[116] *The 9/11 Commission Report*,

[114] Mark M. Lowenthal, *Intelligence: From Secrets to Policy*, 4th edition (Washington, DC: CQ Press, 2009), 77.

[115] Hamilton Bean, "Organizational Culture and US Intelligence Affairs," *Intelligence and National Security* 24 (2009): 483.

[116] See, among others, Philip Shenon, *The Commission: The Uncensored History of the 9/11 Investigation* (New York: Twelve, 2008).

for example, pointed to the limits that a failure to share information between the FBI and CIA placed on the effective transmission of key data prior to the attacks, attributing this failure to competing and incompatible organizational cultures; it also issued the damning "failure of imagination" critique, a thoroughly ambiguous and contemptuous statement.[117]

The issue of internal control of CIA activities is complicated *in stasis*, but additional questions are equally complicated, such as do and should these parameters shift to engage with a continually changing political environment and a set of emerging and evolving threats? One commentator referred to the development of intelligence oversight as the result of "fungible absolute rules"; the rules are in place until they must adapt to a new exigency.[118] Another intelligence officer who had served as a high-level legal counselor in two major intelligence agencies described the difference between private sector law and legal support of the intelligence mission by pointing out the difference in legal focus: in private practice, the attorney's objective is to limit risk by making sure the client stays well within the law. In bounding intelligence, the attorney provides the service of finding how close to the law the client may come before breaking it.[119] This means that as the threat adjusts, the functional constraints on intelligence activities adjust with it. This dynamic is the key to a holistic understanding of oversight. Oversight itself must be forced to adjust to the flexible culture and process of changing intelligence, which, in turn, must adjust to the exigencies of the demands of the threat environment. This is not, however, to suggest that oversight must be diluted or disempowered, but rather that the entire range of relationships between overseen and overseer must be considered when assessing the efficacy of oversight and thus the strength of accountability.

---

[117] *9/11 Commission Report*, see ch. 11, 339–60, for a specific list of criticism regarding the Intelligence Community's behavior leading up to the attacks on 9/11.

[118] Presentation by David G. Brooks, International Spy Museum, Washington, DC, February 7, 2011. While I find the phraseology odd here, the concept is very apt.

[119] Interview with a senior CIA official, November 8, 2010.

3 EXTERNAL ACCOUNTABILITY: THE DEVELOPMENT OF CONGRESSIONAL OVERSIGHT

> As far as Congress is concerned, oversight of the executive branch is motherhood. Oversight of the CIA is motherhood, apple pie, and the 4th of July wrapped into one.
>
> L. Britt Snider[1]

In the executive branch, accountability refers to internal mechanisms responsible for meeting presidential requirements in terms of support for foreign policy objectives, legality, and efficacy. Efficacy in this context is operational: does a specific project meet the particular needs of the executive, and is it legal? Does it fit within the broader panorama of foreign policy requirements and objectives? What could the consequences be if the project fails? What collateral damage could there be from the program?[2] In the early years, it was also asked whether the program could be traced to the president or whether that particular connection could be denied if the program were discovered – in intelligence terms, plausible deniability. Within the CIA itself, internal accountability focuses on internal authority, requiring formal internal hierarchy; established bureaucratic processes; recourse; and, finally, internal autonomy of the mechanism. These processes are in place to constrain the behavior of personnel to align with internal expectations and the overall objective of the CIA's mission. These processes

---

[1] Quote from *Creating a Statutory Inspector General at the CIA* (Washington, DC: CIA, 2001). Available online at https://www.cia.gov/library/center-for-the-study-of-intelligence/kent-csi/vol44no5/html/v44i5a02p.htm.

[2] These questions reflect those asked of the developers of covert projects by internal program reviewers.

are locked firmly in a hierarchical chain of accountability that leads to the director. The one role deviating from this hierarchy is that of the inspector general, statutorily independent from this chain but also responsible to it. External accountability, the focus of this chapter, explores the development of congressional oversight mechanisms that hold the intelligence community responsible for its actions; serve as information conduits for intelligence information among the intelligence community, Congress, and the public; and serve as a check on the activities of the intelligence services.

This friction in the relationship between the executive branch and Congress is one reason oversight has developed incrementally and unevenly, and why it continues to function at a level that is suboptimal. I term this dynamic process *oppositional oversight* – the tension between the branches serving as the *driver* for change in oversight mechanisms, and also, potentially, as a source of credibility in terms of the oversight mechanisms in the legislative branch. Oppositional oversight as a model for interaction highlights how the two branches use specific asymmetric tools to leverage their strengths. For example, the executive manipulates information control as the owner of intelligence, while the legislative branch uses the strengths of its institutions: not only the appropriations process, but also publicity and the public as a lever for gain. The effect is complex, dynamic, and *lasting*. We continue to see the same types of oppositional manipulations used now as we saw in the very earliest years of earnest congressional oversight of intelligence.

To understand the development of external accountability, I will divide what I define as the necessary characteristics of effective accountability into five categories: knowledge conditions; organizational complexity; autonomy; temporality; and transparency. I will explain how external accountability functions in practice and then describe the development of legislative oversight mechanisms, gauging how change affects each of these categories and providing a snapshot of the mechanisms at a series of pivot points. Whereas internal accountability remains relatively robust, external accountability has tended to break down time and again. Overall, this latter problem is due to the inherent information asymmetry that exists between the intelligence community and the external world. In this context, I seek to focus on which of the five categories of accountability are challenged and how this occurs at each pivot point. Doing so will provide not only a more granular view of development, but also allow for more refined and specific prescriptions for change. Change in the relationship between the overseer and the "overseen" is driven by a need to "rebalance" the asymmetry that characterizes the relationship. The friction in this relationship drives development of the oversight mechanism.

LEGISLATIVE OVERSIGHT: HISTORY AND DEVELOPMENT

The National Security Act of 1947, which created the Central Intelligence Agency, also required that the president keep Congress "fully and currently informed of the intelligence activities of the United States, including any significant anticipated intelligence activity ...."[3] Congressional oversight reinforces the ideal view that elected representatives stand in for the public and support their interests, a particularly important task when matters are technical, secret, and ostensibly crucial to national security. It is institutionalized and formal and represents a clear and established example of the balance of powers. Congressional oversight is also responsible for authorizing programs and activities and appropriating funds for them. This long-established *modus operandi* notwithstanding, criticisms of the intelligence community in the wake of 9/11 and the subsequent steps toward reorganization, including the addition of a new agency and the transformation of existing agencies, have all challenged the traditional structure and expectations regarding congressional oversight of intelligence. These changes, as well as the challenges of an emergent threat that requires unorthodox tactics, have increased the pressure to maintain the accountability of the intelligence community to the rest of the government and to the public it serves.

The concept that national security is the purview of the executive is deeply embedded in American culture and governance. Adherence to the "deference theory," the convention that the other branches of

---

[3] 50 U.S.C. § 413 (b) (2006). The National Security Act of 1947, as amended.

government defer to the executive on issues of national security, has been the norm since the founding of the republic and provides the basis for the oppositional concept I am introducing here. Since that time, custom has provided that decision making on foreign policy and security rests in the hands of the chief executive and that intelligence activities are core to both of these functions. The upheavals of the 1970s, however, provided a political context in which the engrained tradition of the exceptionalism of national security issues – with mystery surrounding intelligence activities deeply culturally entrenched – could be challenged. For the first time, secret government activities were considered something to which the public could or should have access. From World War II to 1972, warrantless surveillance conducted by the executive went both unquestioned and unsupervised, so the shift that took place in the 1970s was momentous.[4]

The current form of active, institutionalized intelligence oversight was a direct reaction to the political upheavals and uncertainty of the 1970s. The Vietnam War, public outrage in response to the Watergate scandal, and President Nixon's perceived political misuses of both "national security" and "executive privilege" had, by 1974, created both a charged political environment and a skeptical public attitude toward government.[5] When, in late 1974, revelations emerged of long-term intelligence activities that had not only crossed boundaries of legality but had also focused on the American population, the result was widespread public uproar.[6] In the words of former DCI William Colby: "All the tensions and suspicions and hostilities that had been building about the CIA since the Bay of Pigs, and had risen to a combustible level during the Vietnam and Watergate years, now exploded."[7] The challenge to the sanctity of intelligence operations demonstrated how immediate public reaction could affect the policy

---

[4] Barbara Ann Stolz, "The Foreign Intelligence Surveillance Act of 1978: The Role of Symbolic Politics," *Law and Policy* 24 (2002): 274.

[5] Athan Theoharis, *Spying on Americans: Political Surveillance from Hoover to the Huston Plan* (Philadelphia: Temple University Press, 1978), 9.

[6] Seymour Hersh, "Huge CIA Operation in US against Antiwar Forces, Other Dissidents in Nixon Years," *New York Times*, December 22, 1974.

[7] Colby quoted in Loch K. Johnson, *A Season of Inquiry: Congress and Intelligence* (Chicago: Dorsey Press, 1988), 11.

process regarding issues that had been seen as clearly out of public reach prior to that time.

Investigative journalist Seymour Hersh wrote in some detail of the CIA's involvement in domestic spying against U.S. citizens. The first sentence of his piece set the tone for public response: "The CIA, directly violating its charter, conducted a massive illegal domestic intelligence operation during the Nixon Administration against the antiwar movement and other dissident groups in the United States, according to well-placed government sources."[8] This was the first of several above-the-fold exposés of intelligence activities. Interestingly, the catalogued activities brought to public attention by Hersh's article had been collected and organized by the CIA itself in an effort to understand the depth of its involvement in the Watergate break-in.[9]

Determined to explore the depth of the CIA's involvement in Watergate, and in the midst of a deep reform of the Agency, Director of Central Intelligence James R. Schlesinger and Deputy Director for Operations (DDO) Colby had issued an order on May 9, 1973, requiring CIA employees to report "on any activities now going on, or that have gone on in the past, which might be considered outside the legislative charter of the Agency."[10] Further, they demanded to be informed if any employee received an order that appeared "in any way inconsistent with the legislative charter [NSA 1947]."[11] The DDO asked specifically for listings of events that could potentially have "embarrassment potential" for the Agency.[12] The submissions from CIA personnel were compiled by the inspector general into a 693-page document,

---

[8] Seymour M. Hersh, "Huge C.I.A. Operation Reported in U.S. against Antiwar Forces, Other Dissidents in Nixon Years." *New York Times*, December 22, 1974; Johnson, *A Season of Inquiry*, 11.

[9] The potential connection between the CIA and Watergate was through Howard Hunt, a former CIA employee, who by the time of the Daniel Ellsberg trial for release of the Pentagon Papers in April 1973 had already been convicted of the Watergate break-in. During the course of Ellsberg's trial, it was discovered that Hunt had been a member of the team that burglarized Ellsberg's psychiatrist's office.

[10] Memo from Schlesinger to CIA staff, quoted in Rhodri Jeffreys-Jones, *The CIA and American Democracy*, 3rd edition (New Haven, CT: Yale University Press, 2003), 191.

[11] Daniel L. Pines, "The Central Intelligence Agency's 'Family Jewels': Legal Then? Legal Now?" *Indiana Law Journal* 84 (2009): 641. See also CIA, *Family Jewels* 00418 (1973), available at at http://www.foia.cia.gov.

[12] *Family Jewels*, memorandum, May 15, 1973, 36.

classified, and titled the "Family Jewels" because the substance was considered sensitive and potentially damaging to the CIA if released outside of the Agency.[13] Included were previews of later revelations: descriptions of domestic surveillance, experimentation with drugs on unwitting subjects, surveillance of American journalists, and descriptions of CIA activities in conjunction with other domestic agencies. In a secret annex, the CIA's involvement in assassination attempts against foreign leaders was described.[14] While Schlesinger had ordered the assembling of the "Jewels," he had moved on to become secretary of defense by the time they were complete. His successor, Colby, was left to decide how they should be brought to congressional attention, particularly as he was coming up for confirmation as the new DCI.[15]

The creation of the "Family Jewels" raises an important point with regard to information control within the CIA. The CIA has Byzantine methods for handling information. Information is stored in separate streams within the Agency – the abused term "need to know" describes when an officer attains access to a specific set of data. Information is thus compartmented so that the fewest possible individuals have access to it. This process clearly complicates both internal and external oversight of CIA activities by making internal information opaque even to senior-level managers. This problem would arise again during the Iran-Contra scandal and is continual in terms of the categories included in my accountability framework.

In the face of the period's negative attitude toward intelligence, Colby felt that opening the "Jewels" would protect the CIA, protect his nomination, and hedge against further intrusion from external parties. A voluntary briefing also allowed the CIA to control what information was offered to Congress. Colby briefed senators John C. Stennis and Stuart Symington of the Senate Armed Services Committee and representatives Felix Hebert and Lucien Nedzi of the parallel House Armed Services Committee. Those briefed focused on whether such

[13] The inspector general (CIA) was not statutory at this point. The position was a part of the upper-management structure with no external reporting requirements.

[14] *Family Jewels*, 00418 (1973). William Colby, *Honorable Men: My Life in the CIA* (New York: Simon and Schuster, 1978), 340–2. Much of the literature documenting the CIA's drug experiments was destroyed internally in 1972.

[15] Colby, *Honorable Men*, 345.

activities existed only in the past and whether they would be allowed in the future.[16] Of all four men briefed, Representative Nedzi was the only individual to ask specific questions and to query whether the "Jewels" should be released to the public as a "catharsis of the past and a barrier against their repetition in the future."[17] Nedzi pointed out that at that time, there was little awareness of what the four members of Congress *should* do about the "Jewels" because there was no precedent for formalized congressional involvement in intelligence oversight at that time. In Nedzi's own words in 1973: "It is a bit unsettling that 26 years after the passage of the National Security Act of 1947, the scope of real congressional oversight, as opposed to nominal congressional oversight, remains unformed and uncertain."[18]

Prior to the establishment of the permanent oversight committees in 1976 and 1977, intelligence oversight responsibilities were placed in four subcommittees: the House and Senate Armed Services Committees and the House and Senate Appropriations Committees. These committees seldom met on intelligence issues, submitting the intelligence community to approximately twenty-four hours of "legislative 'probing' " in both House and Senate over the course of an entire year.[19]

In this case, the CIA found preemptive, controlled transparency a method by which to hedge what it viewed as excessive congressional investigation of a purely internal, executive agency matter. Indicative of this point, the seeming congressional unconcern at the time about the potential for scandal embodied by the "Jewels" was not matched by quietude on Colby's part. As DCI Colby later said, "The shock effect of an exposure of the 'Family Jewels', I urged, could, in the climate of 1973, inflict mortal wounds on the CIA and deprive the nation of all the good the agency could do in the future."[20] The "Jewels" would have a particularly strong impact because the CIA had very little public profile. As Colby mentions in his autobiography, if the revelations

---

[16] L. Britt Snider, *The Agency and the Hill: CIA's Relationship with Congress, 1946–2004* (Washington, DC: Center for the Study of Intelligence, 2008), 30–1.

[17] Colby, *Honorable Men*, 346.

[18] Quoted in Snider, *The Agency and the Hill*, 31.

[19] Johnson, *A Season of Inquiry*, 7.

[20] Quoted in Pines, "The Central Intelligence Agency's 'Family Jewels'," 642.

regarded the Army, the FBI, or a local police force, the public would have had a context for understanding these extreme activities. As it was, there was very little sense of what the CIA actually did and thus no real frame of reference for an observer exposed to such things for the first time.[21] While Colby's awareness of public reaction was reasonably astute, his own personal reaction to the content of the "Jewels" bears recounting in its original detail in order to provide a sense of the culture and leadership of the CIA at that time. The following passage from his autobiography further illustrates the continuing challenge of effective oversight of intelligence activities:

> And perhaps I revealed my own long career in, and resulting bias in favor of, the clandestine profession, when I concluded that this list of CIA misdeeds over twenty-five years was really not so bad. Certainly there were activities on it that could not be justified under any rule or by any rationalization, were outside CIA's proper charter, and were just plain wrong whether technically forbidden or not. But I was familiar with the procedures of other intelligence and security services in the world; was aware of the kind of encouragement and exhortations CIA received from government leaders and public alike during the Cold War, to be "more effective, more unique and, if necessary, more ruthless than the enemy"; knew the difficulty of enforcing disciplined behavior in an atmosphere of secrecy and intrigue; and knew personally some of CIA's more bizarre characters ....[22]

While the details of the "Jewels" were not personally scandalous to Colby, their exposure to the public was. Further, his sense that his agency was vulnerable and would be misunderstood by the public turned out to be correct. This sense of vulnerability penetrates internal discussions of CIA matters to the present – protective concern spikes uniquely and sensitively when scandal or failure occurs. The feeling of suspicion and mistrust that stems from external perceptions of the Agency and its activities runs in both directions – internally, officers feel that they must protect their closed society. This was highlighted when extracts drawn from the "Jewels" were published by Hersh, causing outrage and ultimately a general feeling to arise that the CIA

[21] Colby, *Honorable Men*, 342.
[22] Colby, *Honorable Men*, 341.

could no longer be trusted and particularly could not be trusted in its traditional autonomous role.[23] Watergate, of course, contributed to the anxiety that the intelligence community was at risk of manipulation for political ends – as it was generally unclear what role the CIA did, in fact, have in the break-in.[24] This is where the crucial role of covert action comes into play.

COVERT ACTION AND OVERSIGHT DEVELOPMENT

Covert action was only defined clearly three decades ago; thus the executive had used the ambiguity of the CIA's original charter up to that point to forge a mission for it – one clarified in terms of emerging need.[25] Regardless of the safeguards put in place to ensure that laws are not broken, that appropriate individuals are kept informed, and that Americans are not harmed by the action, at root covert action holds a quirky but virtually sacrosanct role in American foreign policy. This role has remained virtually untouched in practice, although external structures for notification of its use have been developed over the decades. This stability – while sound operationally – introduces a broad range of questions in terms of the role of covert action in a democracy, the dialectical tension between executive privilege and legislative oversight responsibilities, and the appropriate level of transparency of the United States government. The relationship between the executive and legislative branches regarding covert action has been core to the development of legislative oversight and fundamental to the safeguards regarding secrecy surrounding active intelligence.

The reasoning behind the importance of covert action is that it can remain unacknowledged publicly and thus can be a tool of exceptional

---

[23] Kirsten Lundberg, *Congressional Oversight and Presidential Prerogative*, Harvard Case Study C14-01-1605.0, 2001, 4. Ironically, the "Family Jewels" were released in their entirety by D/CIA General Michael Hayden in 2007 to signal greater openness and transparency of the Agency. There was very little public reaction to their substance.

[24] *Legislative Oversight of Intelligence Activities: The US Experience*, Report Prepared by the Select Committee on Intelligence, United States Senate, October 1994, 4.

[25] "[Covert action is] an activity or activities of the United States Government to influence political, economic, or military conditions abroad, where it is intended that the role of the United States Government will not be apparent or acknowledged publicly." NSA 503(c).

power. It is also active – that is, its purpose is to change a foreign political environment – and thus stands outside the frame of intelligence
collection, analysis, and dissemination that is core to the usual intelligence process. In terms of political resonance, it also is the type of intelligence activity that can end up on the front page of major newspapers,
obviously potentially embarrassing government leaders. Covert action
is defined as "an activity or activities of the United States Government
to influence political, economic, or military conditions abroad, where it
is intended that the role of the United States Government will not be
apparent or acknowledged publicly ...."[26]

Another description that addresses the operational detail of covert
action states: "It is a program of multiple, subordinate, coordinated,
interlocking intelligence operations, usually managed over a long period
of time, intended to influence a target audience to do something or
refrain from doing something, or to influence opinion (e.g., of the general public, business elites, or political or military leadership)."[27] Covert
action as a category can be further subdivided into propaganda (the dissemination of nonattributable communications to affect foreign political environments); political action (assistance to individuals or groups
in a foreign country – this could be through financial support, advice,
or other assistance); paramilitary assistance (providing secret military
assistance and advice to organizations or forces in foreign countries);
and secret intelligence support (security assistance to a foreign leader
to protect the leader and to protect the leader's government).[28]

Considered a method that cuts between diplomacy and overt military action, covert action has traditionally been a heavily relied-upon
tool for foreign policy decision makers.[29] In the words of Henry

---

[26] Definition in Intelligence Authorization Act of 1991, Pub. L. No. 102–88, 105 Stat. 429 (1991) §503(e).

[27] William J. Daugherty, *Executive Secrets: Covert Action and the Presidency* (Lexington: University of Kentucky Press, 2008), 12.

[28] These definitions are listed in William E. Conner, "Reforming Oversight of Covert Actions after the Iran-Contra Affair: A Legislative History of the Intelligence Authorization Act for FY 1991," *Virginia Journal of International Law* (32: 4, 1991–2), 877. The subdivision of the concept of covert action is drawn from the Church Committee Final Report, Bk 1 at 141, n.2, 445.

[29] John MacGaffin, "Clandestine Human Intelligence," in *Transforming U.S. Intelligence*, eds. Jennifer E. Sims and Burton Gerber (Washington, DC: Georgetown University Press, 2005), 83.

Kissinger: "We need an intelligence community that, in certain complicated situations, can defend the American national interest in the gray areas where military operations are not suitable and diplomacy cannot operate."[30] The reasons for this trend are relatively self-explanatory: covert action appears to allow a decision maker to cut through bureaucratic process while allowing for distance from the activity should the operation fail. It also can be designed to achieve specific, targeted missions, minimizing risk. Because of its flexibility and deniability, it has even been said that covert action became an "addiction" for some policy makers.[31] Further, as one scholar points out, it is not in the interest of the president to use restraint in terms of using covert action. In his words: "Once the hidden hand of the United States had been perceived in one event, it would be assumed to exist in every conceivable case, whether or not a particular president was observing a self-denying ordinance: if such a president did restore good faith, his successors, not he, would be the likely beneficiaries."[32]

Covert action utilizes the full range of human intelligence, including spies, militaries, aspects of the media, paramilitary activity, and more.[33] Many operations have had lasting political effects that have affected regional and international dynamics long after the immediate objective of the action was reached. Early actions with lasting impact include Operation Ajax, which overthrew President Mohammed Mossadegh, the democratically elected leader of Iran. Mossadegh nationalized British oil interests in the region and thus was overthrown through covert actions organized by the British and Americans. Heavily supported by the Americans, the Shah was brought back to head the government. The resulting backlash agreeably provided the groundwork for the rise of the Islamic Republic under Ayatollah Khomeini. Other cases include the overthrow in the 1950s of the government of Guatemala that seemed to be leaning left and, of course, the provision of weapons to the Afghan Mujahaddin during the Soviet war

---

[30] Henry Kissinger, *NBC Evening News* (1978), quoted in Loch K. Johnson, "Covert Action and Accountability: Decision-Making for America's Secret Foreign Policy," *International Studies Quarterly* 33 (March 1989): 82.

[31] Jeffreys-Jones, *The CIA and American Democracy*, 98.

[32] Jeffreys-Jones, *The CIA and American Democracy*, 98.

[33] MacGaffin, "Clandestine Human Intelligence," 84.

in Afghanistan, considered by some to be one of the most successful covert actions.

Other types of covert actions include bribery, attempts to influence elections, and the dissemination of political propaganda. More recently, of course, covert action has grown to include targeted killing by drone.[34] Drone attacks and the use of the CIA for paramilitary purposes are worth highlighting. While paramilitary activities have had a significant role in CIA activities, stemming back to the days when the CIA was the Office of Strategic Services during World War II, there are changing trends in the military use of intelligence officers that could potentially have a significant effect on the conduct of oversight. Covert actions are organized in manifold ways. Programs vary in length and level of risk. The programs can involve large numbers of individuals operating in multiple locations with a single central node, the hub-and-spoke model, or can be simpler, involving a small group focused on a single target.[35] While covert action now has the signal action of the killing of Osama bin Laden as exemplar, many of the programs last for years and are focused on achieving multiple and much more wide-ranging political objectives.

While clearly attractive to policy makers, covert action is a friction point between the executive and legislative branch and thus has led to the creation of increasingly stringent reporting requirements. Covert action is perceived to infringe on the territory of both branches and tends to push the boundaries of what constitutes legitimate government behavior.[36] Thus, covert action contributes to the constitutional tension regarding how power should be shared among the branches and is an inflection point where the asymmetric relationship among branches with regard to foreign intelligence arises. The CIA is the only U.S. agency *officially* permitted to conduct covert action – there are caveats to this that

---

[34] Loch K. Johnson, "Governing in the Absence of Angels," in *Who's Watching the Spies*, eds. Hans Born, Loch K. Johnson and Ian Leigh (Washington, DC: Potomac, 2005), 65. Political assassination has been illegal since 1976, but post-9/11 wartime authorities have authorized it, although questions of definition continue to plague legal analysis.

[35] Interview with Stephen R. Kappes, March 12, 2011.

[36] Americo R. Cinquegrana, "Dancing in the Dark: Accepting the Invitation to Struggle in the Context of 'Covert Action,' The Iran-Contra Affair and the Intelligence Oversight Process," *Houston Journal of International Law* 11 (1988–9): 181.

are discussed later in this book. This role was not explicitly defined by statute until the 1991 Intelligence Authorization Act; prior to this point, covert activity fell into a fifth directive – or "Fifth Function" – of the National Security Act (1947), which ordered the CIA "to perform such other functions and duties related to intelligence affecting the national security as the [NSC] may from time to time direct."[37]

According to Clark Clifford, an advisor to President Truman, this fifth function was left purposely ambiguous to provide room for unexpected contingencies. It also could be argued that it laid the groundwork for the plausible deniability originally built into the concept of covert action. Further, in his words, "We did not mention [covert actions] by name because we felt it would be injurious to our national interest to advertise the fact that we might engage in such activities."[38] Covert action introduces moral ambiguity; as stated by Senator Frank Church in reference to covert action: "I must lay the blame, in large measure, to the fantasy that it lay within our power to control other countries through the covert manipulation of their affairs. It formed part of a greater illusion that entrapped and enthralled our Presidents – the illusion of American omnipotence."[39] Further, "The moral issues attached to covert action are not unique, but they are sharper because of the presumption that the operation itself, not just the decision, can remain unconnected to the United States, thus suggesting that the larger moral questions might be evaded.[40]

While the public may not have been exposed to the activities of the intelligence community until the mid-1970s, Congress had already begun to consider tightening the oversight, at least, of covert action earlier in the decade. This nascent engagement with foreign policy issues included a range of statutes intended to bridge the gap between Congress and the executive branch on foreign affairs issues.[41] In terms

---

[37] 50 U.S.C. § 403(d) (1988).

[38] David F. Rudgers, "The Origins of Covert Action," *Journal of Contemporary History* 35 (2000): 249–62.

[39] Quoted in John Prados, *Presidents' Secret Wars: CIA and Pentagon Covert Operations since World War II* (New York: Morrow, 1986), 337.

[40] Gregory F. Treverton, *Covert Action: The Limits of Intervention in the Postwar World* (New York: Basic Books, 1987), 7.

[41] Harold Hongju Koh, *The National Security Constitution: Sharing Power after the Iran-Contra Affair* (New Haven, CT: Yale University Press, 1990), 46.

of covert action, in 1974 Congress amended the Foreign Assistance Act of 1961 with the Hughes-Ryan Amendment. This amendment required that the president produce a *finding* – a statement – for Congress regarding a potential covert activity asserting that the activity was in the national security interest of the United States.[42] The notification requirement of the Hughes-Ryan Amendment points to the beginning of the establishment of a framework among branches that would supervise and constrain intelligence activities and also lead to an oppositional and complicated relationship at once adversarial and complementary in terms of burden sharing. Hughes-Ryan was the first oppositional move on the part of Congress to claim a stake in the oversight process, forcing the president to be accountable for covert action. This was no small step, considering that the president had not been required to take responsibility for these activities in the past. The term of art for this disconnect between presidential orders for actions and accountability for them is called *plausible deniability*.

One of the most attractive aspects of covert action for any president has always been the freedom it gave him to deny knowledge of the activity, allowing him to distance himself from any scandal and shift the risk to the intelligence agency conducting the operation. Hughes-Ryan installed a firm, triangulated connection to monitor covert action. The connection included responsibility being shared among the CIA, the executive branch, and Congress. It also served to differentiate covert action from other types of intelligence activities. Hughes-Ryan clarified and made explicit the relationship between the president and the CIA, reinforcing the fact that the CIA responds to executive orders. In Loch Johnson's formulation: "The objective of plausible deniability was to brush away footprints in a covert operation to prevent anyone from following the tracks back to the United States and particularly to the Oval Office."[43]

Plausible deniability is still core to the concept of covert action, the sponsorship of which is not externally *owned* by those responsible for it. This disconnect between action and government is crucial

---

[42] Frederick P. Hitz, *Why Spy? Espionage in an Age of Uncertainty* (New York: St. Martins Griffin, 2009), 117.

[43] Johnson, *A Season of Inquiry*, 58.

in many cases to the success of the mission. Until the Hughes-Ryan Amendment, there had in fact been minimal *external* accountability regarding covert action to Congress. The requirements of Hughes-Ryan represent a first step, albeit a weak one, in the development of Congress as supervisor of intelligence activities. First, Hughes-Ryan required the executive to *inform* Congress of covert action – but Congress had no official *in-process* recourse to change activities of which it disapproved. That is, Congress could cut off funding for a particular program, but the process for doing so would be difficult to complete in a timely fashion, particularly given that there has always been ambiguity in terms of the required timeliness of reporting in relation to the commencement of the program. Further, achieving unanimity among U.S. representatives to do so would be difficult given partisanship and diverse ideological claims. An unofficial approach to ending a covert action could be to leak the matter to the press, but there has generally been a norm against doing so, and since leaking is unofficial, it does not have a role in our framework for institutionalized accountability. It should be remembered that Hughes-Ryan was passed prior to the installation of dedicated intelligence oversight committees. Its findings were distributed among six committees with minimal connection to and expertise in intelligence activities. Thus, in terms of knowledge conditions, expertise and focus were thin and variable. When the intelligence committees were established a few years later, the number of committees grew to eight. While a rather diluted step, Hughes-Ryan was instrumental in establishing institutional pathways to facilitate the mechanics of intelligence oversight. The pathways established not only a line of discipline for the relationship between the executive and legislative branches, but also a line that provided the future pathway of controversy and friction that would continue to challenge and catalyze the development of intelligence oversight mechanisms for decades.

Frederick Hitz, the first statutory inspector general of the CIA, makes an interesting point regarding Hughes-Ryan. In his view, the "Agency rank and file were pleased for the most part by the passage of the Hughes Ryan Amendment because it squelched subsequent chatter in the Church Committee that the CIA was a 'rogue elephant' operating on its own in covert action proceedings."[44] This trend toward greater control over intelligence issues was helped by a change of congressional generation – the older, veteran representatives who had conducted oversight informally via personal relationship were replaced by a new generation of young representatives eager to begin a post-Watergate political era by challenging the conventional independence of the CIA.[45] This shift was particularly acute in the House, where seventy-five new reformist members – "the Watergate class" – joined the chamber with a mission to change congressional process. A second change was a new congressional focus on foreign policy expertise in order for Congress to be more involved with the executive branch on foreign policy issues.[46] Both objectives on the part of freshmen representatives pointed toward an interest in rebalancing the traditional asymmetry with the executive in terms of foreign policy and national security.

The rationale for focusing so heavily on covert action within this chapter on the development of external oversight mechanisms within the legislative branch is manifold. First, covert action is an inflection point between the executive and legislative branches when it comes to foreign policy; second, in terms of oversight and control, covert action provides a crucial test of external oversight; third, the friction between external oversight and internal control are at their most manifest within the context of covert action; finally, it is within the realm of covert action that we see the clearest evidence supporting the main thesis of this book, which is that by engaging with mechanisms in the other branches, the executive branch provides an improved system of secrecy in order to protect its intelligence activities.

THE INVESTIGATIONS: PREEMPTIVE, PUBLIC, AND PURPOSEFUL

To understand the depth of intelligence agency malfeasance alleged by the Hersh articles, three investigatory committees were created – two

---

[44] Hitz, *Why Spy?*, 117.
[45] Snider, *The Agency and the Hill*, 49.
[46] Koh, *The National Security Constitution*, 45.

in Congress (one in each chamber) and one in the executive. Congress seized this evidence as proof that the executive branch required checking and took the opportunity to delve into its excesses, with the White House hoping to hedge against inopportune investigation. In 1975, the Pike Committee – originally the Nedzi Committee – was established in the House and the Church Committee in the Senate, while the White House set up the Rockefeller Commission. The three investigatory efforts focused on different aspects of the intelligence enterprise, although all three touched on the appropriateness and legality of intelligence activities. The Church Committee analyzed the range of alleged abuses, both foreign and domestic. Pike did not examine the abuses, but worked mainly on intelligence performance and effectiveness.[47] The Rockefeller Commission analyzed the CIA's role in domestic intelligence activities, as well as oversight and internal CIA control mechanisms.[48]

In terms of the oppositional relationship between Congress and the executive regarding intelligence oversight, the installation, process, and purview of the Rockefeller Commission is instructive. When it became clear that the fallout from the Hersh revelations was to lead to multiple investigations, President Ford acted to preempt invasive congressional inquiries by establishing his own investigatory mechanism. It was thought that responsive presidential reaction to the alleged abuses could curb the other investigations, demonstrate leadership, and allow the president to frame and control criticism. Executive branch views of the potential fallout of the revelations were extreme. In Kissinger's words: "If they come out, blood will flow."[49] The congressional committees' activities were striking because they explored intelligence activities in unprecedented depth, but the mere creation of the Rockefeller Commission was precedent-setting. The Rockefeller Commission marked the first time that a presidential commission had been created to investigate the national security apparatus.[50]

---

[47] Snider, *The Agency and the Hill*, 38.

[48] *Rockefeller Commission Report*, June 1975. See in particular chapters 7–8, 71–95.

[49] John Prados, *Safe for Democracy: The Secret Wars of the CIA* (Ivan R. Dee: Chicago, 2006), 433.

[50] Kenneth Kitts, "Commission Politics and National Security: Gerald Ford's Response to the CIA Controversy of 1975," *Presidential Studies Quarterly* 26, No. 4, Fall (1996): 1081.

Considerations were given as to how to define jurisdiction of the commission's investigations – DCI Richard Helms recommended that the
FBI be included in the White House investigations, but ultimately
President Ford decided that the focus should be on CIA only, and on
a narrow slice of CIA activities at that.

The Rockefeller Commission, under the leadership of Vice
President Nelson Rockefeller, was mandated to investigate alleged CIA
improprieties only *within* the United States. The outcome of the investigation was not far-reaching – or even soul-searching – but clearly an
attempt at an oppositional move to preempt external inquiry into the
activities of the CIA. As one scholar of presidential commissions put it,
"Behind-the-scenes maneuvering shaped the panel's activity throughout the investigation and even altered the content of the final report.
And long after the commission had disbanded, Ford continued to use
the commission's findings as a preemptive tool to argue against the
need for more external controls on the intelligence community."[51] In
further support of the importance of preemption in order to oppose
and limit congressional investigations, Ford asserted in his memoirs
that "unnecessary disclosure" would have been the result of a commission led by Congress.[52] Further, all recommendations from top aides
responsible for decision making regarding the commission mentioned
the need to preempt congressional action. One aide, Jack Marsh, stated
the need baldly. In his words, "The panel's efforts would take the initiative rather than finding ourselves whipsawed by prolonged congressional hearings."[53] Finally, as Colby reported it in his memoirs,
"I was then told that Ford was considering appointing a 'blue ribbon'
commission to conduct an investigation of CIA's domestic activities
to answer *The New York Times* charges, and hopefully to still the outcry and thus prevent a full investigation of intelligence from getting
started."[54]

With the objective of the Rockefeller Commission being to deflect
and/or mitigate critical congressional investigation of the intelligence
community, the outcome was unsurprising. The report focused on the

---

[51] Kitts, "Commission Politics and National Security," 1082.
[52] Kitts, "Commission Politics and National Security," 1083.
[53] Kitts, "Commission Politics and National Security," 1083.
[54] Colby, *Honorable Men*, 398.

history of the Agency and mildly addressed the major charges leveled. It recommended some reforms, such as strengthening the internal CIA oversight role of the inspector general, but the report itself
was considered a whitewash. I would suggest that the installation of
the Rockefeller Commission was a pure tactical oppositional move
that ultimately did not have much strategic bearing on hindering the
development of external oversight mechanisms. This failure to shut
down the congressional investigations was due to the unique political
environment of the time, as well as the deft use of public exposure
on behalf of the congressional committees – particularly Church – to
gain traction on reform. The congressional investigations of the 1970s
changed the environment surrounding intelligence and security issues
by exposing some of the more illegal and extreme programs, but also
by suggesting that deference to the security function must be kept
within bounds and implying that the security apparatus itself was part
of the normal functioning of democratic government. These results
were possible and plausible because of the political environment and
the political pressure that required that information on programs be
forthcoming – although begrudgingly – from the intelligence community at the time. The struggle for intelligence information is a key component of this oppositional relationship and the asymmetry inherent
in intelligence accountability: the executive will always own the intelligence, and the legislative branch will always ask to borrow it.

Although executive efforts were made to head off congressional
involvement in intelligence activities, the most far-reaching and lasting of the investigatory efforts stemming from the Hersh revelations
was that of the Senate committee (the United States Senate Select
Committee to Study Governmental Operations with Respect to
Intelligence Activities, known as the Church Committee after its chair,
Senator Frank Church (D-ID). Its broad impact was partially due to
the fact that its activities were public, widely publicized, and, in some
cases focused on scandal that could be conveyed visually, for example,
through images, such as the infamous photograph of Senator Church
holding a dart gun.

The Church Committee hearings were also a very organized public spectacle, and thus the committee had leverage over the executive's
more private investigatory undertakings and therefore leverage over

the final objective of institutionalized oversight.[55] The committee's activities were more often in the public light than the Pike Committee and Rockefeller Commission due to the fact that Senator Church launched a presidential campaign for the 1976 election immediately after accepting the chairmanship. As L. Britt Snider, who served both on the Hill and in the CIA, put it: "This inevitably led to an investigation that was more sensational, more controversial, and more political than it otherwise would have been."[56] Church's attempt to use the committee's investigations as a political lever seems apparent in his desire to hold as much of the investigations in public as possible. This plan contradicts his rather disingenuous statement, made directly to the press after his appointment as chair, in which he said: "I would not see this inquiry as any type of television extravaganza. It's much too serious to be a sideshow." According to him, his objective was to "safeguard the legitimate security interests of the country" while uncovering abuses of power "lest we slip into the practices of a police state."[57]

In addition to Senator Church's personal role in publicizing the proceedings of the Church Committee, the more systemic consideration was the stated and restated objective of the congressional hearings: they were intended to restore legitimacy of government, underscoring the assertion that at least one branch of government, Congress, was willing to be honest with the public. They were to provide an aperture for the public into the internal workings of the intelligence agencies, and they were to provide symbolic legitimacy to the institutions of government. They were a public oppositional move to executive obfuscation and denial regarding intelligence activities, and their public nature was a symbolic and pointed gesture to the executive. The public was engaged so that the intelligence community would be responsive to congressional demands.[58] According to this argument, the public was to be marshaled as a pressure point to force the intelligence community to reform. To mobilize public sentiment in this direction, some of the more lurid

---

[55] The Ford administration did not even want to release the final report of the Rockefeller Commission until public outcry forced its release.

[56] Snider, *The Agency and the Hill*, 49. Johnson also speaks at length about the politicized nature of the committee proceedings in his memoir *A Season of Inquiry*.

[57] Senator Frank Church, quoted in Johnson, *A Season of Inquiry*, 15.

[58] Johnson, *A Season of Inquiry*, 13.

intelligence program details – such as the IC's involvement in political assassinations – were to be disclosed openly. The staff supporting the committee's work were strongly in favor of this approach. As F. A. O. Schwarz, Jr., the general counsel to the committee, stated: "It was vital to make the politicians and the American people really *believe* that reform was necessary. You couldn't speak in abstractions; you had to have something real and concrete. This the assassination report provided, in memorable, horrifying detail."[59]

The Church Committee delved into a wider range of alleged abuses than the Rockefeller Commission, including domestic activity by the FBI.[60] In terms of seeking transparency, the objectives of the Church Committee were in direct opposition to the goals of the Rockefeller Commission. Further, while the main functional goal of the Senate committee was to explore the stories of abuses and open these activities to congressional scrutiny, more importantly the result of its recommendations was to be the basis of a new charter for the intelligence community that would redefine its responsibilities and boundaries in light of the flagrant civil liberties infringements of the FBI and CIA.[61] This charter would *specify* the responsibilities of the intelligence community and place constraints on how it would conduct its duties. This may seem a weak goal for so much investment of political time and money during that period, but the intelligence community's activities remained unspecified for decades and in many ways still are.

In concept, the goal of the Church Committee investigations was to restore accountability and public trust in government, but it was also an oppositional move to differentiate control over intelligence from the executive branch. According to conventional wisdom, the Church Committee investigations "opened" intelligence to the public and began the process of integrating intelligence back into "normal" government.[62] What the Church Committee discovered was wide-ranging

---

[59] Johnson, *A Season of Inquiry*, 55.

[60] Americo R. Cinquegrana, "The Walls (And Wires) Have Ears: The Background and First Ten Years of the Foreign Intelligence Surveillance Act of 1978," *University of Pennsylvania Law Review* 137, no. 3 (1989): 806.

[61] Johnson, *A Season of Inquiry*, 227.

[62] Arthur S. Hulnick, "Openness: Being Public about Secret Intelligence," *International Journal of Intelligence and Counterintelligence* 12, no. 4 (1999): 467.

and particularly damning of both the CIA and FBI, although it was the CIA that was rightly blamed for operating outside of its jurisdiction. The CIA, strictly forbidden from operating domestically by NSA (1947), launched Operation CHAOS, using intelligence methods to gather over one million files on American citizens. CHAOS was focused on gathering information particularly on student dissident groups in order to expose foreign – that is, Communist – involvement in their activities.[63] Local police departments took part in some of these activities, either on their own initiative or in tandem with federal agencies. Interestingly, the main outcome of these programs tended to be needless harassment of the public; they did not tend to be terribly effective in terms of operational intelligence gathering. CHAOS, for example, led to the collection of huge amounts of "useless intelligence, all of which had to be analyzed in a vain attempt to persuade a disbelieving president that it did not contain evidence of a vast international conspiracy."[64]

Programs, such as COINTELPRO – organized by the FBI – infiltrated groups perceived by domestic law enforcement as politically unsavory or potentially threatening to the United States government. The FBI infiltrated these organizations and disrupted their activities. FBI agents directed targeted harassment of individuals – for example, political leaders and journalists – and even the blackmail of high-profile public figures, one of the more bizarre examples being Martin Luther King, Jr., whose alleged extracurricular sexual activities the FBI threatened to expose if he did not commit suicide. Individuals and groups were subjected to surveillance, mail was opened and read, and assassinations of foreign leaders were deemed acceptable in dealing with the domestic threat.[65] Other programs focused on intercepting mail and telegrams, such as the National Security Agency's Operation MINARET.

Reading over the operations conducted by the intelligence agencies of that period, it is difficult to avoid being struck by their simultaneous outrageousness and banality. In addition to the FBI's attempts

---

[63] Christopher Andrew, *For the President's Eyes Only: Secret Intelligence and the American Presidency from Washington to Bush* (New York: Harper Collins, 1995), 354–5.

[64] Andrew, *For the President's Eyes Only*, 355.

[65] See Johnson, *A Season of Inquiry*.

to disrupt a range of usually peaceful social groups, the CIA experimented on unwitting civilians with LSD in order to test what effect the drug had. One person died from the tests, resulting in the creation of new criteria prohibiting the use of drug testing on unknowing individuals (!). The issues and problems of that period are poignantly addressed in a series of rhetorical questions listed in the Church Committee's final report:

> What is a valid national secret? What can properly be concealed from the scrutiny of the American people, from various segments of the executive branch or from a duly constituted oversight body of their elected representatives? Assassination plots? The overthrow of an elected democratic government? Drug testing on unwitting American citizens? Obtaining millions of private cables? Massive domestic spying by the CIA and the military? The illegal opening of mail? Attempts by an agency of the government to blackmail a civil rights leader? These have occurred and each has been withheld from scrutiny by the public and the Congress by the label "secret intelligence."[66]

According to the lore about the issue, the Church Committee's revelations were shocking on several levels. They came on the heels of specific evidence of executive branch misdeeds, but they also shattered complacency regarding intelligence on two sides. Post–World War II, the public had grown accustomed to the primacy of national security issues, in specific the ambiguity of the outcome of nuclear war and the doctrine of mutually assured destruction (MAD) required a certain level of faith in government decision making and problem solving.[67] As F. A. O. Schwarz, Jr., the chief counsel to the Church Committee, explains it, the political environment prior to this period had been very different, with an ingrained sense of "cultural trust."[68] As the country

---

[66] *Church Committee Final Report*, Book I [45A, 12].

[67] Much of the RAND Corporation's nuclear scenario planning of that period was based on the ambiguity of potential nuclear outcomes. This penetrates deeply both the decision making and political culture surrounding security decision making of that period. See Fred Kaplan, *The Wizards of Armageddon* (Palo Alto, CA: Stanford University Press, 1991), for an interesting discussion of this issue. The extreme but related version is, of course, Herman Kahn, *On Thermonuclear War* (Princeton, NJ: Princeton University Press, 1960).

[68] Interview with F. A. O. Schwarz, Jr., April 19, 2010.

drew away from the McCarthy era, citizens had a complex relationship with the agencies although they still respected, feared, and to some degree loved the security apparatus. Some of this trust was based on the fact that these activities were almost completely opaque to the public. There was generally never even a consideration of what the intelligence agencies were doing and if there were, it would be inferred that the agencies were protecting "us" against "them" and that the activities were conducted abroad against a clear threat – the Soviet Union. Questioning the agencies was not done by individuals, or even by Congress, which focused on learning as little as possible about intelligence activities.

The attitude underlying this absence of active oversight prior to the investigations is reflected well in this statement by a Senate overseer: "The difficulty in connection with asking questions and obtaining information is that we might obtain information which I personally would rather not have, unless it was essential for me as a member of Congress to have it."[69] It has been argued that other reasons for this lack of congressional interest in intelligence activities were, in addition to the deference theory, a strong culture of trust in intelligence officers; lack of time to understand fully the highly technical details of intelligence; and the absence of the oft-mentioned true motivator of congressional activity: activities open to the public that could provide support for reelection.[70] Another observer commented: "The mechanism for oversight clearly existed; what was missing was an interest in using it – or more properly speaking, a consensus that would legitimize its use."[71]

---

[69] David M. Barrett, *The CIA and Congress: The Untold Story from Truman to Kennedy* (Kansas City: University Press of Kansas, 2005), 230.

[70] This series of reasons for disinterest in oversight is laid out in Johnson, *A Season of Inquiry*, but the congressional focus on reelection as a prime motivator is deeply rooted in the literature on Congress. See Richard F. Fenno, Jr. *Congressmen in Committees* (Boston: Little, Brown, 1973), for a solid, if dated, discussion. See Roger H. Davidson, "Congressional Committees as Moving Targets," *Legislative Studies Quarterly* 11, no. 1 (1986): 19–33, for an updated discussion. This topic is also touched upon in the oversight classic, Joel D. Aberbach, *Keeping Watchful Eye: The Politics of Congressional Oversight* (Washington, DC: Brookings Institution Press, 1990).

[71] Robert M. Gates, "American Intelligence and Congressional Oversight," *World Affairs Council of Boston*, January 15, 1993.

Further environmental conditions that contributed to an attitude of oversight avoidance stemmed from the Manichean ideology of the post–World War II era – the concept of a very distinct good versus evil conflict that had resulted in resounding victory for American administration and values. This era of heroism demonstrated American exceptionalism in terms of strength and ideology and also reinforced the legitimacy of government won by long-term successful warfare. The postwar prosperity and the blossoming of the middle class formed the basis of conformity in terms of obedience and trust in government during the early Cold War period. Conformity was reinforced by civil defense exercises intended to organize the distributed population, as well as by threat communication that focused on the prospect of nuclear war.[72]

In terms of accountability and the tools of oversight, the investigations ushered in a modern era in terms of the relationship between the executive and legislative on issues of intelligence. In the scholarship about this period – and about intelligence oversight overall – this era ushered in a changed political environment for oversight. Academics assessing the 1970s point out that the investigations marked the "opening of government" and the reintegration and normalization of intelligence activities. The feeling across the board, from both intelligence operators and overseers, was that the 1970s scandals were a turning point. Some scholars argue that this was a brand new era of intelligence in the United States; I would argue that none of the steps in the development of the American security environment have been "brand new," but rather have built incrementally upon the past, with grand objectives on both sides being subject to the normal mitigation of the political environment, the limitations of resources, and the boundaries the American public places on outsize efforts made by its government in unorthodox and, perhaps, illegal directions.

Important themes for accountability emerged from these discussions: for example, the fundamental question about all of the abuses, but particularly such egregious programs as assassination, was how

---

[72] A fascinating description of how civil defense worked to instill particular values and trust under the continual threat of nuclear war is Andrew Grossman, *Neither Dead nor Red: Civil Defense and American Political Development in the Early Cold War* (New York: Routledge, 2001).

much did the president know about the proceedings? Did he order the programs, or was the CIA operating under its own authority without executive branch supervision or involvement of any kind? These were shades of the discussions on plausible deniability that had led to the Hughes-Ryan Amendment. Additional questions included, what should be done about providing a systematic framework for future intelligence activity? And, if approval is given for a project, how long does that approval last before the activity must be reviewed again? While seemingly basic among the range of broader excesses of that period, in terms of oversight control, many of these questions had not been thoroughly addressed in any kind of public forum. It is difficult to grasp how opaque the entire world of intelligence was, and just how shocking the revelations were to both public officials and private citizens. Further questions included how congressional review and approval of programs should be structured, how reform of the intelligence community should be organized, and who should take charge of the process.

All three investigatory bodies delivered answers to these questions in one form or another, but the most lasting in terms of oversight structural development stemmed from the recommendations of the Church Committee. As mentioned previously, while the Rockefeller Commission was an interesting development for our model of oppositional oversight, in reality it turned out, as expected, to be generally a presidential whitewash, although it did touch upon some suggested reorganization recommendations. The Pike Committee, the House's effort at investigating poor intelligence performance, became mired in politics and sloppy handling of classified material, including allowing the report in its entirety to be leaked to the *Village Voice*. Interestingly, in a direct oppositional move, in the wake of the debacle brought on by the mishandling of the Pike Committee report, President Ford attempted to regain control over intelligence oversight by making a stern statement about the direction of intelligence reform. His executive order on intelligence activities was intended to establish a line of authority over intelligence reform.[73] His address regarding the issue was, interestingly, presented publicly on television, and he stated that

[73] Andrew, *For the President's Eyes Only*, 419.

he was conducting "the first major reorganization of the intelligence community since 1947" in response to what was perceived as the irresponsible release of the secrets of the Pike Committee report.[74] Thus, he preempted congressional recommendations about intelligence reform *and* did so publicly; he pulled tools from both sides of the oppositional relationship in making this statement. While the move was deft in terms of an attempt at regaining the operational high ground, the Church Committee recommendations contributed to reform and to the permanent installation of institutionalized oversight mechanisms within Congress. Congress won that round.

The Church Committee concluded its assessment with ninety-six recommendations for change within the intelligence community and to intelligence oversight.[75] Recommendation ninety-six was the creation of a permanent Senate intelligence oversight committee, with the bulk of the recommendations focusing on processes for overseeing domestic intelligence activities via internal methods.[76] This period marked a very real transition for the intelligence agencies and their dealings with the other branches, or a "metamorphos[is] into an entirely new operating environment for the intelligence community."[77] The creation of the intelligence committees centralized supervision of intelligence activities. It also allocated resources to staffing and coordinating intelligence oversight with other types of oversight, requiring that intelligence oversight processes be standardized, for example, with set terms of appropriations and authorization. By fiscal year (FY) 1979, the Intelligence Authorization Act placed intelligence agencies in the same authorization and appropriations cycle as other federal agencies.[78] It also shifted the role of intelligence from being a service dedicated almost totally to the needs of the executive branch to one that also served the legislature. As Hitz points out, the creation of the committees added additional consumers of intelligence information, diluting to some degree the proprietary executive control over intelligence that had existed up

[74] Andrew, *For the President's Eyes Only*, 419.
[75] Interview with David Aaron, task force leader, Church Committee, April 6, 2010.
[76] *Intelligence Activities and the Rights of Americans*, Book II (Church Committee Final Report), April 26, 1976.
[77] Lundberg, *Congressional Oversight and Presidential Prerogative*, 4.
[78] Lundberg, *Congressional Oversight and Presidential Prerogative*, 6.

to that point.[79] In former senator David Boren's (D-OK) words: "The activities of the [intelligence] oversight committees … are inherently controversial; the mere existence of them in some ways circumscribes the power of the Presidency."[80]

The committees were installed in the Senate and House in 1976 and 1977 respectively. The Senate committee, approved by a vote of eighty-seven to seven, was based on the structure of the Church Committee. Not only did the Senate absorb many of the Church Committee recommendations in its development of a permanent intelligence oversight mechanism, but the new oversight committee hoped to minimize partisanship by keeping the ratio of majority to minority members close – eight to seven – and requiring a vice chair from the minority party.[81] This mirrored the composition of the Church Committee. As a "select" committee, members are chosen by the Senate majority and minority leadership to serve in the new committee. Members were chosen from the standing committees with experience in intelligence: Judiciary, Armed Forces, Foreign Relations, and Appropriations. In a step to avoid capture or cooptation on the part of the oversight committee members, tenure on the committees was initially limited to eight years in the Senate and six years in the House.[82] Based on Senate Resolution 400, intelligence agency heads would be required to keep the committee "fully and currently informed with respect to intelligence activities, including any significant anticipated activities."[83]

The House Permanent Select Committee on Intelligence (HPSCI) was established in 1977, a year after the Senate committee. The original committee had thirteen members chosen by the majority and minority leadership (nine Democrats and four Republicans) and was subdivided into four subcommittees: Oversight, Legislation, Evaluation, and Program-and-Budget Authorization. Unlike the Senate committee,

---

[79] Hitz, *Why Spy?* 118.
[80] David L. Boren, "The Winds of Change at the CIA," *Yale Law Journal* 101, no. 4 (1992): 853.
[81] Frederick A. O. Schwarz, Jr., and Aziz Z. Huq, *Unchecked and Unbalanced: Presidential Power in a Time of Terror* (New York: New Press, 2007), 52.
[82] Hitz, *Why Spy?* 117.
[83] S. Res. 400; *Legislative Oversight of Intelligence Activities: The US Experience*, Report Prepared by the Select Committee on Intelligence, United States Senate, October 1994, 5.

the House committee's membership reflected the party proportion in the House as a whole.[84] HPSCI was tasked with developing new charter legislation for the intelligence agencies, reviewing their administrative guidelines, analyzing their requests for annual funding, assessing management structure, evaluating intelligence results and methods, conducting cost-benefit analyses on hardware innovations, and providing a safe haven for whistleblowers and their concerns.[85] HPSCI's genesis is slightly more removed from its investigatory committee forebear, the Pike Committee, because the House committee's tenure was plagued with disorder and leaks, including the leak of the final committee report.[86] HPSCI's authority is reinforced not only by congressional institutional authority, but also the authority to determine intelligence agency budgets. Further, structural requirements mandate specific types of interaction between HPSCI and the agencies. Examples of such interaction include specific types of statutory reporting requirements, such as receiving presidential findings or the mandated reports by the statutory inspector general.[87]

Interestingly, while the Senate Committee was given the authority to authorize funds for all "intelligence activities" annually, specific appropriations regarding "tactical foreign military intelligence activities serving no national policymaking function" were excluded from the Senate Intelligence Committee's purview.[88] In contrast, HPSCI maintains authorization and appropriations authority over "tactical intelligence and intelligence-related activities" (or TIARA, a marvelous acronym coined by the military). TIARA was an interesting divergence from the rather more limited jurisdiction ascribed to the Senate committee, as well as a testament to the strength of the Senate Armed Forces Committee, keen at that time on retaining its turf.[89] This

---

[84] Snider, *The Agency and the Hill*, 53.

[85] Loch K. Johnson, *America's Secret Power: The CIA in a Democratic Society* (Oxford: Oxford University Press, 1989), 210.

[86] Johnson, *A Season of Inquiry*, 190–1.

[87] The CIA statutory IG was installed later than in the other agencies – in 1989 – but I include this account here to provide a sense of the realm of HPSCI responsibilities.

[88] Snider, *The Agency and the Hill*, 51.

[89] Frederick M. Kaiser, *Congressional Oversight of Intelligence: Current Structure and Alternatives*, (Washington, DC: Congressional Research Service, 2011), 5; Snider, *The Agency and the Hill*, 51.

division has tended to create a lopsidedness in conference committees' processes for integrating intelligence authorization bills. To highlight the novel role of the committees, referring to HPSCI, Representative Richard Bolling (D-MO) mentioned during discussion of the legislation to create the House committee, "This is a select committee, a permanent select committee. It is basically a committee of the leadership."[90] The selectivity of both HPSCI and SSCI can be encapsulated by a sense of prestige but also by the reality that these committees have privileged information and are not only the providers of framework and responsibility to the intelligence community, but also the primary interlocutors regarding matters of security to their colleagues. As a former HSPCI staff director pointed out, the committees are the guarantors to the rest of the members that responsibility is being taken for these matters.[91]

In terms of the analytical framework for accountability, the installation of the oversight committees marked a giant step forward in all categories. The most important aspect of the framework for the strength and efficacy of an oversight mechanism is external autonomy. In the case of the two committees, they were installed by statute in the House and Senate in 1977 and 1976 respectively and, of primary importance, were given the authority to authorize and appropriate funds for the intelligence community. Although there were term limits in the early years, dedicated committees gave overseers a unified forum for the investigation of intelligence activities as well as institutional processes, such as hearings and briefings, which gave the committees external independence from the executive. Knowledge and expertise were centralized and the committees were staffed and provided with the specialized resources necessary, such as secured sites to read classified documents. One aspect of external autonomy that began weak and still remains troublesome is *recourse*. In this case, the problem of recourse links to another category in the framework, temporality. Both of these categories are somewhat more complicated in the legislative branch than in the others because the committees are charged with supervising

---

[90] Quoted in Frank J. Smist, Jr., *Congress Oversees the United States Intelligence Community, 1947–1995*, 2nd edition (Knoxville: University of Tennessee Press, 1994), 215.

[91] Interview with a former HPSCI staff director, June 28, 2011.

a wider range of intelligence activities than, for example, the judiciary. The weakness of these two categories also provides the groundwork for the creation of a closed system of secrecy in that while the institutions were novel and unprecedented in their access to intelligence information, they had limited recourse to change the behavior of the overseen.

In terms of covert action, for example, the executive is required to issue a finding and provide it to the committees in a timely fashion. Other types of intelligence do not require such specific reporting, other than the general mandate that the committees be kept "fully and currently" informed. This lack of specificity adds ambiguity to the process. Further, there is the question of recourse: what can the committees do if they disagree with a proposed program? The most strenuous measure would be to curtail funding. Programs are reviewed every year, and budgets for them can be cut, amended, or extended. Less formally, representatives can express their dismay in an advisory capacity and, less formally, can leak information about the proposed program to the media. The complications of each of these methods of recourse are somewhat obvious. In terms of funding, timeliness plays a role. It would be difficult to cut funding unilaterally and immediately upon hearing about a dissatisfactory program. Further, covert actions do not require approval of the committees in order to be conducted; the requirement is only that the committees be informed. This leaves the issue of the authority to exact consequences somewhat ambiguous. Secondly, any change in behavior would be dependent on personal suasion – not the most reliable or institutionally sound approach to changing behavior. Thirdly, in my discussions with both intelligence officers and overseers, leaking to the media is uniformly frowned upon, not only due to potential endangerment of intelligence operatives, but the potential further damage to sources and assets. Finally, the norm of patriotic support for the country's national security apparatus post-9/11 has generally curbed congressional leaking on these matters.

The final category – transparency – must be viewed relatively. That is, the installation of the intelligence committees greatly enhanced the transparency of the process from the backroom-dealings approach that had preceded it. Within Congress, the members of the committees stood in symbolically for their peers and thus, by extension, for the public. Some hearings were public, and redacted reports began to be filed every year. On the other hand, the committees were and are still heavily dependent on the executive branch for intelligence information. Although they were, by statute, allowed access to this material, it was still owned by the executive branch, and thus dissemination was and has continued to be contingent on the goodwill and judgment of the administration.

The development of these congressional intelligence oversight mechanisms was catalyzed by the loss of government legitimacy that characterized the Vietnam War/Watergate era, the revelations of widespread, long-term intelligence abuses, and newfound political willingness in Congress to engage with issues long believed the sole purview of the executive branch. From the perspective of the executive branch, the committees also connoted a deep incursion into its territory and provided the basis for continuing struggle between the two branches. As has been mentioned throughout this book, the relationship between the executive and other branches regarding intelligence is characterized by information asymmetry. Control of intelligence information is core to authority over its operations. Development of oversight mechanisms to ensure accountability of the intelligence community is an attempt on the part of the legislature to rebalance the asymmetry toward an equilibrium, while the executive branch, broadly, works to keep the informational tilt in its favor.

4   CONGRESS AND OPPOSITIONAL OVERSIGHT

The old tradition was that you don't ask: It was a consensus that intelligence was apart from the rules ... that was the reason we did step over the line in a few cases, largely because no one was watching. No one was there to say don't do that.

William Çolby, DCI, 1973–76[1]

The previous chapters described the history of the CIA and the legislative oversight committees respectively. They show how the CIA developed in light of a wartime requirement and then was left to find its own way over the subsequent decades. Its wartime roots, specialized mission, and isolation from regular government created a unique and demanding institutional culture that regulates how the agency interacts with the outside world and how its personnel behave. Challenges to behavioral expectations – particularly divulging internal information – are met with swift internal consequences. This institutional culture and the rules and regulations that contribute to it are the central functional method for managing secrecy – for protecting the core of the Agency's technical mission. Chapter 3 focused on the origins of legislative oversight mechanisms that emerged out of scandal and discussed how they developed to take an unprecedented role in supervising intelligence activities.

This chapter explores the dynamics of the relationship between the executive and legislative branches regarding the oversight of intelligence. Similar to development in other parts of the government,

---

[1] Quoted in Loch K. Johnson, *A Season of Inquiry* (Chicago: Dorsey Press, 1988), 7.

change has been driven by tension – or opposition – between the branches and has occurred incrementally. Tension has developed at particular pivot points – in several cases due to political scandal – and the oversight mechanisms have adapted to engage with each set of emergent issues. What has developed out of this relationship can be termed a collaboration – as counterintuitive as this may sound. Over time, a system has developed that incorporates both sides of this oppositional relationship. Rather than being deemed "apart from the rules," as the quotation at the beginning of this chapter mentions, intelligence information – and thus secrets – are organized and institutionalized together in a closed system.

OPPOSITIONAL BEHAVIOR IN THE EXECUTIVE: PRIORITIES AND SPECIFICITY

President Ford's overt attempt at staking a claim on intelligence reform and reorganization demonstrates a secondary trend in the development of intelligence oversight (both legislative and executive). The trend is characterized by overstatement of objectives and, in actuality, only incremental change – not surprising within an adversarial political environment. This is a function of both the oppositional relationship and internal countervailing political trends. The former is a creation of the interbranch relationship; the latter is an intrabranch phenomenon. The argument addressed in this chapter focuses on the former dynamic. This outcome is not novel for political scientists accustomed to analyzing incentives for compromise, but the process of underachieving within this context is worthy of analysis. The trend is political and rhetorical. For example, for the most part, broad and vague terms such as "reform" or "change" touch upon reorganizing a committee or redefining specific intelligence terms, such as what constitutes "covert action" or "timeliness." Wide conceptual claims resulting in minor advancement become one of the goals of the executive side of the oppositional relationship when it comes to specifying the role and limits of the intelligence function. The reason for this is that a primary objective of the executive is to maintain as large an arena for the intelligence services to maneuver as possible. This objective obviously contrasts with congressional desires to broaden Congress's oversight purview and increase legislative control over intelligence activities. Executive oppositional intentions, thus, require keeping the structure of constraints as underspecified as possible or keeping the constraints so limited as to be almost valueless. Further, the executive must maintain a clear focus on its requirements in terms of *internal* accountability of the intelligence services – to the president and his or her foreign policy objectives. President Ford's executive order (EO) 11905 of February 1976 illustrates this point.

EO 11905, in a series of sweeping and authoritative statements, established "a new command structure for foreign intelligence" and established "a comprehensive set of public guidelines" that would be "legally binding charters" for intelligence activities.[2] Ford replaced the 40 Committee – the intelligence oversight committee within the NSC – with a smaller five-person Operations Advisory Group, comprised of senior members of the White House, CIA, State, and Defense.[3] The executive order established the Intelligence Oversight Board (IOB) within the executive branch, consisting of three presidentially appointed members. Members were able to receive reports from the inspectors general and general counsels of the intelligence agencies and were "instructed to report possible illegalities to the attorney general and improprieties to the president."[4] At a press conference, President Ford explained the context for EO 11905:

> What we have sought to do in this case is to make the process and the decision-making fall on the shoulders of the President, and he will be held accountable by the American people. In each of the cases – of the Director of the Central Intelligence or any of the other intelligence agencies – the directives or the guidelines will hold special individuals accountable for what happens in their particular area of responsibility. But the final and ultimate responsibility falls on the shoulders of the President.[5]

---

[2] Bretton G. Sciaroni, "The Theory and Practice of Executive Branch Oversight," *Harvard Journal of Law and Public Policy* 12, no. 2 (1989): 404.

[3] Christopher Andrew, *For the President's Eyes Only: Secret Intelligence and the American Presidency from Washington to Bush* (New York: Harper Collins, 1995), 419.

[4] Andrew, *For the President's Eyes Only*, 419.

[5] Sciaroni, "The Theory and Practice of Executive Branch Oversight," Fn 207, 404.

This presidential responsibility for accountability is reiterated in an interesting critique of that period. In a remarkable piece, published interestingly in the CIA's internal, classified journal *Intelligence Studies*, we read that:

> [An] intriguing aspect of the emphasis on accountability is that it should have become the focus of Executive Branch intelligence reform after the revelations that many of the abuses of the intelligence agencies were caused not by too little, but rather by too much, *accountability to the President*. [emphasis added]. Often the agencies had wandered from their statutory roles precisely in an effort to be responsive to Presidents who sought (or ordered) their help either in covert actions overseas or in dissident surveillance on the home front .... It was perhaps symptomatic of the Ford Administration's image of itself – and indeed largely its reality – that no doubt would ever enter its mind that Presidents could be trusted, were honest, and always proceeded by legal means.[6]

This quotation highlights the competing definitions of accountability that are core to the oppositional relationship. It also challenges, as its authors intend, the common belief of that period that the CIA was rogue, instigating actions far removed from the appropriate constraints of governmental regulation, when, in fact, it was tightly linked to presidential decision making. This statement should, of course, be taken with several grains of salt, as the CIA was locked in a long-term endeavor to explain its overreach in some places and actual crimes in others.

Further, William Colby, the DCI during that period, made several attempts to clarify to Congress the actions of the CIA. His attempts at disclosure earned him a varied response, but it is important to note here that his personal attempt to clarify the activities of the Agency is representative of a definitive CIA trend that lasts until this day. The CIA, unlike other agencies, relies on the voice of one man to defend and protect its actions. Colby's response to the criticism of the CIA was to make selective disclosures to his interlocutors.[7] His statements were startling to many within the Agency – not exactly because of their

---

[6] Timothy S. Hardy, "Intelligence Reform in the Mid-1970s," 11, DDRS, 1989, no. 1247, quoted in Andrew, *For the President's Eyes Only*, 419.

[7] Rhodri Jeffreys-Jones, Rhodri Jeffreys-Jones, *The CIA and American Democracy*, 3rd edition (New Haven, CT: Yale University Press, 2003), 199.

content, but because they were inconsistent with the Agency's culture of secrecy and the expectations of the president up to that point. In fact, they resulted in his firing. Colby's words in his memoir of the period are indicative of the oppositional dynamic and the expectations placed on the players who were obviously expected to support the executive side. He says:

> I believe I was fired because of the way I went about dealing with the CIA's crisis. My approach, pragmatically and philosophically, was in conflict with that of the President and his principal advisors. From their point of view, I had not played the game during that turbulent year as a loyal member of the White House "team."
>
> My strategy quite simply had been to be guided by the Constitution, and to apply its principles. This meant that I had to cooperate with the investigations and try to educate the Congress, press, and public, as well as I could, about American intelligence, its importance, its successes and its failings. The Agency's survival, I believed, could only come from understanding, not hostility, built on knowledge, not faith.[8]

While the executive orders always focus on supporting the executive side of the oppositional dynamic, they are also reflective of the individual administration's perspective on the use of covert action, which can evolve from reaction to previous covert activity, political ideology, stance, and environment and/or the exigencies of the threat environment. When President Ford's successor, Jimmy Carter, having campaigned on a platform very critical of covert action, superseded Ford's executive order on January 26, 1978, with Executive Order 12,036, he focused it on constraining intelligence activities by instituting a more rigorous decision cycle for covert action. Under Carter, two committees were established in the NSC with responsibilities for intelligence activities: the Policy Review Committee (PRC), focused on setting the requirements for foreign intelligence collection and monitoring resource allocation and intelligence product; and the Special Coordination Committee (SCC), which was to be responsible for authorizing covert action proposals prior to advancement to the

---

[8] William Colby, *Honorable Men: My Life in the CIA* (New York: Simon and Schuster, 1978), 14–15.

president for his approval.[9] In addition to having a primary responsibility for covert action, the SCC reviewed and approved particularly sensitive intelligence collection and counterintelligence programs. The members of the SCC were high level, including the secretary of state, secretary of defense, attorney general, director of the Office of Management and Budget (OMB), assistant for national security affairs, chair of the Joint Chiefs of Staff, and the director of the CIA.

Arguably, however, President Ronald Reagan's order, signed in 1981, was the most important of them all, not least because it is still in place in amended form today, but also because it marked a more strenuous foreign policy and commitment to the use of covert action. Reagan's Executive Order 12333 defined covert action as follows:

> Special activities conducted in support of national foreign policy objectives abroad which are planned and executed so that the role of the United States Government is not apparent or acknowledged publicly, and functions in support of such activities, but which are not intended to influence United States political processes, public opinion, policies, or media and do not include diplomatic activities or the collection or production of intelligence and related support functions.[10]

EO 12333 is important for a number of reasons. First, clarification of covert action brings a level of basic transparency to a very secret activity that even the Hughes-Ryan Amendment didn't address fully, while it also firmly keeps the power of specificity in the hands of the administration. To clarify, the focus of activity, whether it is collection or covert action, has a significant impact on the level and procedure of oversight. For example, the D/CIA (at that point, the DCI) is empowered by EO 12333 with the positive authority to initiate intelligence collection within specific bounds, but does require presidential approval in the form of a finding for any covert activity.[11] Second, the order reinforced the point that covert action occurs at the behest of the White House and is not something instigated by the CIA. This is key to many operations officers in the CIA, who point out that the CIA is not "rogue"

---

[9] Loch K. Johnson, "Covert Action and Accountability: Decision-Making for America's Secret Foreign Policy," *International Studies Quarterly* 33, no. 1 (1989): 92–3.

[10] E.O. 12333 text.

[11] Personal communication with a former senior congressional staffer, August 18, 2014.

and is not plotting illegal activities, but rather is providing an operational service upon demand within an institutionalized oversight process and in accordance with specific foreign policy objectives. This is reinforced by the actuality of the covert action initiation process, which is rather different from common perceptions of it. As former deputy director (CIA) – also a former director of operations – Stephen R. Kappes pointed out, "Covert action is owned by the NSC and implemented by the CIA. Covert action is a tool of the president."[12] Finally, Reagan's own words firmly confirm presidential accountability over intelligence activities:

> These orders [EO 12333 and 12334] have been carefully drafted … to maintain the legal protection of all American citizens …. Contrary to a distorted image that emerged during the last decade, there is no inherent conflict between the intelligence community and the rights of our citizens. Indeed, the purpose of the intelligence community is the protection of our people.
>
> This is not to say mistakes were never made and that vigilance against abuse is unnecessary. But an approach that emphasizes suspicion and mistrust of our own intelligence efforts can undermine this Nation's ability to confront the increasing challenge of espionage and terrorism …. As we move into the 1980's, we need to free ourselves from the negative attitudes of the past and look to meeting the needs of the country.[13]

In an interesting foreshadowing of the challenges of Iran-Contra, EO 12333 stipulates that all covert action be conducted by the CIA, with the dual exceptions that the armed forces may conduct covert activity during a time of war declared by Congress or during a period covered by a report from the president to the Congress consistent with the War Powers Resolution. Under this order, these are the only bodies that may act in a covert fashion officially unless the president determines that another agency is more likely to achieve a particular objective.[14]

---

[12] Interview with Stephen R. Kappes, April 6, 2011.

[13] Pub. Papers, Ronald Reagan, 1981 1126 (1982); quoted in Sciaroni, "The Theory and Practice of Executive Branch Oversight," 409.

[14] William J. Daugherty, *Executive Secrets: Covert Action and the Presidency* (Lexington: University of Kentucky Press, 2008), 14.

Reagan's statement contributes to the oppositional argument because, as asserted in the previous chapter, presidential ownership is not only fundamental to the process of covert action, it is also critical to the legal ramifications of the activity and eventually, in some cases, the public perception of it. While congressional oversight is usually where the aperture to the public resides regarding intelligence activities, covert action has a unique position in the oppositional relationship upon which even Congress is wary of encroaching. Public awareness of covert action has increased, a function of both an attempt to defend against misinformation about CIA actions and the increased media penetration of government activity overall.[15] A clear example of this trend is President Obama's overt ownership of the covert action that led to the capture and killing of Osama bin Laden. While this particular situation plainly differs from most covert actions, the president pointed out clearly that that he had ordered then–CIA director Leon Panetta to develop a plan to remove bin Laden and that "he had given the order to execute."[16] This is a new and interesting use of the covert function; formerly shrouded in black, the function is currently an ongoing source of political credibility, strength, and proof of activity on the part of the administration. This is particularly the case because although the executive is required to inform Congress of the action, that is the extent of executive's requirement; it need not garner Congress's approval for the actions, at least in the immediate term.

EO 12333 was amended numerous times post-9/11 to reflect both the changing threat environment and the reconfiguration of the intelligence community, but changes to the text have been minimal over the years, reflecting a firm belief in the use of executive control. While the congressional committees have not developed a charter for the intelligence community and have not focused on generating one for some time, the executive has long held to a general set of guidelines, particularly regarding covert action.

---

[15] Interview with a former staff director for the Senate Select Committee on Intelligence (SSCI) and former staff director for the President's Foreign Intelligence Advisory Board (PFIAB), April 29, 2011. Personal communication with a former senior congressional staffer, August 18, 2014. See also the televised presidential press conference of President Barack Obama on the death of Osama bin Laden, May 1, 2011.

[16] Press conference of President Obama on the death of bin Laden, May 1, 2011.

We have seen how the executive worked at reclaiming authority over intelligence activities through both asserting presidential authority over intelligence accountability on a public level while also focusing on specifying the terminology regarding intelligence activities. The next section will return to an analysis of the development of congressional oversight. Although the administrations discussed here were of both political parties, the trends in maintaining control over intelligence and intelligence oversight varied very little among them. The presidents defined accountability in terms of the intelligence services' responsibility to the executive, defined the intelligence activities most relevant to external oversight, and specified the terms used to constrain or expand the intelligence function. All three of these functions are virtually unassailable by the adversary – Congress – and thus the congressional committees have developed their own processes through which to gain traction on the relationship. Evidence of this state of affairs can be seen in the bureaucratic procedures brought to bear on the intelligence community, particularly as the mechanisms developed out of the immediate scandal era of the mid-1970s.

INTERMEDIATE DEVELOPMENT: FRICTION AND LEGISLATIVE OVERSIGHT

By the late 1970s, the committees had become institutionalized with developed procedures. Intelligence agencies were subjected to an annual legislative budget review, required to attend hearings on the Hill, submit reports, brief politicians, and generally acquiesce to the requirements of their overseers.[17] Further, pressure to refine intelligence information processes were brought to bear by Congress. The two major pieces of legislation that demonstrate this trend are the 1980 Oversight Act and the 1991 Authorization Act. These two statutes bookend the Iran-Contra scandal; the first provided loopholes that may have facilitated the illegal activities of the Reagan

---

[17] Loch K. Johnson, *America's Secret Power: The CIA in a Democratic Society* (Oxford: Oxford University Press, 1989), 208.

administration, while the second attempted to shore up any oversight vulnerabilities. Combined, both acts created the current oversight structure.

The foundations of the 1980 Oversight Act involved a 263-page charter for the intelligence community, the development of which had been a core objective of the Church Committee's original recommendations. By the end of the debate over the charter, after intrabranch negotiations and compromise, the bill had been reduced to two pages.[18] This period also introduced more leverage on the part of regular political dynamics. Not only did the political allegiances of the chairs matter to the focus of the committees, but the political and threat environments also played a role in where the committees stood in the balance of the intelligence community in terms of constraints. The political context during this period provided some impetus for slimming down exceptional needs on the part of the oversight committees. Senator Birch Bayh (D-IN) was chair of the SSCI and initially was engaged with fulfilling the recommendations of the Church Committee, such as completing the aforementioned charter. With the onset, however, of the Soviet campaign in Afghanistan, the emphasis shifted away from post–Church Committee constraints and more toward opening the options of the intelligence community. This period also a saw the onset of the Iranian revolution, which in the eyes of American leadership increased the need for security strength. However, Senator Bayh did champion both the Intelligence Oversight Act as well as, prior to that, the Foreign Intelligence Surveillance Act, which delimited the role of the judiciary in intelligence oversight, albeit only over foreign intelligence collection within the United States.[19] The SSCI began to take a swing back toward championing the intelligence community when Barry Goldwater (R-AZ) took over as chair upon the Republican Senate takeover of 1980.

[18] Harold Hongju Koh. *The National Security Constitution: Sharing Power after the Iran-Contra Affair* (New Haven, CT: Yale University Press, 1990), 58.

[19] Frank J. Smist, Jr, *Congress Oversees the United States Intelligence Community: 1947–1994*, *2nd* edition (Knoxville: University of Tennessee Press, 1994), 96–7.

The end result of Senator Bayh's last days as chair and the waning moments of the Church Committee era was the Intelligence Oversight Act, which streamlined the process of oversight, solidifying the reporting requirements and narrowing the committees to whom the intelligence community had to report to two. In addition to the requirement to keep the committees "fully and currently informed," stated in an executive order signed by President Carter, the Intelligence Oversight Act required the executive to give prior notice to Congress on all important intelligence activities, including covert action. When the president did not inform Congress of covert action before the operation, he was to inform the committee of the action in a "timely fashion" and explain why advance notice was not given. Interestingly, while considered a step forward in streamlining and focusing the oversight process, the final act was a diluted version of the original bill, which had attempted to require *advance* notice of all activities, but ended up with the ambiguous "timely" notice.[20]

As the accountability framework highlights, this issue of the timeliness of reportage is key to an understanding of the characteristics of accountability. It was quite controversial in the early years of institutionalized intelligence oversight and remains so. The requirement of timeliness gradually narrowed from "the occasional report" to Congress regarding covert action through the early 1970s, to reports "in a timely fashion" following Hughes-Ryan Amendment (1974), to prior notice of covert activity, according to the 1980 Oversight Act.[21] On a conceptual level, timely reporting is an issue of both legitimacy and efficacy in the relationship between the intelligence services and Congress. It means that the oversight function is meant to guide intelligence and thus is both proactive and reactive. It allows congressional committees to have a voice in how projects are developed, how they are funded, and whether they should continue to be funded. These are all fundamental components of effective oversight and effective maintenance of the chain of accountability. Further, timeliness can be a factor in the level of legitimacy of an issue. For example, if time allows a number of actors to support an activity, this lends

[20] Koh, *The National Security Constitution,* 127.
[21] Johnson, *America's Secret Power,* 225.

credence to that project if it becomes public, even if it is, ostensibly, secret. And, as we know, covert action projects are increasingly becoming overt in the current technological and political environment.

In addition to this crucial factor of temporality, an important variable was, and is, to whom this information is ultimately reported. I define the audience for intelligence briefings as *reporting recipients*. The reporting recipients fit in the external independence category of the accountability framework and are crucial to oversight efficacy. The Oversight Act of 1980 streamlined the process of intelligence oversight by changing the reporting mandate. Thenceforth the intelligence community would only be required to report to the two intelligence oversight committees, thereby keeping tighter control over intelligence information and centralizing authority over intelligence activities. The act, while framed in efficient, corporate, and positive terms such as "streamlined," limited the number of members of Congress who would have access to intelligence information and thus narrowed the number of those who would have a voice in oversight of the agencies. When the number of recipients is limited, alongside the usual limitations regarding classified material, external autonomy of the oversight mechanism can easily be compromised.

This issue of controlling the number of recipients has been key throughout the development of congressional oversight mechanisms. Arguments that members could potentially be irresponsible and leak critical intelligence information, either purposely or accidentally, have imbued the debate about the role Congress should play in intelligence oversight for decades. One informal approach to limiting access to intelligence information was to limit briefings to four people, the "Gang of Four." The participants in the Gang of Four are the chairs and ranking members of the two intelligence oversight committees. Gang of Four briefings are not based on statute, but they do provide an avenue for the agencies to brief on matters perceived as being of such sensitivity that briefing the full committees could risk disclosure. Gang of Four briefings deal only with *noncovert action* intelligence activities and, in terms of formality, were overtaken by this Oversight Act.[22]

---

[22] Alfred Cumming, *"Gang of Four" Congressional Intelligence Notifications* (Congressional Research Service [CRS] Report R40698, January 29, 2010).

The limited notification provision was formalized but increased to eight congressional members in the act by the following statement:

> If the President determines that it is essential to limit access to the finding to meet extraordinary circumstances affecting vital interests of the United States, the finding may be reported to the chairmen and ranking minority members of the congressional intelligence committees, the Speaker and minority leader of the House of Representatives, the majority and minority leaders of the Senate, and such other member or members of the congressional leadership as may be included by the President.[23]

The eight individuals listed are informally known as the Gang of Eight. While this issue of limited notification may seem arcane and irrelevant in light of the broader issues of intelligence and the requirements of thorough oversight, it has become a key operational factor in understanding how oversight is conducted as well as a methodological problem for researchers, because it limits any record of the transmission of intelligence information from the agencies to Congress.

At root, in terms of oversight, the notification limitation provision has its basis in the fear that extremely sensitive intelligence information distributed to the full memberships of the two intelligence oversight committees could be prone to leaks or other congressional misuse. An integrated assumption when the act containing the Gang of Eight limited-briefing provision was passed was that the committee leadership would decide the procedures for notifying the remainder of the committee membership. Limited notification was not considered a permanent bypass of congressional committee procedure; it was a midstep based on the understanding of the importance of sensitivity to timeliness in reporting covert activities.[24] In the words of Senator Walter Huddleston (D-KY): "The intent is that the full oversight committees will be fully informed at such time the eight leaders determine is appropriate. The committees will establish the procedures for the discharge of this responsibility."[25] At the time, limiting the number

---

[23] 50 U.S.C. § 413 (b) (2006). The National Security Act of 1947, as amended.

[24] Alfred Cumming, *Sensitive Covert Action Notification: Oversight Options for Congress* (CRS Report R40691, January 29, 2010), 5.

[25] Cumming, *Sensitive Covert Action Notification*, 3.

of those briefed on a specific mission was a reasonable compromise between congressional oversight, on the one hand, and executive expectations and requirements of secrecy in the conduct of covert action, on the other. It does, however, appear to be a solid victory for the executive in terms of the oppositional relationship between the branches regarding intelligence oversight.

Obviously, from the legislative perspective, the oversight concern is that limited hearings enforce opacity with regard to active oversight. This matter, while discussed in depth in the late 1970s, continues in almost exactly the same format to this day. Records of these limited hearings are generally not kept, staff members are not allowed to attend, and notes are not taken. Further, and vital to the functioning of the institutional culture of Congress, it remains ambiguous as to what degree those briefed are allowed to discuss these issues with their committee colleagues, and this limitation tends to be decided by the executive branch.[26] The complexities of this type of briefing were exemplified in 2009 by questions over whether House Speaker Nancy Pelosi was indeed briefed on the enhanced interrogation techniques then in use by the CIA. As expressed by a former congressional staff member, who had also served as a CIA attorney:

> As a former legal counsel for both Republican and Democratic leaders of the House and Senate intelligence committees, I'm well aware of the limitations of these "gang of eight" sessions. They are provided only to the leadership of the House and Senate and of the intelligence committees, with no staff present. The eight are prohibited from saying anything about the briefing to anyone, including other intelligence panel members. The leaders for whom I worked never discussed the content of these briefings with me.
>
> It is virtually impossible for individual members of Congress, particularly members of the minority party, to take any effective action if they have concerns about what they have heard in one of these briefings. It is not realistic to expect them, working alone, to sort through complex legal issues, conduct the kind of factual

---

26 This list of concerns is drawn from a letter from Representative Jane Harman (D-CA) to President George W. Bush, January 4, 2006 regarding the National Security Agency's Terrorist Surveillance Program (TSP).

investigation required for true oversight and develop an appropriate legislative response.[27]

Although the 1980 Oversight Act seems in retrospect not only to be heavily skewed in the favor the executive but also to have caused hindrances to effective and active oversight to this day, President Carter went even a step further when he signed the act. He stipulated: "There are circumstances in which sensitive information may have to be shared only with a limited number of executive branch officials, even though the Congressional oversight committees are authorized recipients of classified information."[28] Rather than being a bold step toward intensified oversight, the Act simply codified the practice of the Carter administration from the last four years.[29] Interestingly, although the act contained much of the language from Carter's 1978 executive order on intelligence, the administration did not want to enact its provisions through legislation "because the President did not want to give those restraints the force of law."[30]

INSTITUTIONAL CHALLENGE: THE IRAN-CONTRA SCANDAL

In the preceding section, I briefly outlined the incremental development of legislative oversight mechanisms stemming from the pivotal moment of the 1975 congressional investigations of intelligence ending with the last relevant oversight legislation prior to Iran-Contra. In this section, I describe the second turning point in the development of intelligence oversight: the Iran-Contra scandal. The Iran-Contra scandal was important to the development of oversight because it was the first major test of the oversight mechanisms. It was also the source of tremendous upheaval in terms of the balance among the branches of government. It required investigators to assess whether the system and institutions were at fault for the scandal or whether individuals had taken advantage of loopholes and lax systems within the system to attain their

---

[27] Suzanne E. Spaulding, "Power Play: Did Bush Roll Past the Legal Stop Signs?" *Washington Post*, December 25, 2005. Interview with Suzanne E. Spaulding, April 6, 2011.

[28] Johnson, *America's Secret Power*, 209.

[29] Koh, *The National Security Constitution*, 58.

[30] Koh, *The National Security Constitution*, 58.

objectives. It generated questions, again, of what role the other governmental branches have and, normatively, should have in terms of placing constraints on the executive, particularly on covert action.[31]

In brief, the Iran-Contra scandal centered on an elaborate scheme for advancing the Reagan administration's interest in supporting the Nicaraguan Contras, the opponents of the left-leaning Sandinista government. The Iran-Contra scheme emerged out of a complex set of geopolitical beliefs. Reagan and his director of central intelligence, William Casey, strongly believed that the Soviets would threaten American security by gaining a toehold in Central America.[32] While they felt that the Marxist Sandinista government was an emergent threat, the real fear was that a joint Cuba–Soviet incursion could threaten the United States. In Ronald Reagan's words:

> Although El Salvador was the immediate target, the evidence showed that the Soviets and Fidel Castro were targeting all of Central America for a Communist takeover. El Salvador and Nicaragua were only a down payment. Honduras, Guatemala and Costa Rica were next, and then would come Mexico.[33]

By December 1981, Congress had begun supporting the venture, supplying materiel, clothing, and advice to the Contras via the CIA. However, congressional backing for the Contras was short-lived, mainly due to waning public support and general feelings that deep engagement in Central America could lead to another quagmire similar to the Vietnam War.[34] Reacting to these political trends, Congress prohibited funding for the specific purposes of overthrowing the Sandinista government in 1983 and then limited all aid to the Contras to $24 million in fiscal year 1984.[35] A key moment in the development of congressional aversion to continuing funding the Contras came when it was discovered that the CIA had been involved in mining the harbors in Nicaragua without informing Congress appropriately.[36]

---

[31] Koh, *The National Security Constitution*, 2.

[32] Andrew, *For the President's Eyes Only*, 461.

[33] Ronald Reagan, *An American Life*, 238–9, quoted in Andrew, *For the President's Eyes Only*, 461.

[34] Executive Summary, *The Iran-Contra Majority Report*, issued November 18, 1987, 1.

[35] Executive Summary, *The Iran-Contra Majority Report*, 1.

[36] Executive Summary, *The Iran-Contra Majority Report*. Interview with a former staff director of the SSCI and former staff director of the PFIAB, April 29, 2011.

The mining incident served to highlight the role of the CIA in the later scandal, even though the core of the questionable activity happened within the NSC. This led to Congress cutting off all funding for the Contras, including both military and paramilitary operations, in fiscal year 1985. Signed into law by President Reagan on October 12, 1984, this congressional act, the Boland Amendment, marked the beginning of a series of amendments limiting and finally curtailing support for the Contras.

Committed to continuing support for the Contras, President Reagan, however, ordered the NSC to find a means to do so. In early 1984, with funding to the Contras drying up, William Casey and Robert McFarlane began exploring different options for continuing their support of the rebel group.[37] They looked abroad for potential sponsors in Saudi Arabia and Israel, with Saudi Arabia eventually providing millions of dollars in aid. Critical to the progression of the engagement is the fact that as congressionally appropriated funding was cut off in the summer of 1984, operational responsibility for the Contras switched from the Directorate of Operations in the CIA to Lieutenant Colonel Oliver North in the NSC. The rationale behind this change was the fact that because the law forbade any U.S. "agency or entity ... involved in *intelligence activities*" from supporting the Contras, the NSC, as a nonintelligence component and thus apparently not covered by the statute, would provide an acceptable base for such activities.[38] Thus, secret activity was removed from the traditional home of covert activity, the CIA, in order to evade a congressional statute and placed in an agency that was created to advise the president on national security matters but conduct no operations of its own, all without letting Congress know about the entire operation. The process that ultimately developed – as is widely known – was to mark up drastically the cost of weapons to be sold to Iran in order to divert the excess funds to support the Contras. In house, this illegal process was known as "the Diversion."[39]

---

[37] Robert M. Gates, *From the Shadows: The Ultimate Insider's Story of Five Presidents and How They Won the Cold War* (New York: Simon and Schuster, 1996), 391.

[38] Gates, *From the Shadows*, 392. Emphasis added.

[39] Interview with Charles E. Allen, July 7, 2011.

The outcome of the scandal, which resulted in a largely ruined relationship between Congress and the executive branch and a fundamental questioning of the president's capability to lead, had severe repercussions for the Agency, not least because some CIA officers were implicated in the scandal itself, but more because Congress viewed the scandal as the outcome of an incomplete picture of covert action in the country. The CIA itself was only specifically statutorily tasked to conduct such missions in 1991. While this statutory permission arrived many years after the National Security Act of 1947 had given the Agency authorization by default, the activities of the NSC under President Reagan challenged the newly installed congressional oversight mechanisms and forced a recalibration of intelligence oversight from that point on. The irony of the Iran-Contra scandal is that the key pivotal moment that demonstrated a compression of the relationships between government branches and the public, leading to a leap forward in intelligence oversight, had very little to do with the actual intelligence agencies.

The outcome of the critique weighed heavily on senior administrators. Congressional inquiries faulted Director of Central Intelligence Robert Gates for not objecting more strenuously to the ongoing Iran affair, especially regarding the nonnotification of the intelligence oversight committees. He was criticized for not demanding that Casey go to the attorney general and for not insisting on full disclosure to the intelligence committees after being informed by senior CIA officer Charles Allen of his suspicions of the diversion.[40] In his words, "A thousand times I would go over the 'might-have-beens' if I had raised more hell than I did with Casey about non-notification of Congress, if I had demanded that the NSC get out of covert action, if I had insisted that CIA not play by NSC rules, if I had been more aggressive with the DO in my first months as DDCI, if I had gone to the Attorney General on Allen's suspicions of a diversion, if ...."[41] In terms of the CIA, rising star Allen was reprimanded due to his failure to report apparent malfeasance immediately. This reprimand was later removed from his record.

---

[40] Gates, *From the Shadows*, 416.
[41] Gates, *From the Shadows*, 417.

Interestingly, the final report of the Iran-Contra Committee had only had one recommendation regarding executive branch intelligence oversight, namely that the president's appointees for the offices of IG and GC be confirmed in the Senate before assuming office. While seemingly minor, this recommendation has implications for our accountability model and the importance of understanding the different types of accountability and the various processes inherent to each type. First, the executive branch is generally perceived of as monolithic in terms of intelligence programs. Intelligence is a tool of the presidency, according to the spies themselves. Iran-Contra shattered the inviolability of presidential decision making regarding covert action that had, ultimately, survived even the scandals of the 1970s. To suggest officially that other internal mechanisms should have supervised the activities of the presidency is to invite scrutiny of internal activities. In terms of this project, the mention of the importance of internal control mechanisms and the stated importance of the internal independence of mechanisms from the overseen reinforce the theoretical approach to accountability that forms the core of my approach.

Among the changes were several that focused explicitly on reporting on covert action, the crux of the Iran-Contra issue and an ongoing theme in the development of intelligence oversight. The congressional committee that investigated the Iran-Contra affair recommended that notification be required within forty-eight hours after a covert action finding had been approved. Additionally, it was recommended that all findings be in writing and personally approved by the president, retroactive findings should be prohibited, findings should specify their funding sources, and all findings should lapse after one year unless the president renewed them.[42] While the executive malfeasance during the Iran-Contra scandal period was egregious, the changes to intelligence oversight were ultimately minimal. Focusing on the prerogatives of the president as commander-in-chief, the George. H. W. Bush administration refused to be bound by the forty-eight–hour time limit and for the first time ever vetoed the Intelligence Authorization Bill. An agreement

---

[42] *Report of the Congressional Committees Investigating the Iran-Contra Affair*, 423–7, quoted in L. Britt Snider, *The Agency and the Hill: CIA's Relationship with Congress, 1946–2004* (Washington, DC: Center for the Study of Intelligence, 2008), 66.

was reached eventually, however, in which the earlier strenuous deadline was diluted to require the president to provide "timely notice," explained in the conference committee notes to mean "within a few days" of the signing of a finding.[43]

The legislation that eventually arose from the investigation of the Iran-Contra affair, the Intelligence Authorization Act (1991), outlawed retroactive presidential findings and required that any third-party participation in covert activity be reported to the congressional oversight committees.[44] Almost a decade after the committees were put in place, post–Iran-Contra measures were enacted to statutorily codify rules that had previously been agreed upon tacitly. During that interim period, there was still a level of ambiguity as to what degree Congress could compel the intelligence agencies to provide information. As a thirty-year veteran of the Hill and former House Permanent Select Committee on Intelligence (HPSCI) staffer put it, prior to the Iran-Contra revelations, oversight of covert action had been conducted based on a "gentlemen's agreement."[45] It was *assumed* that notification of covert action would be timely and appropriate, but actual measures to enforce diligent reporting were slow to follow this assumption.

Iran-Contra, according to some arguments, was the second act to the original congressional investigations of the 1970s; it forced a reinvestigation of the oversight relationship between the agencies, particularly the CIA, and Congress.[46] It is true that the 1991 act served to strengthen the areas that seemed to have allowed for the loopholes that resulted in the Iran-Contra episode. While the investigations, both in the 1970s and 1980s, were titillating and involved the press and public to an unusual degree in intelligence operations, what do they – and the legislative decisions made in response to them – mean for the accountability framework? Essentially, the soul-searching of that period produced some change in terms of our categories of effective accountability, but the changes themselves were minor in comparison to the deep distrust between the legislature and executive that

[43] Snider, *The Agency and the Hill*, 67; David L. Boren, "The Winds of Change at the CIA," *Yale Law Journal* 101, no. 4 (1992): 856.

[44] Boren, "The Winds of Change at the CIA," 857.

[45] Interview with a former HPSCI staffer, May 5, 2011.

[46] Smist, *Congress Oversees the United States Intelligence Community*, 269.

the scandal itself engendered. The process of reporting was tightened, but even the small step to try to force a time window on the executive failed. Taking the choice of temporality of reporting away from the executive would have reinforced the congressional mechanism's external independence. Interestingly, the focus on timely reporting once again highlights the importance of temporality in accountability. Transparency of the congressional oversight mechanism was not in play, but conversely the investigations shed light on the range of executive control mechanisms that had not been functioning appropriately during this episode.

I would argue that even though the Iran-Contra scandal did not lead to strong congressional legislation, it proved a pivotal moment in legislative oversight, mainly because it showed, once again, that while the mechanisms of the 1970s were deemed important, real effective oversight is almost impossible in light of an executive that is determined to pursue a specific agenda. Thus, in terms of analysis, it is important to assess the asymmetrical relationship between the two branches rather than try to engage in the fallacy that congressional oversight can provide a constraining mechanism without executive branch buy-in. Once again, the 1991 Authorization Act started with a large objective and, following the trend developed within this chapter, was minimized throughout the process to provide only a microstep in the development of the overall matrix of oversight mechanisms. I would also argue that the scandal tightened control over covert action. It greatly reinforced the importance of closely monitoring this exceptional tool of foreign policy. In the sections that follow, I describe briefly how covert action is developed, coordinated, and monitored within the executive branch. This demonstration will also contribute to understanding how complicated overseeing this particular type of activity from the outside has proven to be.

COVERT ACTION, EXECUTIVE CONTROL, AND CONGRESS: THE NATIONAL SECURITY COUNCIL

Iran-Contra shook political legitimacy nationally and caused the public to question its leaders much like the Watergate scandal had more than a decade before. A fascinating feature of the Iran-Contra scandal, however, was the role of the security services, particularly the CIA, and the use of covert action. The scandal raised questions of what covert action is, how it has developed, who does it, and who controls it.

The National Security Council is the highest – and closest – advisory body for the president on national security matters. It is underestimated how important this distance was to early intelligence activities and thus what a large step it was to tighten this relationship and remove the ambiguity concerning its activities, even if the circle of individuals privy to the most secret matters remained extremely small. Characterizations of rogue, ungoverned – and ungovernable – covert action run throughout coverage on the issue, both in fiction and non-fiction treatments. The truth of control and oversight of covert action is somewhat different from its portrayal, according to the operators, with strict protocols in place to govern program development and approval, regular reviews and audits by numerous supervisory bodies, and layer upon layer of legal review. As Gregory Treverton writes, "... I have been struck by the contrast between the free-wheeling image of covert action and the accountant-like auditing that is CIA practice."[47] Increased oversight and multifaceted project management have developed alongside the development of statute to clarify the practice and ensure lines of communication about covert activities. A theme that runs throughout this project is very prevalent here: that the ends of covert action may be unsatisfactory to many on moral, ethical, or legal grounds, but the process of planning, coordinating, and undertaking a covert action is currently conducted in bureaucratic lockstep. This was not always the case, and I will illustrate this by describing briefly the history of National Security Council covert action supervision before turning to the modern implementation of executive control over covert activity.[48]

---

[47] Gregory F. Treverton, *Covert Action: The Limits of Intervention in the Postwar World* (Basic Books: New York, 1987), 138; interview with Stephen R. Kappes, March 12, 2011.

[48] As a point of interest, I asked one of my interviewees, a senior CIA officer who had served in the NSC as senior management over covert action, what term was used for the executive branch supervision over covert action. The term "oversight" was never used; in its

The NSC and CIA have worked closely together on covert action since shortly after the National Security Act (1947) was passed. As early as 1948, the CIA's Office of Policy Coordination provided a forum where representatives from external departments such as the departments of Defense and State could convene to discuss covert action proposals.[49] Covert activities were authorized through Function V as well as a series of NSC directives that usually passed without much external commentary.[50] As Loch Johnson points out, during this early period it was not assumed that the NSC had approval authority, but rather that the CIA had appropriate approval through NSC directives such as NSC-4 and NSC-4a, which focused on the importance of covert action in defeating international communism, as well as subsequent directives. The forum provided by these directives was perceived as one in which ideas could be exchanged and external members could offer whatever guidance they felt appropriate, but did not give them veto power over a particular action.[51]

In 1954, Eisenhower created the 5412 Committee (known as the Special Group) to coordinate covert activity and review major covert actions. The Special Group was succeeded by a range of similar but differently named groups, such as the 303 Committee and, up to the Ford administration, the 40 Committee. These secret committees, composed of representatives usually from the State and Defense departments and relevant agencies, "oversaw" the development of covert action plans, but their impact as actual oversight seems to have been minimal. Rhodri Jeffreys-Jones argues that the objective behind the new incarnations of the same mechanism was a function of its hybrid nature: it was intended to be secret, but also intended to carry the burden in place of the president if the action failed and became public. He argues that the changing names and composition of this mechanism was intended to deceive public opinion. If the group in one guise was exposed, it was quickly replaced by a reconfigured one with a new name but roughly the same participants.[52] This, however,

---

place, "management" or "control" was used. Interview with s former NSC director of intelligence programs, November 14, 2011.

[49] Johnson, "Covert Action and Accountability," 90.

[50] Function V of the National Security Act of 1947 directs the CIA "to perform such other functions and duties related to intelligence affecting the national security as the National Security Council may from time to time direct." (P. L. 80-253) Sec. 102(d)(5).

[51] Johnson, "Covert Action and Accountability," 90.

[52] Johnson, "Covert Action and Accountability," 90.

never proved to be very effective; the president could not usually turn to his amorphous NSC committee to take the blame when an action failed. The entity conventionally blamed for any such failure was and continues to be the CIA. This is, at least, partially due to the unique and dependent relationship the CIA has with the president.[53] In support of this point, former DCI Gates put it:

> The CIA is a uniquely presidential organization. Virtually every time it has gotten into trouble, it has been for carrying out some action ordered by the president – from Nicaragua to Iran. Yet few presidents have anything good to say about CIA or the intelligence received.[54]

In terms of how effective early NSC mechanisms were at actually overseeing covert action, participation in them generally was uneven and guidelines and expectations about their performance were unclear. For the most part, internal advice on covert action would be provided by a small group of close confidants of the president, and this advice was usually only given in the case of a major operation. The president and his staff, including the NSC, tended to be included only in deliberations regarding major, or particularly risky, covert actions. For the most part, the CIA had authorization to develop and conduct programs without even notifying the president, as long as the programs were in line with the administration's foreign policy objectives.[55]

As the Church Committee pointed out, "loose understandings rather than specific review formed the basis for CIA's accountability for covert operations."[56] Mirroring to some extent the path of legislative oversight of intelligence, this looseness and dependence on the CIA to develop and conduct covert actions with little external input seems to have lasted until the 1970s. According to the Church Committee's findings, about 14 percent of covert actions between 1961 and 1975

---

[53] Johnson, "Covert Action and Accountability," 90; interview with Stephen R. Kappes, March 12, 2011. This issue of blame being directed at the CIA due to convenience is repeated so often that it is impossible to cite the complete range of sources. More currently, this trend was very apparent during the investigation into the perceived intelligence failure on 9/11.

[54] Gates, *From the Shadows*, 567.

[55] Daugherty, *Executive Secrets*, 98.

[56] *Church Committee* 1976b, 50.

had been approved by the NSC.[57] An objective behind this lack of connection between the CIA and the president on covert action was to protect plausible deniability to ensure that the president could distance himself should an action go wrong. In fact, rather than constituting a check on covert activities, these early mechanisms were actually a convenient mechanism through which to deflect presidential responsibility for covert action.[58] In the words of former DCI Richard Helms, the early special group, under Eisenhower, "was the mechanism ... set up ... to use as a circuit-breaker so that [covert operations] did not explode in the president's face and so that he was not held responsible for them."[59]

Much like within the other branches of government, this loose "gentleman's agreement" format for intelligence oversight began to change in the early 1970s. During this period, the activities of the CIA and the relationship of the Agency to the domestic population were very heated and contested political issues.[60] Part of this stemmed from the overall lack of faith in government during that period; another part was due to the opacity of the intelligence community itself. Most people knew very little about the purview and activities of the CIA or the other intelligence agencies. Thus, when stories of domestic experimentation on unwitting individuals, harassment programs, and attempted assassinations began to percolate through society, it was difficult to understand the limits of this secret agency, particularly in terms of what the CIA was permitted to do domestically. As an example, when the issue of political assassinations was discussed in the committee hearings, even members of Congress were not entirely sure whether this type of assassination of political leaders was being conducted domestically in addition to abroad. (It was not.)

This pivotal moment in the history of control of the CIA began with President Ford being forced to cope with the Nixon resignation and an extremely tense political environment, replete with allegations of the administration having misled the public and Congress regarding CIA operations in Chile. Faced with this environment, Ford exposed the

[57] *Church Committee* 1976b, 56–7.
[58] Jeffreys-Jones, *The CIA and American Democracy*, 93.
[59] Quoted in Jeffreys-Jones, *The CIA and American Democracy*, 93.
[60] Jeffreys-Jones, *The CIA and American Democracy*, 194.

existence of the internal NSC oversight committee, the 40 Committee, while also focusing on the congressional role, not only in oversight but also in the design of executive branch oversight mechanisms. Both of these moves were unprecedented in their inclusion of the public and Congress into the process of intelligence supervision. In Ford's words:

> That Committee reviews every covert operation undertaken by our Government, and that information is relayed to the responsible Congressional committees where it is reviewed by House and Senate committees.
>
> It seems to me that the 40 Committee should continue in existence, and I am going to meet with the responsible Congressional committees to see whether or not they want any changes in the review process so that the Congress, as well as the President, are fully informed and are fully included in the operations for any such action.[61]

While this statement was intended to assuage any anxieties about inappropriate foreign intelligence conduct, it was released just prior to the biggest upheaval to hit the intelligence community ever: the 1974 Hersh disclosure of decades of intelligence abuses and malfeasance conducted both *domestically* and internationally. The details of the disclosures as well as the revelations found in three separate government investigations will be described in depth in the next chapter, but what is crucial to the current discussion is how the political environment began to catalyze and shape legislative action with regard to oversight, as well as how the executive branch responded to encroachments on its perceived national security and, particularly, foreign intelligence territory.

Over the course of the decades following the National Security Act of 1947 (NSA 1947), covert action has been gradually defined and clarified through a series of statutes and executive orders. Development of oversight institutions in Congress has tended to be in reaction to public scandal that has occurred generally as a function of both perceived deviant intelligence activities and political environment, whereas the executive branch has organized control based on administration policy objectives and political ideology. Executive guidance has also responded mildly to accusations of intelligence malfeasance.

[61] *Presidential Papers Ford, 1975, 150–1, quoted in Andrew, For the President's Eyes Only, 400.*

The following description vacillates between focusing on the development of legislative mechanisms and on executive policy decisions and orders in order to illustrate how the strands of control and oversight are intertwined.

Executive branch control of intelligence activities tends to focus on several main points. First, it usually endeavors to define covert action, including pointing out in detail what it is and who should conduct it. Second, it usually clarifies the particular administration's view of the role of the NSC vis-à-vis the CIA. This is a close relationship; the NSC is charged under NSA 1947 with responsibility for intelligence activities. Thus, beyond review responsibilities that are standard among legislative oversight mechanisms, the NSC is an equal partner, usually, in developing, monitoring, and correcting covert action programs.[62] The development of executive orders on covert action shows remarkable consistency even between widely divergent administrations. As is to be expected, they all fiercely guard executive privilege with regard to intelligence activities by carefully defining the activities conducted, limiting oversight within the executive branch, and carefully delimiting the terms by which they will allow outsiders access to intelligence information.

Most of the tension between the branches regarding oversight stems from the argument over how much, when, and to whom this information is provided – that is, in terms of the accountability framework, knowledge conditions. Overall, this isn't a fair debate, because the relationship is entirely asymmetrical: the executive branch controls policy and the tools that inform policy – intelligence information – and thus the argument is really not who is more effective at "overseeing" intelligence activities, particularly covert action, but rather how the apertures of information that others are provided are used to provide external controls and whether and how this information is transformed into a useful flow for extra-executive decision making regarding these types of activities. All of the explanations of policy choices regarding intelligence oversight discussed in this section are deeply embedded within each president's policy framework.

While the executive branch is protective of its purview over intelligence, after the early 1970s, when intelligence activities were forced to

<hr>

[62] Interview with a former NSC director of intelligence programs, November 14, 2011.

be more transparent, the executive has also tended to pander slightly to the public mood of respective administrations' eras. Presidential statements regarding constraints on intelligence, particularly on covert action, could be considered almost a public relations device designed to communicate to the public diligent presidential control over intelligence activities, particularly over covert action. This nod to the requirement of public acceptance of intelligence activities appears in public statements but also in the executive orders themselves, and it all begins in the 1970s. Thus, there are two dominant themes when it comes to the information regarding covert action emanating from the executive branch: on the one hand, there is the extreme executive prerogative to control this perceived natural tool of the executive branch; on the other, there is a sense that the executive should bend slightly not to the will of the people, which remains, as ever, ambiguous in terms of national security matters, but to a norm of responsibility and responsiveness to American democracy and the populace. This latter effect stems from the broader political environment, whereas the former stems from embedded executive privilege and the threat environment. I will illustrate this dual dynamic later in this chapter in a brief exposition of relevant executive orders regarding covert action and intelligence. For this I have chosen to focus on three administrations – those of Ford, Carter, and Reagan – because they are the most relevant in terms of understanding the foundations of intelligence oversight. Their relevance stems from the fact that the turbulence of the 1970s catalyzed engagement with intelligence oversight that had ramifications for all three administrations during their respective tenures.

The NSC holds a pivotal role with regard to the process of developing and approving covert actions; as mentioned throughout the text, the NSC is the highest executive branch institution responsible for guiding the president on intelligence matters, but the process itself varies – much like the NSC itself – depending on the administration. Control over covert action is an involved process and – based on my research – a careful and rigorous one, involving a wide range of stakeholder groups, with each step in development being carefully monitored by attorneys from the CIA, NSC, and Department of Justice.[63]

---

[63] Interview with Stephen R. Kappes, April 6, 2011.

It is very important to understand how the process of covert action approval functions in order to understand not only how intelligence oversight operates, but also to have a clear idea of the role that covert action plays in achieving foreign policy objectives, not only from the perspective of the policy makers, but especially from the side of the operators themselves.

Pre-1970s NSC control over covert action was relatively *ad hoc*, but began to be tightened incrementally after the scandals of the 1970s. According to current operators, the process is now regularized with tight iterations on proposed projects between the NSC and CIA. Authority is clear and the process of program development and review is thorough, disciplined, and painstakingly reviewed by legal staff in both the CIA and the NSC. There are at least two facets to this tight relationship: budget and legal structure. In the first case, solid support from the White House via the NSC is key to funding covert actions out of special budgets. The second aspect of this situation is more central to the oversight of covert action. Initiation of covert action projects stems from a range of agencies; it could be from a department such as State, from the NSC, or as the result of a larger, intelligence communitywide problem such as terrorism. Program initiation is usually never from the CIA itself, although this is a common misconception. While seemingly basic, the point of origin of covert action projects is a source of contention. Most of the controversy about from where the idea for an action stems is rooted in the idea that the CIA operates separately from normal modes of governmental control; that is, the assumption is that operations are impromptu and conducted without review or oversight. In actuality, covert action is generated from a range of government policy *needs*, and the program is developed to solve the problem that is embedded within those needs.

The first step after initiation is the passage of the proposal to Operations (now the National Clandestine Service) for project development. Operators develop a plan to carry out the mission in a process that involves numerous CIA components, most notably the continual involvement of CIA attorneys. The actual practice of developing covert programs debunks two further misconceptions: that programs are unconstrained by legal structure and that the DCIA is not involved. In fact, lawyers are embedded throughout the Agency to determine at multiple levels where the legal line stands with regard to appropriate activity. A constant trend in all current analysis of the internal activities of the CIA is the role of attorneys and a pervasive culture of legality. Lawyers are present at all meetings. This leads all the way up to the Office of the General Counsel. One operator commented that it is not uncommon to have several lawyers from different layers of the Agency present in a meeting disagree about the legality of a particular program. Further, after review by CIA lawyers, the proposed action is reviewed by NSC lawyers and then, most likely, by lawyers in Congress after the finding is sent to the Hill. The DCIA and DDCIA are integrally involved in the development of all programs. As the program passes up the layers of the CIA hierarchy, the director and deputy director of the CIA are integrally involved in the review and "scrubbing" of the proposal.

In terms of internal mechanisms, covert actions are considered, analyzed, and tested in two specific locations: the Covert Action Planning Group (CAPG) and the Covert Action Review Group (CARG). CAPG – a directorate-level working group – is convened by the deputy director for operations or the associate deputy director for operations and includes representatives from all of the components potentially involved in the action. This includes the component chief, the operations officer in charge of program management, an attorney assigned by the general counsel's office, component attorneys, budget managers, and other covert action specialists.[64] This group reviews the covert action proposal for goals, feasibility, costs, risks, coherence, and adherence to the tenets of administration foreign policy goals.[65]

Once any necessary adjustments are made to the program, it is then shipped up to the Agency-wide level of covert action review. The CARG is particularly pertinent to the development of intelligence oversight mechanisms as, in addition to demonstrating critical and thorough involvement in the controlled development of covert action at the highest level, it was also the creature of the fallout surrounding the Iran-Contra scandal. It demonstrates the addition of another layer of internal check and control over covert action, and its creation

[64] Daugherty, *Executive Secrets*, 104.
[65] Daugherty, *Executive Secrets*, 104.

seems to point to a high-level understanding of the need for this check. Established by former DCI Gates in 1986, the group was originally intended to provide coordinated advice to the DCI and DDCI on "all aspects of proposed findings for covert action and changes to existing findings."[66] At that time, the group included the executive director, DDO, DDI, general counsel, comptroller, and director of congressional relations. In Gates' words:

> While the group was created to streamline and improve the internal CIA coordination process, it was also intended to bring more intrusive oversight of covert action. Later, when he became DCI, Bill Webster would further strengthen this group and formalize its procedures. In any event, the clandestine service – I would later learn – was neither comfortable nor happy with such involvement by other parts of the Agency in its activities.[67]

Again, rooted in the covert action and political scandal of Iran-Contra, this group is still critical to the development and review of covert action. Currently, it is composed of the relevant members of a range of internal CIA offices, which, in addition to Operations Division officers, includes the Office of General Counsel, the Office of Science and Technology, and Support Division staff. The Support Division staff plays a key role here, being the personnel required to provide logistical and other material support to the proposed operation. Congressional Affairs and Public Affairs representatives are also present, as are briefers pulled in from the relevant specialties. These members are voting members of the board, and they are responsible for approving, rejecting, or altering the operational plans presented to them by the Operations Division.[68] Plans are subjected to detailed scrutiny, revised if necessary, and in some cases sent back to the National Security Council with concerns detailed.

As Kappes mentions, the CARG is a place of professional candor and is meant to be challenging and a rigorous test of potential operational plans. Core to the deliberations, according to former DCI William Webster, were answers to the following questions: "Is it [the proposed

---

[66] Gates, *From the Shadows*, 379.

[67] Gates, *From the Shadows*, 379.

[68] Interview with Stephen Kappes, April 6, 2011; interview with General Michael Hayden, March 9, 2011.

covert action] entirely consistent with our laws? Is it consistent with American values as we understand them? And will it make sense to the American people?"[69] Kappes revises this statement to suggest that the focus of program development is very much on whether the objectives of the proposed operation reflect policy objectives correctly. While legality is fundamental to the analysis of the feasibility of an operation, Kappes argues that worry about public perception is less of a concern for the operators, as they leave this aspect to the policy makers. Pragmatically, questions of feasibility and effectiveness in meeting operational and policy goals are the critical issues of covert program review.

One reason for the detailed scrutiny is in the nature of the type of activity. As Kappes put it, there is a level of uncertainty inherent to the conduct of covert activity. The best plans can go awry, and the activities are dangerous. In his words, "A lot of people can tell you how covert action starts, but no one can tell you how it ends."[70] After approval by the CARG and the director, the proposal is passed to the NSC. In process, NSC monitoring of covert activities fits into a normal bureaucratic pattern. Covert programs developed, traditionally by the CIA, come to the NSC "scrubbed" already by the CIA's process of internal review. Covert action is perceived by the NSC, much like the NSC itself, as the "president's program."[71] Programs begin in the NSC with a working group review; upon refinement and approval, the proposal moves upward in the institutional hierarchy to the Deputies' Committee; to the Principals' Committee; and, finally, upon approval, to the president for his signature and issuance of a finding of covert action to be sent to Congress.[72] As has been pointed out throughout this section, attorneys are involved in every step of this process, beginning with the CIA's lowest level; continuing up to the director before heading through the NSC's process; and, upon issuance of the president's finding, finally through congressional committee and, perhaps, legal review.[73] According to a senior CIA official, who had served as

---

[69] William Webster quoted in James A. Barry, "Managing Covert Political Action: Guideposts from Just War Theory," *Studies in Intelligence* 36, no. 5 (1992): 19–31, at 21.

[70] Interview with Stephen Kappes, April 6, 2011.

[71] Interview with a former NSC director of intelligence programs, November 14, 2011.

[72] Interview with a former NSC director of intelligence programs, November 14, 2011.

[73] Interview with a former NSC director of intelligence programs, November 14, 2011; interview with Stephen R. Kappes, May 12, 2011.

a director of intelligence programs at the NSC, this careful process was due to the political traumas involving the intelligence community of the 1970s and 1980s, meaning the congressional investigations of abuses in the mid-1970s and the Iran-Contra scandal of the 1980s.[74] The action can be denied at each of these levels, making the internal process toward approval more onerous, detailed, and controlled than is sometimes assumed.[75]

Findings, as has been discussed throughout this book, are a key component of intelligence oversight. As mentioned previously, findings were a crucial step to the beginning of the institutionalization of a clear process for oversight, but also, and extremely important, the cornerstone of a weakening of plausible deniability. Findings themselves outline the scope and goals of the proposed activity. They outline who will be involved and the government agencies upon which the operators are authorized to call for assistance. The key to the writing of a finding is to find a middle ground between too broad and too specific and narrow. According to an NSC program reviewer, findings also build in processes for internal review and status reporting as the program proceeds.[76] To integrate all relevant parties, opinions are sought from those potentially impacted – for example, cabinet secretaries – and amendments are made for incorporation into the finding. The finding is a critical legal document and is usually briefed to the president in person. Findings include four sections: Policy Objectives, Plan of Action, Risk Assessment, and Resources Required. If there could be loss of life of non-CIA personnel during the operation, the finding is known as a "Lethal Finding," and this information is conveyed to Congress.[77] Clear themes of iterative cleansing of programs through different levels of responsibility, overlapping responsibilities for the programs, and ultimate presidential control emerge from this description drawn from senior intelligence officers in control of covert action in the NSC. In terms of our broader argument about

---

[74] Interview with a former NSC director of intelligence programs, November 14, 2011.

[75] William E. Connor, "Reforming Oversight of Covert Actions after the Iran-Contra Affair: A Legislative History of the Intelligence Authorization Act for FY 1991," *Virginia Journal of International Law* 32 (1991–2): 885.

[76] Interview with a former NSC director of intelligence programs, November 14, 2011.

[77] Interview with Stephen Kappes, May 12, 2011; Daugherty, *Executive Secrets*, 110; Jeffrey T. Richelson, *The US Intelligence Community* (Boulder, CO: Westview Press, 2011), 509.

the opposition between the executive and legislative branches, covert action proves once again to be an inflection point. The asymmetric relationship is at an acute point with covert action. While mechanisms have developed slowly to monitor these activities, and the power of the purse can eventually halt them, they still are the tightly controlled purview of the executive, with congressional overseers as merely – albeit important – witnesses.

9/11: REORGANIZATION, BLAME, AND ORGANIZATIONAL CHANGE

Intelligence oversight slipped out of the public eye – and interest – for close to two decades after the Iran-Contra affair. In the post–Cold War world, intelligence activities waned in importance. In a time of perceived diminished worldwide threat, there was even talk of dismantling the CIA. The next great attention paid to the intelligence community came in the wake of the attacks on 9/11.

While it is clear that the Church Committee investigations and the Iran-Contra scandal led to a clarification of the relationship between the executive and legislative branches and a recalibration of where checks should be placed on the executive branch, the changes after 9/11 have turned out to be a different matter altogether. This is partly a function of the characteristics of the different crises: the first two were political scandals, while the third was an operational failure calling for a different type of potential solution. The reaction to the attacks – as well as to the failure to find weapons of mass destruction in Iraq – led to unprecedented change and reorganization of the intelligence community. While the changes were wide-ranging, cutting across cultural and institutional boundaries, the oversight committees remained surprisingly supine in reaction to 9/11 Commission criticisms that they were part of the problem. This section touches very briefly on the activities of the 9/11 Commission, as they provided the basis for the organizational change that occurred within the intelligence community. I describe two results of the recommendations and discuss briefly the ramifications of those changes for intelligence oversight.

The attacks on 9/11 were an unexpected shock that shook American perceptions of safety and insularity. The attacks did not introduce a new type of threat to the world; they simply brought immediacy to an age-old tactic, but the impact was immediate.[78] The result of the attacks was, as intended, societywide fear and cascading economic effects, but the United States never faced an existential threat and probably never will. What the attacks on 9/11 did shatter was the exceptionalism born of incredible relative strength in the international arena and hubris arising not only from this strength, but also from motivated ignorance of the dynamics of the world. The reason I mention ignorance is to illustrate that much of the response to the attacks in terms of institutional reorganization of the national security apparatus was in response to the political environment rather than the exigencies of the threat. It is true that the audacity of the attacks was unprecedented, and the fact that U.S. infrastructure could be used so effectively against itself was striking. All talk of brilliant mastermind terrorists, however, is overblown. In the case of 9/11, the dual keys to the project were timing and an awareness of American structural vulnerabilities. But, instead of reacting proportionally to the attacks, both in terms of return strikes against the purported adversary and hardening of American targets, the U.S. government under the George W. Bush administration rushed to reorganize the sprawling intelligence community.

A concerted effort was made to discover what had gone wrong – what had been missed to allow the 9/11 attacks to occur. A joint congressional investigation into the causes of 9/11 as well as a second commission, the 9/11 Commission, investigated where the fault for 9/11 lay and where to place blame. The 9/11 Commission became famous and popular in a way unique for an investigatory commission. Partially this was because of the outsized personalities eventually chosen to participate, particularly the chair and vice-chair, former New Jersey governor Thomas Kean and former U.S. representative Lee Hamilton; and secondarily because of

---

[78] A quote from Martha Crenshaw, a renowned terrorism scholar with years of experience prior to 9/11, counters the "break from the past" theory succinctly: "… [T]he departure from the past is not as pronounced as many accounts make it out to be. Today's terrorism is not a fundamentally or qualitatively 'new' phenomenon but grounded in an evolving historical context." Quoted in Paul R. Pillar, *Intelligence and U.S. Foreign Policy: Iraq, 9/11, and Misguided Reform* (New York: Columbia University Press, 2011), 209.

the nature of the topic, *owned* by the American people and represented in the personae of the families of the 9/11 victims, whose influence on the proceedings proved to be enormous. Scholar and former CIA official Paul R. Pillar summarizes the impact of the commission in a commonly accepted view within Washington circles:

> The 9/11 Commission would attain – in part because of the salience of the event it was charged with investigating and in part because of its own prodigious salesmanship – prominence and influence that would make it the envy of ad hoc panels everywhere. It would come to be listened to as the arbiter of all that is good and bad in counterterrorism. Its word would be accepted and replayed again and again as the last word on everything about 9/11, including everything involving intelligence.[79]

Unfortunately, a determination to be politically sensitive to the families of the victims, and the need to smooth bipartisan divides diluted the end product, requiring removal of some data and the watering down of interpretation.[80] The partisanship issue was particularly fraught, because the 9/11 Commission was investigating a highly charged political issue that sat exactly at the inflection point between the Clinton and Bush administrations. Who failed at counterterrorism? Both were eager to protect their colleagues from specific blame, leading to bargaining and deal-making on how the individuals would be investigated and presented in the final text of the report. Thus, the ultimate report does not particularly blame individuals. In text delicately worded for a government publication, the blame was placed on the intelligence community for a series of ambiguous sins, including "failure of imagination." Anyone who has ever worked in a bureaucratic organization should chuckle at this censure. Further, biases and assumptions on the part of specific commission staffers had an effect on the final conclusions of the investigation. All of this not only affected the outcome of the report, but also the subsequent recommendations for intelligence community reform. One such issue was the creation of a director of

---

[79] Pillar, *Intelligence and U.S. Foreign Policy*, 234.

[80] Pillar, *Intelligence and U.S. Foreign Policy*, 235. See also Philip Shenon, *The Commission: The Uncensored History of the 9/11 Investigation* (New York: Twelve, 2008). This sentiment also appeared in my interview with a former 9/11 Commission staffer, April 14, 2011.

national intelligence, a pet project of the extremely strong-willed 9/11 Commission staff director Philip Zelikow.[81]

The 9/11 Commission's role in determining the appropriate approach to intelligence reform is an interesting phenomenon in its own right. First, the commission grew out of a combination of issues, including the tepid response to the congressional investigation and the prolonged public demands for further investigation on the part of groups representing the victims' families. In many ways, the 9/11 Commission's genesis mirrored those of the investigations after the 1970s scandals and in response to the Iran-Contra scandal. It was, as were the others, a public display of governmental thoroughness and earnestness in the wake of a national scandal or, in this case, tragedy. The outcome of the commission's investigation was an anodyne, well-written best-seller that served to soothe the partisan conflict that characterized discussions of the issue.[82]

Blame was placed on the intelligence community for its failure to share information and build an accurate-enough mosaic of the looming attack that might have enabled its prevention and overall for a failure to adapt. Drawing upon the range of opinions expressed both in the media analyses and among the intelligence officers I interviewed, as well as my own analysis, the truth of the failure was actually much more basic than the hearings and commission reports would suggest. The intelligence community is a series of hierarchically organized agencies. These agencies use standard procedures to shift an incredible amount of information through the system and into the hands of policy makers. Failures will happen. Some of the vulnerabilities of the system should have been fixed years prior to the attacks, among them the different spheres of influence within the community, the turf wars, and the unwillingness to share. Other major issues included the absence, in some cases, of unifying objectives for the overall intelligence community; structural atomization; and the uneven relationship between the director of central intelligence – in theory the head of the

---

[81] Pillar, *Intelligence and U.S. Foreign Policy*, 239. See also Shenon, The Commission, for detail on how Zelikow's management style, personal political connections, and analytical predelictions influenced the outcome of the 9/11 Commission's work.

[82] Interview with Bill Harlow, CIA public relations officer under George Tenet, March 28, 2011; interview with a former 9/11 Commission staffer, April 14, 2011.

community at that time – and the secretary of defense, who controlled, and still controls, the lion's share of the intelligence budget. This does not even begin to address the layers upon layers of political and policy failings that contributed to the attacks, from the Bush administration's alleged failure to take warning of potential Al-Qaeda attacks from Presidential Daily Briefs (PDBs) to President Bush's lack of interest in foreign policy matters. Of course, on the other side, accusations were made that President Clinton's administration was soft on national security – "swatting at flies" – and terrorism, thus allegedly leaving the Bush administration with the prior administration's mess to clean up.[83]

The 9/11 Commission recommended a series of organizational changes to the intelligence community in the politicized environment of the period. They were wholeheartedly embraced by Congress and contributed heavily to the legislation guided quickly through Congress by the Senate Governmental Affairs Committee. There was also a political push behind the recommendations in that the report appeared during the final stages of the 2004 presidential campaign, and neither candidate wanted to appear weak on national security at such a crucial juncture for American safety. The bill was passed by the Senate two weeks after it was introduced; the House bill also passed in two weeks.[84] One of the main points of the legislation, of course, was the creation of a director of national intelligence to sit atop the intelligence community. This move reduced the former putative head of the community, the director of central intelligence, to the level of a mere agency director. Judge Richard Posner described the plan for the role of DNI: "... [T]he DNI, shorn of responsibility for running the CIA, would become not the chairman but the chief executive officer of the intelligence community."[85] The idea behind the hierarchical change was that coordination and information sharing were the key problems leading to 9/11 and thus a very senior official could unite the sixteen agencies of the community, as well as serve as the point person and central intelligence advisor to the president.

---

[83] National Commission on Terrorist Attacks upon the United States (Philip Zelikow, Executive Director; Bonnie D. Jenkins, Counsel; Ernest R. May, Senior Advisor), *The 9/11 Commission Report* (New York: W. W. Norton, 2004), 202.

[84] Richard A. Posner, *Preventing Surprise Attacks: Intelligence Reform in the Wake of 9/11* (Lanham, MD: Rowman and Littlefield, 2005), 53.

[85] Posner, *Preventing Surprise Attacks*, 37.

As described previously, since NSA 1947 clarified the role of the CIA, the director of central intelligence (DCI) has held two responsibilities: he has directed the CIA and has also been charged with the direction of the entire intelligence community, at least in terms of the IC's coordination with the requirements of the president. This bifurcation of roles has always carried many inherent caveats and drawbacks. Mainly, the DCI, while formerly the key reporter to the president about intelligence issues, did not have control over the bulk of the intelligence budget, which is under the purview of the secretary of defense. Further, the tension between the military and national intelligence program agencies was exacerbated by the military's fear that a strong DCI could hinder military intelligence agencies' responsiveness to the needs of the military.[86]

Over the course of many years, it has been suggested that an overall coordinator of the entire intelligence community could be useful in streamlining information stemming from the awkwardly atomized intelligence community. While the creation of such an office had been discussed for several decades, the attacks on 9/11 and the analyses after these attacks led to the realization of such an office. As a result of the recommendations of the 9/11 Commission, the Intelligence Reform and Terrorism Prevention Act (IRTPA) of 2004 established the Office of the Director of National Intelligence with the responsibility of serving as the president's advisor on intelligence with purview over the national intelligence program, excepting the military-focused agencies, which remain in the Department of Defense.

In addition to the position of the DNI, intended to centralize intelligence, another specific criticism brought by the 9/11 Commission was the failure to "connect the dots" – the failure to share information among agencies enough to put the pieces of the plot together. In theory, proposals to create centralized locations where analysts drawn from throughout the community could work together on a specific issue, such as counterterrorism or counterproliferation, would centralize information, thinking, and analysis and could help with the problems of group-think, lack of alternative analysis, and stovepiping that

[86] Richelson, *The US Intelligence Community*, 453.

led to the failure to foresee the attacks on 9/11. In actuality, the result of the pressure to build additional components and units whose focus was to share and integrate information was to cause a massive pro-liferation of the entities charged with overlapping duties. While these new institutions at the top level have created confusion with other longer-entrenched components, these problems have also dropped down to the local and state levels and caused the number of agencies to multiply drastically. The push for increased interagency coopera-tion and information sharing led the federal agencies – particularly the Department of Homeland Security (DHS) and the FBI as the two agencies focused on domestic security issues – to begin to integrate local-level agencies, such as local law enforcement, into the intelli-gence gathering process.

Investments using federal funds were made to increase the num-ber of "fusion centers," locations where members of various agencies would be co-located to analyze intelligence information. These usually all have a DHS officer detailed to serve as a point person to the fed-eral level. Joint Terrorism Task Forces (JTTFs) were organized by the FBI through their field offices to bring collaborating agencies together to work on terrorism issues. Thus streams of information have been increasing in all directions. Local-level agencies began to get the atten-tion of their "betters" in Washington, while the federal agencies started to consider local-level expertise on communities and practice useful to the overall intelligence enterprise. Thus the network of agencies linked together has grown, as has the number of components dealing with counterterrorism.

As is noted throughout the literature on the 2004 intelligence reforms, these reforms have not proven exceptionally successful, for several reasons. They were devised in haste to serve political constit-uents not normally a part of the oversight process; they were based on the assumptions and quick analysis of the 9/11 Commission; and they were not realistic about the successes and failures that are nor-mal to the intelligence process as a regular bureaucratic function. The political imperative to find fault and to highlight the faults of the IC allowed observers to ignore the many successes of the agencies. This is not to apologize for the community, but rather to point out that rash and dramatic reorganization was its own failure of foresight, leading to the disruption of the many components of the community that had worked effectively.[87]

The intelligence failure on 9/11 was the product of a bureaucratic process that is large, overlapping, and beset with conflicting objectives. It also involved individuals – and thus potential human failure – as well as linkages between operators, analysts, and decision makers. As pointed out in Chapter 2, the Agency and the intelligence community are easy to blame. The secrecy inherent to their work, their lack of public profile, and the fact that they do not have a natural constituency within the policy debates to support their claims, such as the Pentagon does, make them an easy target. As former DCI Helms put it, "I am the easiest man in Washington to fire. I have no political, military or industrial base."[88] One can, however, go too far with assertions of unfair blame and accusations of habitual scapegoating of the intelligence community. My assertion is that blame for the attacks was misaligned with the actuality of which changes could have been beneficial to the intelligence apparatus. Scores of books have been written on 9/11, analyzing what enabled the attacks to succeed, and arguing for a range of different solutions to the problems these analyses unearth. My objective here is not to add to this list, but rather to point to how the 9/11 Commission's own goals, and the political context within which it released its recommendations, enabled a specific, narrow type of reorganization of the intelligence community.

The creation of a new position atop the intelligence community and the dispersion of intelligence gathering authorities raise conflicting questions for accountability. On the one hand, centralizing intelligence decreases apertures for oversight, while on the other, the increase of intelligence-focused components dilutes the attention overseers would be able to give to the individual intelligence activities. An issue that has arisen in the post-IRTPA period is what role the director of national intelligence and his office play in the oversight of active intelligence operations. The DNI is not an actual "overseer" in the terminology that I use throughout this book. A question often

---

[87] Richard K. Betts, *Enemies of Intelligence: Knowledge and Power in the American National Security* (New York: Columbia University Press, 2007), 2.

[88] Quoted in Pillar, *Intelligence and U.S. Foreign Policy*, 179.

asked in terms of the DNI is whether the position possesses oversight authority and how that functions. The DNI is not perceived as "external" to the remainder of the intelligence community. Rather, as stated previously, he is the CEO, the coordinator, and figurehead, and not generally involved in the operational level of intelligence. This creates an extra layer of bureaucracy for the intelligence community, but does not, in fact, affect traditional oversight mechanisms to any great extent. Thus, although we may want to add the DNI to the mechanisms studied, the position added bureaucratic complexity, but not any degree of greater accountability. The sheer magnitude of the responsibilities of the DNI would make any additional "external" task not only impossible, but also inappropriate. The DNI is the president's closest advisor on intelligence matters. He is, thus, responsible for bringing together the thoughts of the community and presenting those to the president daily. He presents a unified voice, but the task of ensuring internal adherence to executive policy requirements rests far below him. One specific challenge to accountability could be a changing role for the inspector general (CIA), who has held a special role in terms of oversight due to the position's statutory basis and reporting responsibilities. This could feasibly change if the DNI chooses to coordinate communitywide inspectors general under his or her authority or under the authority of the inspector general within the Office of the Director of National Intelligence (ODNI).

The proliferation of intelligence components has challenged the unified approach that the DNI represents. While the intelligence community was developing new bureaucratic processes to cope with new agencies, responsibilities, and a new communitywide director, oversight has been challenged to keep up with this change, on both functional and political levels. The two committees have generally not kept up with change in the intelligence community, but the adaptation and growth of the IC has engendered overlapping jurisdictions for security and intelligence-related activities among other committees. The responsibility is currently distributed among seventeen committees, each claiming a particular piece of the intelligence mosaic. Currently, in the House, the House Permanent Select Committee on Intelligence as well as the House Appropriations, Armed Services, Budget, Energy and Commerce, Government Reform, Homeland

Security, International Relations, and Judiciary committees all supervise some aspect of intelligence. In the Senate, Appropriations, Armed Services, Budget, Energy and Natural Resources, Foreign Relations, Homeland Security, and Government Affairs committees as well as the Judiciary Standing Committee and the Senate Select Committee on Intelligence Committee all provide oversight. Further, three members of the HPSCI are on a newly created Select Intelligence Oversight Panel on the Appropriations Committee.

This dispersion brings up intelligence oversight issues of old, when the fear was that briefing numerous committees could lead to leaks of extremely sensitive information. In this case, also, the question arises of what level of expertise regarding intelligence matters each of these committees is expected to attain. It has been proven to be very difficult to understand the intricacies of highly technical programs quickly, hence the reason the Senate abolished term limits within its intelligence oversight committee. This situation becomes even more complex when the intelligence issues stem, for example, from new agencies, such as DHS or ODNI, where processes of reporting are just being established and where senior staffers may be in short supply to provide needed expertise on arcane intelligence matters. This distributed approach to intelligence oversight demonstrates the uneven historical process that congressional intelligence oversight has taken to get to this point and also reflects the increasing number of overlapping issues that have relevance to intelligence in the post-9/11 security environment. These include, among others, issues of civil liberties when law enforcement and intelligence information are integrated, the emergent problem of cyber-security, issues of government-controlled information and access, the amorphous sphere of homeland security, the role of the private sector, and military affairs.[89] The challenge of overseeing such a multitude of atomized and distributed intelligence units is clear. This also comes at a time when the numbers of congressional staffers on the oversight committees are actually *shrinking*. In the words of one scholar, the intelligence community has achieved "an extraordinary rate of growth ... which has not been matched by a comparable increase in

---

[89] Frederick M. Kaiser, *Congressional Oversight of Intelligence: Current Structure and Alternatives*, Congressional Research Service (2011), 1.

the size of the oversight committee staffs or a corresponding expansion of other oversight mechanisms."[90]

Many recommendations have been advanced post-9/11 to improve congressional oversight. For example, increased attention in the Senate has been focused on improving the relationship between the intelligence committee (SSCI), which handles the authorizations for the intelligence community, and the appropriations committee, responsible for any appropriations for the IC.[91] Other relevant systemic measures to increase oversight have engaged with the role of the inspectors general and the potential insertion of a statutory IG in an IC-wide capacity, who would be charged with coordinating and strengthening the reporting among the various agency IG offices. This step would not be uncontroversial, particularly if it conflicted with the authority of the statutory IG in the CIA. At the committee level, the Senate Intelligence Committee has abolished the limits on the number of terms that its members may serve, although the House has not. This, in itself, is an interesting shift in the priorities of the constitution of the committees. The issue of tenure on the committees is rooted in the original debates about them in the 1970s and is based on one of the fundamental complexities of regulation and oversight: how to avoid "capture" by the agency one is charged with overseeing. Secondarily, it was thought that increasing the number of viable candidates for membership on the intelligence communities could increase the opportunities for members to learn about intelligence matters.

This fear of members being coopted by the priorities of the intelligence agencies led term members to be limited to eight years in the Senate and six in the House. This requirement was lifted according to S. Res. 445 in 2004 in response to the recommendations of the 9/11 Commission. While term limits may seem a banal issue, they have been a crucial consideration since the committees were originally established, and were considered a change of immense importance by members of the Senate committee staff.[92] On an analytical level, it is important that members and their staff have adequate time to

---

[90] Steven Aftergood, quoted in Amy B. Zegart, *Eyes on Spies: Congress and the U.S. Intelligence Community* (Stanford, CA: Hoover Institution Press, 2011), 99.

[91] Kaiser, *Congressional Oversight of Intelligence*, 3.

[92] Interview with a former senior SSCI staffer, June 16, 2011.

understand the arcane issues of intelligence, particularly as technological advances make intelligence a much more involved process. Further,
there is an implicit trust that must be placed in the overseers not to be
captured by their agencies. Thus, trust in the committees has apparently grown, or efficiency in maintaining skill in intelligence has outweighed doubts about members' bias in this more controversial threat
environment. In terms of the accountability framework, unbounded
service on the committees contributes a great deal to a wider expertise and authority on the increasingly arcane and technical matters of
intelligence.

Post-9/11 criticism of the intelligence oversight committees also
recalls the pre-Church Committee era, when Congress chose not to
engage rather than delve into unpleasant details of intelligence activities. In a 2007 statement before the Senate Select Committee on
Intelligence, Lee Hamilton articulated in strong terms his perspective
on the current state of intelligence oversight:

> To me, the strong point simply is that the Senate of the United
> States and the House of the United States is [sic] not doing its job.
> And because you're not doing the job, the country is not as safe as
> it ought to be .... You're dealing here with the national security of
> the United States, and the Senate and the House ought to have the
> deep down feeling that we've got to get this thing right.[93]

It has been argued that the level of fear engendered by the 9/11 attacks
greatly challenged the stature of overseers, as the Bush administration made increasingly greater inroads on their purview. As Church
Committee staffer Treverton points out, "... The process of congressional oversight of intelligence, including covert action, so carefully crafted
in the 1970s, is now regarded as something of a joke in Washington.
Terrorism is frightening enough to the body politic to justify almost any
action in response ...."[94] This is an interesting point in terms of how
anxiety and public reaction can cause extreme effects in the perception

---

[93] SSCI Hearing on Congressional Oversight, 110th Cong., 1st sess., November 13, 2007,
quoted in Amy B. Zegart, "The Domestic Politics of Irrational Intelligence Oversight,"
Political Science Quarterly 126 (2011): 1.

[94] Gregory F. Treverton, *Intelligence for an Age of Terror* (Cambridge: Cambridge University
Press, 2009), 232.

that security outweighs concerns about civil liberties that are ostensibly protected by careful oversight of the intelligence process. I find, however, the quip too facile to grasp adequately the complexities of the post-9/11 security and intelligence environment. Rather, I would argue that political concerns – including an unwillingness on the part of Congress to cross partisan ideological lines, as well as an overall reluctance to be seen as unsupportive of defense and security issues – are more to blame for the laxity of congressional oversight post-9/11. Although this chapter describes opposition between the executive and legislature regarding intelligence, it was only in the last decade or so that partisanship within the committees began to actively impact intelligence oversight. At this point in our incremental development of intelligence oversight, progress has stalled somewhat. The complexities of the changes in overseeing the post-IRTPA environment are clear, but questions remain. For example, why has partisanship within the oversight committees begun to play such a strong role in the current environment? On a theoretical level, what does partisan rancor mean for the accountability framework? That is, does internal conflict hinder the provision of adequate external accountability? In the next section, I will investigate these questions through explorations of specific moments of post-9/11 partisanship. I will look at a particularly concrete case, the "power of the purse" – congressional authorization and appropriations for the intelligence function – and the failure to enact Intelligence Authorization Acts, which highlights this dynamic particularly clearly.

THE POWER OF THE PURSE: PROCESS AND THE CONGRESSIONAL INTELLIGENCE OVERSIGHT COMMITTEES

As the core of this chapter discusses, the legislative and executive branches are locked in an oppositional relationship that was designed purposely to dilute absolute power on the part of an individual branch. In terms of the legislative oversight of intelligence, this dynamic becomes the most concrete when attention turns to the funding of intelligence activities. The "power of the purse" is vital to the attempt at balancing power between Congress and the executive, and particularly fundamental to congressional control over executive behavior. As a former CIA officer states:

The centrality of the budget to oversight should be obvious. In reviewing the president's budget submission and crafting alternatives or variations, Congress gets to examine the size and shape of each agency, the details of each program, and the plans for spending money over the next year. Congressional overseers have total access to the agencies and their activities. No other activity offers the same degree of access or oversight. Moreover, given the constitutional requirement for congressional approval of all expenditures, in no other place does Congress have as much leverage as in the budget process.[95]

The details of the intelligence budget remained very opaque to outsiders until very recently, but they are crucial to understanding whether and how congressional oversight is and can be effective. It was only in 2006 that the top line – the overall amount spent on intelligence activities – was released to the public. This was followed by the leak of the entire black budget by Edward Snowden via the *Washington Post* in August of 2013. At this point, the public first got an inkling of the amounts spent on each of the agencies, as well as the vast increases that some agencies had received in the post-9/11 era. The exposed budget showed how much money was being spent on previously inaccessible budget areas such as data collection, analysis, processing, and exploitation. The budget was broken down into further detail in terms of programs, such as covert action; human intelligence operations in the CIA; and cryptanalysis, exploitation, and sensitive data collection in the NSA.[96] The leaked budget also showed that the budgets for both the CIA and NSA had increased by more than 50 percent each – 56 percent and 53 percent respectively. This leak marked the first time that the public had access to the numbers involved in supporting the intelligence enterprise. The budget is the crucial external control mechanism over the intelligence community and is the crucial point where legislative overseers bring the most power to bear over the community.

[95] Mark M. Lowenthal, *Intelligence: From Secrets to Policy*, 4th edition (Washington, DC: CQ Press, 2009), 207.

[96] See http://www.washingtonpost.com/wp-srv/special/national/black-budget/ (August 29, 2013).

To explore this question further, I describe how the budget process works and examine where potential hindrances within that process to effective oversight stand. On a more granular level, I explore the variables, both in terms of process and politics, that affect how the two components of funding – authorization and appropriations – function. This delineation between approval and the disbursement of funds has proven to be a point of friction at specific points over the past decade.

To begin, the intelligence budget is divided into separate programs. The Military Intelligence Program (MIP) budgets finance all of the defense-related intelligence activity, while the National Intelligence Program (NIP) budgets support national intelligence agencies, including the CIA. NIP programs are managed by program managers within the intelligence agencies. The program managers develop and monitor budgets and allocate funds.[97] TIARA, as was mentioned earlier in this chapter, is a subset of defense intelligence programs mainly dealing with immediate tactical force support. NIP funds can be reprogrammed within the CIA to another NIP program within the CIA. The DNI is also authorized to reprogram and transfer funds.[98]

After the president submits his budget, usually in February, it is then briefed to the congressional oversight committees. The briefs begin at the top level; in terms of the NIP, the director of national intelligence briefs it and then as interests become more specific and localized, briefings drill down into individual agencies' activities and programs.[99] This process evolves from the more formal hearings to individual interactions among committee staff, particularly the program managers and budget directors, and the representatives from the individual intelligence agencies. As a former HPSCI staff director put it, the staffers have "an all-access pass" to go to the agencies and request information.[100] They gather information, visit agencies, ask granular questions about agency programs, and interact closely with

---

[97] Gordon Adams and Cindy Williams, *Buying National Security: How America Plans and Pays for Its Global Role and Safety at Home* (London: Routledge, 2009), 131.

[98] Personal communication with a former senior congressional staffer, August 18, 2014.

[99] Interview with a former senior congressional staffer, November 26, 2013.

[100] Interview with a former senior congressional staffer, November 26, 2013.

their counterparts in the agencies. It is important to note that a deeply significant part of legislative oversight of intelligence occurs though these back-channeled methods. While hearings are crucial, much of the specific information regarding plans and programs comes through these other, rather more informal, means.[101]

After the preliminary briefings over the initial budget are conducted, the next stage involves justifications for budget requests in the form of Congressional Budget Justification Documents (CBJDs). At this time, all of the agencies brief on their particular projects, providing members the opportunity to ask questions and also delve into the particulars of specific pet projects. After several hearings, the committee staff begins to generate a bill presented in two parts: the unclassified version; and the much more important classified annex, which breaks down by agency, and then by program, the budgetary allocations decided upon by the committee. The final stages of the bill involve including members' changes, particular issues, and amendments. The bill is marked up with any additional changes, reported out, and then goes to the full House after the Rules Committee. The classified annex to the bill is the crucial information regarding the intelligence budget. This separate document is sometimes overlooked in analyses of the activity and attention of the intelligence oversight committees. The annex is available to House members, but it must be read in a secure setting – a Sensitive Compartmented Information Facility (SCIF) located in the basement of the Capitol.[102] As would be expected, congressional focus on the specific issues of intelligence waxes and wanes with the political and public attention these issues are receiving at any particular time. As whose responsibility for which programs varies among the chambers, leading to differing constellations of committees responsible for developing authorization bills, in addition to the normal requirements of conferencing bills between the committees in both chambers to calibrate differences, the varying jurisdictions require additional committees, such as the Senate Armed Services

---

[101] Joel D. Aberbach in his *Keeping a Watchful Eye* makes a similar point about all types of congressional oversight. Aberbach, *The Politics of Congressional Oversight* (Washington, DC: Brookings Institution Press, 1990).

[102] Interview with a former senior congressional staffer, November 26, 2013.

Committee (SASC) and House Armed Services Committee (HASC), to weigh in on military intelligence issues. This in itself can create a logjam in terms of agreement on appropriate guidance for the intelligence agencies.[103]

A further consideration that links to the knowledge conditions component of the analytical frameworks is the fact that since the budgets are classified and processes regarding appropriate handling of sensitive material are onerous, very few members of the committees actually engage in thorough analysis of budget requests. This suggests that recourse is limited even in this area, where it should be assumed that concrete consequences are the norm. In the words of one congressional staffer: "There's lobbying in intelligence, but not nearly as much and it's all done behind closed doors .... What are you going to do if you're an authorizer who doesn't like what's in the appropriations bill? Hold up the entire defense appropriations bill? No way. There's not much recourse for intelligence authorizers, but there is in other areas."[104]

Some also point to the intervention of the executive branch at several levels of the budgeting and oversight process, citing at the most obvious level attempts to lobby members to change particular programs and, at a more discreet level, the failure to provide necessary intelligence information and/or to limit excessively the distribution of information.[105]

When it comes down to the crucial methods of recourse that have formed a large component of the discussion of strength of accountability throughout this book, the two strongest methods that Congress has to force behavioral change on the part of the intelligence community are its convening authority – for example, its authority to call a hearing to address a particular issue – and its budget authority. As a former HPSCI staff director put it with regard to the anxiety induced by a committee hearing: "The ability to call a hearing [is] a frightening thing–the ability to call someone in for a public shaming in a open hearing; to get questions and get yelled at, and [receive] media attention. Every hearing that Congress has forces the executive branch to

[103] Interview with a former SSCI staffer, July 17, 2011.
[104] Quoted in Zegart, *Eyes on Spies*, 104.
[105] Interview with a former SSCI staff director, July 17, 2011.

get prepared; to get their act together on a particular issue. The White House may act to organize immediately."[106] The second method – the power of the purse, that is, the power to authorize and appropriate funds – is, of course, the most crucial.

As per normal congressional procedure, authorization and appropriations for intelligence are separated into two different processes.[107] While this overall process is standard across different issues areas, one difference from standard procedure when it comes to intelligence is that while the authorization bills received from the administration are public, the levels of personnel and funding regarding intelligence are appended to the open budget in a classified annex.[108] Some argue that a core problem of intelligence oversight lies with this process of one body authorizing appropriations but dependent on the appropriators for actual budget action.[109] There can be friction between these two sets of mechanisms. For example, programs may be approved but the appropriators may not fund them or fail to fund them to the level to which they were originally authorized. Termed "hollow budget authority," the appropriators are superseding the wishes of the authorizers. In another example of authorizers' wishes not being respected, appropriators can appropriate funds not authorized. This is called "appropriated but not authorized."[110] The crucial issue here is how oversight can break down over this mismatch between authorization and appropriations. Although the intelligence community will continue to be funded under the Defense Department Appropriations Act even in the case of no authorization bill, oversight in this context is much weaker – such as it was from FY 2006 to FY 2011, when no authorization bill was enacted. There is no deep dive into the details of intelligence programs and thus weaker guidance from the oversight committees. Having said this, regardless of whether a detailed bill is passed, the committees still do have the authority to call intelligence officers and other members of the executive to Capitol Hill to explain themselves.

[106] Interview with a former HPSCI staff director, November 26, 2013
[107] Johnson, *America's Secret Power*, 218.
[108] Loch K. Johnson, Appendix A, in *Strategic Intelligence: Windows into a Secret World*, eds. Loch K. Johnson and James J. Wirtz (Los Angeles: Roxbury, 2005), 216.
[109] This was the standard argument provided by the 9/11 Commission, in particular.
[110] Lowenthal, *Intelligence: From Secrets to Policy*, 206. Also interview with a former senior congressional staffer November 26, 2013.

What does the process of authorization and appropriations mean for the framework of accountability? I have introduced authorization and appropriations here in order to provide more concrete examples of how intelligence oversight could achieve actual consequences on the activities of the intelligence community. What we find, however, is that although the power of the purse is Congress's strongest avenue of recourse, it still provides fractured leverage over the intelligence community. In terms of the framework, knowledge conditions still suffer from the information asymmetry inherent to all relations between these two branches. External autonomy develops, but has become entangled in politics in the post-9/11 era. Temporality has remained largely the same, and transparency has only begun to grow stronger, most likely in light of the pressure of the Snowden revelations and the SSCI's investigation of the CIA's Detention and Interrogation Program. Prior to these emergent issues, transparency seemed weak. Further, the proliferation of intelligence components and the use of contractors dealing with intelligence matters have resulted in increased obscurity of intelligence activities and their oversight.

CONCLUSIONS

In the period immediately following the attacks on 9/11, congressional involvement in security and intelligence activities carried a cachet of public service and responsibility in terms of profile among constituents. On the other hand, the issues have been controversial and politically risky.[111] An example is former House speaker Pelosi's conflict over having been briefed about the use of enhanced interrogation techniques several years ago, or the debate over the "Torture Report" in the Senate. Additionally, some types of intelligence activities have turned increasingly domestic. Examples include federally compiled terrorist watch lists; increased searches; fusion centers, which integrate intelligence and law enforcement information; and government surveillance. The Snowden revelations also brought the concept of

---

[111] Loch K. Johnson, "The Church Committee Investigation of 1975 and the Evolution of Modern Intelligence Accountability," *Intelligence and National Security* 23 (2008), 209.

mass domestic surveillance to the fore. Constituents could conceivably be directly affected by intelligence activities more often.

Other issues – such as enhanced interrogation techniques, extraordinary rendition, and CIA secret prisons ("black sites") – have focused public attention on the "spooky" aspects of intelligence, operations perceived by most as conflicting with democratic values and national culture mores. These variables may change the reactions of overseers to their duties or may, in fact, reinforce the trends witnessed continually – of attention and then reversion to inattention as the immediate crisis passes – but with the added complications of the secret information, technical complexity, and marginal paranoia of intelligence. The pivot points mentioned are the moments of attention given to the intelligence enterprise. Catalyzed by scandal or operational failure, development of congressional mechanisms has been incremental, hindered by executive opposition; internal political dynamics; or a political environment that supports "unleashing" the intelligence services, such as developed after 9/11.

Congressional oversight committees themselves were the outcome of political scandal and are viewed as stand-ins for the public, in order to assure the public that an established process exists for dealing with secret government activities. Thus, committee operations, whether they are public hearings, press releases, or wider investigations into potential problems, are leveraged apertures that allow for controlled transparency about secret government activities. Intelligence oversight is not static; its efficacy ebbs and flows along a continuum as the result of friction, the political environment, *and* the threat environment. As happens with all institutions, the congressional oversight mechanisms have changed over time. Set up to assuage political outrage, they have grown to become part of a system that guides the nation's secret programs toward fruition. As has been mentioned throughout this chapter, at each point of deep change in the mechanisms, their mandate has been refined to create a clearer trajectory for their work. The outcome of this process has been a cleaner process and model for intelligence oversight – as well as a superlative measure on four of the accountability criteria – but also a narrower vision for the role of transparency.

5 AN INDEPENDENT JUDICIARY? THE DOMESTIC IMPLICATIONS OF INTELLIGENCE AND THE POLITICS OF SECRET OVERSIGHT

This concept of "national defense" cannot be deemed an end in itself, justifying any exercise of ... power designed to promote such a goal. Implicit in the term "national defense" is the notion of defending those values and ideals, which set this Nation apart. For almost two centuries, our country has taken singular pride in the democratic ideals enshrined in its Constitution. It would indeed be ironic if, in the name of national defense, we would sanction the subversion of those liberties, which make the defense of the Nation worthwhile.

Supreme Court Chief Justice Earl Warren[1]

You have no civil liberties if you're dead.

Senator Pat Roberts (R–KS)[2]

Very few issues regarding intelligence and accountability have come so suddenly into public view as the role of judiciary and its role in the oversight of intelligence. This began with questions about decisions made during the George W. Bush administration, when changes to the statutory framework were implemented in the name of expeditiousness and executive authority. This concern also increased under the Obama administration, as the breadth, depth, and targets

---

[1] *United States v. Robel* (389 U.S. 258, 264 (1968)), quoted in Fletcher N. Baldwin, Jr., and Robert B. Shaw, "Down to the Wire: Assessing the Constitutionality of the National Security Agency's Warrantless Wiretapping Program: Exit the Rule of Law," *University of Florida Journal of Law and Public Policy* 17 (2006): 430.

[2] Opening statement as chair of the Senate Select Committee on Intelligence (SSCI), on the occasion of the confirmation hearing of General Michael Hayden to be director, CIA, May 18, 2006.

of domestic surveillance programs became publicly known because of extensive leaks. Most recently, the Edward Snowden leaks have led to wide-ranging consideration of whether the National Security Agency (NSA) programs described in his leaked materials are legal, and if so, how; and if vetted through the Foreign Intelligence Surveillance Court, how were the legal questions answered? Concern about the legality of statutory changes and effectiveness of intelligence oversight in the judiciary has significant merit, and the discourse about it has always been extremely polarizing. The concern tends to be due to a lack of clarity and information and an absence of balance in the narratives regarding this issue.

Technological advances and the characteristics of conflict with non-state actors have forced changes in judicial oversight that are not present to the same degree in congressional oversight. I begin this chapter by describing the legal decisions prior to the Foreign Intelligence Surveillance Act (FISA) – all of which excluded judicial review of foreign intelligence activities. Then I discuss how the advent of FISA changed this relationship among the branches. Finally, I explain how changes in technology and the threat environment have challenged FISA and affected the trajectory of its development, arguably weakening it. Although FISA introduced a radical change in terms of how active judicial supervision of foreign intelligence could be, it still did not create "balance" among the branches of government. Asymmetrical access to foreign intelligence information continues to create disequilibrium in the relationships among all three branches of government, and the balance cannot be rectified even through strenuous oversight. Finally, I will address how the Snowden leaks have changed the discussion of judicial oversight, causing its process to be deeply questioned for the first time in decades. A core component of this final discussion is a consideration of what level of secrecy is appropriate in terms of accountability in a democracy and how this particular oversight mechanism must adapt to the requirements of enormous technological development and change.

The Church Committee, as well as the parallel committee in the House and the White House Rockefeller Commission, explored different angles on the problem of intelligence and society, abuses, and executive overreach that came to a head in the mid-1970s. The outcome is well known and widely discussed in the earlier chapters of this book – oversight committees were established in the Senate and House, after the investigations were concluded and recommendations for change, particularly by the Senate's Church Committee, were enacted. The Foreign Intelligence Surveillance Act (1978) stemmed from similar concerns, but had a different genesis. FISA takes a slim slice of the intelligence enterprise and creates a singular judicial oversight mechanism to oversee it. The concerns surrounding this singularity are evident even in the congressional hearings regarding the act. Core to FISA is the concept that U.S. persons must have their rights protected in cases of foreign intelligence surveillance. This concern stemmed from the loosely controlled surveillance conducted by the NSA in particular, but also by other agencies, against the domestic populations in the decades prior to the investigations of the mid-1970s. This focus on U.S. persons raised crucial questions then regarding the potential limit of constitutional rights as well as where executive authority, even over national security issues, should be supervised.

The majority of this book focuses on the CIA, its relationship to external oversight mechanisms, and the requirements of accountability. This chapter, however, includes the NSA because it is important to understand how oversight works when electronic surveillance is being used to pursue foreign intelligence, which can cross rather easily into the domestic arena, regardless of institutional constraints. Signals intelligence (SIGINT) – the intelligence discipline of the NSA and the slice of intelligence most supervised by the judiciary – is increasingly dominant because it is simply more efficient and wide-reaching in many ways than traditional forms of human intelligence (HUMINT) and is a creature of the burgeoning technological environment of the past few decades. It has also been the focus of intense scrutiny since Snowden's June 2013 leaks of documents portraying the NSA's domestic collection programs.

All enterprises depend on some level of communication to function, and signals intelligence provides a view of a vast range of human interaction. Information can be gathered at breathtaking rates of speed. While vast quantities of raw data create their own difficulties for analysis in terms of sifting for relevant facts, in an increasingly technological and globalized era, both electronic surveillance and data collection are necessary to handle the increasingly sophisticated adversaries of the United States. This then requires increasingly sophisticated oversight mechanisms to understand and supervise these activities. The extensive and expedited legislative changes implemented to increase the power of federal law enforcement and counterterrorism capacity after 9/11 had a significant impact on the specific arenas supervised by judicial oversight. Such legislation – for example, the USA PATRIOT Act – broke down boundaries between separate spheres, between law enforcement and intelligence and between domestic and foreign activities, that had developed through legislation and custom over the course of several decades.[3] Further, a historically strong division regarding how U.S. persons are treated in contrast to foreigners has begun to crumble with increased intelligence collection directed against the domestic population. As the Obama administration, Congress, the intelligence community, and the public cycles back to first principles on issues of privacy, secrecy, citizens' rights, and intelligence, in part catalyzed by the Snowden leaks of broad-reaching NSA programs, the developmental trajectory of the only judicial mechanism to oversee foreign intelligence surveillance activity has become increasingly important.

INTELLIGENCE OVERSIGHT AND THE JUDICIARY: FOREIGN INTELLIGENCE AND THE CONSTITUTION

The conventional argument about intelligence oversight is that change is caused by two countervailing impulses. When there is an operational intelligence failure, analysis focuses on improving performance, providing additional resources to the intelligence community, and loosening restrictions on agencies' activities. Oversight becomes contracted. The reverse occurs when there is a political scandal regarding intelligence – evidence of misbehavior on the part of intelligence agencies results in expanded oversight, insistence on improved transparency,

---

[3] Maintaining the separate spheres has been core to the mission of the NSA for decades. Overlapping mechanisms are in place to make sure that foreign does not conflict with domestic in terms of targeting and surveillance, as well as between law enforcement and foreign intelligence.

and a requirement that intelligence integrate itself further into the mainstream of government processes. This is often termed a "pendulum" cycle in the discussions on intelligence; what is not so clearly described is the elaborate framework of laws and practice that must adjust to every swing of this pendulum.

One of the architects of the legal structure under the Bush administration, Jack Goldsmith, characterizes this pendulum as alternating between "timidity" and "aggression," as the intelligence community (IC) responds to executive and congressional expectations that it "engage in controversial action at the edge of the law [but then] fail to protect it from recriminations when things go awry."[4] His explanation for this behavioral bipolarity is that intelligence sits at the nexus between, as he defines it, "related Washington pathologies: the criminalization of warfare, the blame game, and the cover-your-ass syndrome."[5] I agree that this pendulum exists, but also argue that this theory has been tested minimally, particularly in terms of judicial oversight. A reason for this is that the judicial branch can respond only to the cases brought before it by a party with standing; it is not able to initiate action, and standing is difficult to prove within the realm of national security and intelligence. It is a convenient and political argument for those who choose to believe they were caught up in a movement rather than responsible for independent and reasoned arguments in terms of the boundaries of appropriate intelligence gathering. As it stands, FISA was the first check on executive authority; the series of statutory changes emanating from 9/11 are still in process and will no doubt change further in the wake of the Snowden leaks. We can assert that there is a pendulum swing, but we have not yet seen the end of its trajectory.

This explanation introduces the impact of the threat environment on change in judicial oversight and shows how the judicial branch can be more responsive to the changing threat environment as well as to technological development. If so, the different *types* of intelligence activity overseen must be added into the equation. Obviously, electronic collection will change much more dramatically than covert action with the advancement of technology, taken as a whole. During each "swing,"

---

[4] Jack Goldsmith, *The Terror Presidency: Law and Judgment inside the Bush Administration* (New York: W. W. Norton, 2007), 163–4.

[5] Goldsmith, *The Terror Presidency*, 164.

further, deeper, underexplained political trends occur that place intelligence, as well as intelligence oversight, in the center of this dynamic. These involve the trade-offs that occur within Congress, as the result of both partisan negotiations and an oppositional stance to the executive. While Goldsmith's argument has a cast of self-exculpation, he describes the incentives of the players well: the executive wanting action, but as much plausible deniability as possible; Congress demanding to be informed, "but not in a way that will prevent them from being critical when things go badly"; and the intelligence agencies wanting explicit instructions from both branches – and, I would add, legal cover in both technical terms and in the public eye.[6] The tension that this cycle of expansion and contraction introduces into the relationships among the branches as well as the efficacy of intelligence performance is complex. Operationally, this tension affects the information that is shared between agencies; the lengths to which the intelligence agencies are willing to go, for better or for worse, in undertaking risky ventures; and the overall structural framework that serves to guide national security activities in the United States. In terms of oversight, the cycle introduces tension between the branches and a political dimension to decision making.

Developed formally in the wake of the Church Committee investigations, judicial oversight focuses on a narrow set of foreign intelligence matters that can cross over into the domestic realm. Secrecy and a narrow purview distinguish judicial oversight. Judicial oversight is conducted almost entirely outside of the public eye. Constitutional executive authority over foreign intelligence meant that there was no supervision from the judiciary until the radical institutional changes of the 1970s. In decision after decision, the Supreme Court decided that the judiciary had no purview over foreign intelligence and thus intelligence was left to chart its own course, generating programs with the tight cooperation of executive branch components, but with very little external check on its actions from either Congress or the judicial branch.

Congressional oversight has a wide scope and handles a range of intelligence policy issues, whereas judicial oversight is quite narrow and focused.[7] Congressional oversight committees also have multiple roles

---

[6] Goldsmith, *The Terror Presidency*, 164.

[7] Fred F. Manget, "Intelligence and the Rise of Judicial Intervention," in *Handbook of Intelligence Studies*, ed. Loch K. Johnson (London: Routledge, 2009), 330.

when it comes to oversight. They receive some information regarding potential programs – for example, through findings on covert action, about which they are informed but not required to consent – but the majority of their work concerns retroactive examination of programs in process. Congressional control over the budget is the most concrete conduit through which recourse over intelligence activities can be exercised. This contrasts with judicial oversight, which occurs prior to the intelligence activity – in the form of the FISC court orders discussed throughout this chapter.

Prior to the intelligence investigations of the 1970s, there was no active judicial supervision of electronic surveillance for foreign intelligence purposes. Although the Department of Justice (DoJ) possessed the power to initiate prosecutions of criminal misconduct, this statutory responsibility was mitigated prior to the investigations by an agreement between the DoJ and the CIA that allowed the CIA to conduct its own internal investigations of wrongdoing on the part of CIA officers and agents. Most important for the trajectory of judicial oversight development, the judiciary adhered to the custom of respecting the president's perceived "higher authority" in terms of issues touching upon national security drawn from Article II of the Constitution.[8] Every judicial decision up to the creation of FISA in 1978 held an exception for executive authority over the national security function.

While Congress had originally battled for greater supervisory authority over intelligence, the judiciary has ostensibly adhered to a narrower interpretation of its role regarding the supervision of foreign intelligence activities.[9] This relationship fits under the framework established by the "deference theory," the convention that the other

---

[8] Manget, "Intelligence and the Rise of Judicial Intervention," 330.

[9] This would suggest that for all of the post–Church Committee conventional wisdom on the "opening" of intelligence and the reintegration of those activities into "normal" government, that process is either incomplete or has begun to turn in the opposite direction. See Gregory F. Treverton, "Intelligence: Welcome to the American Government," in *A Question of Balance: The President, the Congress and Foreign Policy*, ed. Thomas Mann (Washington, DC: Brookings Institution, 1990). See Loch K. Johnson, "The Church Committee Investigation of 1975 and the Evolution of Modern Intelligence Accountability," *Intelligence and National Security* 23 (2008): 198–225, for a discussion of the range of levels of responsibility congressional intelligence oversight committee members have applied to their task.

branches of government defer to the executive on issues of national security. This idea has a deep foundation in the relationship between the judicial and executive branches. It is commonly accepted that in times of crisis, war, or emergency, American courts defer to the executive regarding matters of national security.[10] The "war on terrorism" has challenged many of the precepts of war and the expectations of what constitutes an appropriate balance between security and civil liberties. The current state of war could be unending, potentially resulting in a permanent state of quasi-emergency. After the attacks on 9/11, in a national environment imbued with political urgency, legislators loosened procedural constraints on law enforcement in order to expand domestic law enforcement and intelligence powers rapidly.

The president's constitutional authority over national security matters extended to foreign intelligence, and thus no other oversight of that function was considered to be required until after the post-Watergate congressional investigations instigated sweeping oversight changes. From World War I to 1972, in fact, surveillance conducted by the executive was both unquestioned and unsupervised.[11] Foreign intelligence collection was always explicitly left out of any legislation as an exception based on the acceptance of the president's constitutional authority over national

---

[10] Jeremy Waldron, "Security and Liberty: The Image of Balance," *Journal of Political Philosophy* 11 (2003): 191. The conventional case upon which to base the deference assertion is *Korematsu v. United States* (1944), which established that in times of war or national emergency, it could be acceptable to limit individuals' civil liberties in protection of national security. In this case, it was decided that Japanese-Americans could be removed from their homes in response to the military threat of Japan. In the words of the decision, "When under conditions of modern warfare our shores are threatened by hostile forces, the power to protect must be commensurate with the threatened danger." *Korematsu v. United States*, 323 US 214 (1944), discussed in Natsu Taylor Saito, "Whose Liberty? Whose Security? The USA PATRIOT Act in the Context of COINTELPRO and the Unlawful Repression of Political Dissent," *Oregon Law Review* 81 (2002): 1077. A counterbalance to *Korematsu* is *Ex parte Milligan*, which focuses on the responsibility of the Supreme Court to stand as a guardian of rights and a guarantor of the promises of the Constitution. Rather than deferring to the executive, as is the conventional argument during crisis, according to this argument, the Court provides a bulwark against extreme measures, even when they do concern issues of national security.

[11] Barbara Ann Stolz, "The Foreign Intelligence Surveillance Act of 1978: The Role of Symbolic Politics," *Law and Policy* 24 (2002): 274; Americo R. Cinquegrana, "The Walls (and Wires) Have Ears: The Background and First Ten Years of the Foreign Intelligence Surveillance Act of 1978," *University of Pennsylvania Law Review* 137 (1988–9): 795.

security matters. In the area of potential judicial oversight, judges perceived their role as 'hands-off' in terms of foreign intelligence gathering and were wary of even defining terms that could potentially infringe on executive authority over foreign intelligence. In terms of the role of the judiciary, "There is even a historical hint of an argument that, to the extent that intelligence activities are concerned with the security of the state, they are inherent to any sovereign's authority under a higher law of self-preservation and not subject to normal judicial review."[12] Deputy Assistant Attorney General Kevin T. Maroney testified on behalf of the Ford administration that the president had "unilateral constitutional authority to use electronic surveillance ... to protect important security interests."[13]

When the courts did issue decisions that touched upon security matters, between the 1920s and 1970s, the issue of intelligence gathering for national security was not considered a constitutional issue; it was simply the purview of the president. The 1928 *Olmstead vs. United States* decision determined that electronic surveillance was not covered by the Fourth Amendment.[14] The case itself involved bootlegging operations, evidence against which was gathered by wiretapping eight telephones. The defense argued that this constituted unreasonable search and seizure as described by the Fourth Amendment. Interestingly, adhering to a literal interpretation of the Constitution, Chief Justice William H. Taft decided in the *Olmstead* decision that the Fourth Amendment pertained only to situations in which a technical trespass or seizure of tangible items occurred. It thus exempted any electronic – or "intangible" – surveillance from Fourth Amendment protections.[15] In language drawn from the majority decision, "voluntary conversations secretly overheard" could not be equated with material 'things' seized by the government."[16]

---

[12] Frederic F. Manget, "Another System of Oversight: Intelligence and the Rise of Judicial Intervention," in *Strategic Intelligence: Windows into a Secret World*, eds. Loch K. Johnson and James J. Wirtz (Los Angeles: Roxbury, 2005), 408.

[13] Gordon Silverstein, *Imbalance of Powers: Constitutional Interpretation and the Making of American Foreign Policy* (New York: Oxford University Press, 1997), 142.

[14] 277 U.S. 438 (1928).

[15] Michael Goldsmith, "The Supreme Court and Title III: Rewriting the Law of Electronic Surveillance," *Journal of Criminal Law and Criminology* 74 (1983): 8.

[16] Quote from majority decision, drawn from Cinquegrana, "The Walls (and Wires) Have Ears," 795.

Olmstead and the series of decisions that followed reinforce the primacy of the executive over intelligence gathering for the purposes of national security; in practice, this meant judicial decisions differentiated domestic law enforcement from foreign intelligence matters.[17]

A series of decisions intervened in the decades after *Olmstead,* but the seminal one challenging *Olmstead* was *Katz vs. United States* (1967), which reversed the *Olmstead* decision and demonstrated a shift in Fourth Amendment jurisprudence, from physical trespass to protection of individual privacy.[18] In this case, Katz was convicted partly based on evidence gleaned by bugging a public telephone booth. This case found that Katz's Fourth Amendment rights had been violated based on the infringement of Katz's reasonable expectation of privacy.[19] The ruling stated that "the Fourth Amendment protects people, not places."[20] *Katz* extended Fourth Amendment protections to cover *privacy expectations,* no longer focusing on property, tangibility, and trespass. As Americo Cinquegrana, an attorney/scholar formerly of the CIA, points out, "Fourth Amendment protection now focused on individuals, not locations, and extended to surveillance techniques not requiring a physical intrusion."[21] But, having broadened the inclusivity of Fourth Amendment rights, *Katz* still did not include national security issues within its purview. A footnote offered that the decision did not state that an order be required for electronic surveillance for the purposes of national security. To quote Cinquegrana again: "Justice White emphasized this point in a concurring opinion dwelling on the unique requirements of electronic surveillance for national security purposes. *He noted the authorization of such activities by a succession of Presidents, concluding that no prior judicial review should be required if the President or Attorney General found surveillance reasonable under the circumstances* [emphasis added]."[22]

---

[17] Cinquegrana, "The Walls (and Wires) Have Ears," 800.

[18] J. Christopher Champion, "The Revamped FISA: Striking a Better Balance Between the Government's Need to Protect Itself and the 4th Amendment," *Vanderbilt Law Review* 58 (2005): 1677.

[19] Goldsmith, "The Supreme Court and Title III," 29.

[20] Cinquegrana, "The Walls (and Wires) Have Ears," 800.

[21] Cinquegrana, "The Walls (and Wires) Have Ears," 800.

[22] Cinquegrana, "The Walls (and Wires) Have Ears," 800. Original text in 389 U.S. 347, 353 (1967) (overruling *Olmstead* and *Goldman*).

The next step in differentiating the law enforcement from national security objectives came in a congressional move. In a shift toward statutory reform, Congress reacted to the guidance of the courts in these earlier decisions and enacted Title III of the Omnibus Crime Control and Safe Streets Act (1968). This act established a judicial framework for orders related to criminal investigation, while again still maintaining the exceptionalism of national security. "[Title III] was designed to provide a framework for regulating all so-called *nonconsensual* electronic surveillance except national security eavesdropping [emphasis added]."[23] Title III authorized electronic surveillance through wiretapping and bugs for the purposes of law enforcement, but required adherence to statutory requirements as well as prior judicial approval.[24] Title III was intended to focus and contain the benefits of wiretapping while constructing a framework of privacy safeguards, including a requirement of high-level responsibility on the part of both the executive and judiciary in terms of application and granting of the order. With regard to judicial responsibility, in addition to being responsible for ensuring adherence to the legal statute, judges under Title III were empowered to deny applications, alter them, or monitor through mandatory progress reports.[25]

Title III, concerned with criminal investigation, is bound by carefully constructed legal structure and practice. "These safeguards, together with the expectation that compliance would be monitored closely by the courts, served to alleviate the fear of many that Title III was synonymous with the arrival of Big Brother."[26] It also left out of consideration the requirements of intelligence gathering in explicit language:

> Nothing contained in this chapter or in section 605 of the Communications Act of 1934 shall limit the constitutional power of the President to take such measures as he deems necessary to protect the Nation against actual or potential attack or other hostile acts of a foreign power, to obtain foreign intelligence information deemed essential to the security of the United States, or to

---

[23] Goldsmith, "The Supreme Court and Title III," 39. It is important to take a moment here to note the irony in the concept of "nonconsensual electronic surveillance."

[24] Goldsmith, "The Supreme Court and Title III," 4.

[25] Goldsmith, "The Supreme Court and Title III," 44.

[26] Goldsmith, "The Supreme Court and Title III," 4.

protect national security information against foreign intelligence activities.[27]

Congress deferred to the executive in exempting national security purposes from the purview of Title III, stating that it in no way attempted to infringe on the president's constitutional authority to protect the United States, to obtain foreign intelligence information, and to protect it from any other "clear and present danger."[28]

The right of the executive to authorize electronic surveillance in internal security matters without prior judicial approval was challenged for the first time in *United States v. United States District Court ("Keith")*, decided in the Supreme Court in 1972. Three defendants were charged with conspiracy to destroy government property; one of them was also charged with bombing a CIA office. As stated in the decision, '"[The] Fourth Amendment contemplates a prior judicial judgment," and although the task of ensuring national security presented special circumstances, it was argued that "[t]he circumstances described do not justify complete exemption of domestic security surveillance from judicial scrutiny."[29] But, again, it was also made clear in the decision that the *Keith* case concerned itself only with domestic surveillance – it did not include entities with significant connections to foreign powers or their agents.[30] Thus, although *Keith* challenged exclusive executive authority over surveillance, foreign intelligence still remained outside the scope of the decision. The Court's perception of its appropriate jurisdiction limited the application of this decision, narrowing it to provide discretion to executive decision making. The *Keith* decision contributed to the separation between foreign and domestic realms for the purposes of intelligence surveillance and to the acceptability of different standards being used in these two separate arenas.[31] An odd passage from the decision rather ambiguously reinforces this separation:

---

[27] 82. Stat. 213 (1968), quoted in Robert M. Pallitto and William G. Weaver, *Presidential Secrecy and the Law* (Baltimore: Johns Hopkins University Press, 2007), 166.

[28] Cinquegrana, "The Walls (and Wires) Have Ears," 801.

[29] Matt Bedan, "Echelon's Effect: The Obsolescence of the U.S. Foreign Intelligence Legal Regime," *Federal Communications Law Journal* 59, no. 2 (2007): 428.

[30] Cinquegrana, "The Walls (and Wires) Have Ears," 802.

[31] *Keith*, 407 U.S. at 320. Quoted in Bedan, "Echelon's Effect," 429.

Different standards may be compatible with the Fourth Amendment if they are reasonable both in relation to the legitimate need
of Government for intelligence information and the protected
rights of our citizens. For the order application may vary according
to the governmental interest to be enforced and the nature of citi-
zen rights deserving protection.[32]

The preceding history is intended to place FISA and current judicial oversight of surveillance – the next section of this chapter – in
a historical context. The judiciary has deferred to a great degree to
the president's constitutional authority on matters of national security
and intelligence. This relationship brings up ancient issues of presidential power, the question of appropriate judicial review that is rooted
in *Madison*, and the difficult trade-offs that are made in a context of
national emergency. FISA, seen through this lens, was a monumental
shift in the relationship among the branches regarding foreign intelligence. The impetus for FISA was drawn from the intelligence abuses
that were exposed in the investigations of the 1970s. The objective was
not only to establish a control mechanism over this type of collection
activity, but also specifically to differentiate the rights of the U.S. persons from those not conferred those rights, foreign nationals.

THE FOREIGN INTELLIGENCE SURVEILLANCE ACT (FISA): JUDICIAL OVERSIGHT, FOREIGN INTELLIGENCE, AND SURVEILLANCE

The aforementioned decisions, while not comprehensively addressed
in this brief summary, demonstrate that active judicial oversight over
foreign intelligence gathering has been a relatively recent development.
They illustrate, too, how complex the installation of FISA would be,
intruding on what had always been presidential prerogative. FISA
strikes a delicate balance between the ongoing demands of the intelligence community and the requirement that there be a structure for
these demands to flow through in order to maintain order and protection for those being investigated. The structure of this oversight

---

[32] 407 U.S. 297 (1972), at 322–2. Quoted in Breglio, "Leaving FISA Behind," 184.

mechanism is different – with different expectations of efficacy – than those we are accustomed to in the legislative branch. The statute not only clarified the terms of judicial oversight, it acted directly to constrain presidential activities that up to FISA's inception had been entirely unfettered by external oversight. In the words of legal scholar David Cole:

> ... [T]he President's authority before FISA was enacted was radically different from his authority thereafter. As is clearly demonstrated by the judicial history described above, before FISA was enacted, Congress expressly recognized the president's 'constitutional power ... to obtain foreign intelligence information deemed essential to the security of the United States.' When Congress enacted FISA in the wake of demonstrated abuses of that power, however, it repealed that provision and ... made it a crime to conduct wiretapping without congressional authority.[33]

FISA emerged out of a process similar to the development of congressional oversight mechanisms. It was the product of an oppositional relationship between Congress and the executive regarding the questions of how electronic surveillance could be controlled and what mechanisms should be put in place to monitor this type of activity. Discussion between Congress and the executive regarding the genesis of FISA centered on how to set the standard for targeting U.S. persons with surveillance and – once again, as the central theme of this book – on the status of the president's inherent authority to conduct foreign intelligence operations.[34] Further, FISA was the product of intra-Congress deliberation and conflict. While FISA is usually touted as the natural outcome of the Church Committee recommendations, there were extensive negotiations in Congress about whether tethering the NSA and FBI to any type of judicial oversight was indeed appropriate. Some legislators argued that the intelligence agencies should be bound to the standard law enforcement procedure of obtaining a court order prior to surveillance, while on the other side of the divide, legislators argued that the agencies should

---

[33] David Cole, "Reviving the Nixon Doctrine: NSA Spying, the Commander-in-Chief and Executive Power in the War on Terror," *Washington and Lee Journal of Civil Rights and Social Justice* 13 (2006): 17–18.

[34] Cinquegrana, "The Walls (and Wires) Have Ears," 810.

remain unregulated.[35] Other concerns centered on whether FISA itself was unconstitutional, as it encroached on executive authority. There was concern that limiting the executive in this way could harm the national security of the country.[36] FISA is the primary judicial mechanism for supervising foreign intelligence gathering through surveillance.[37] More explicitly: "[FISA provides] the exclusive means by which [foreign intelligence] electronic surveillance ... and the interception of domestic wire, oral and electronic communications may be conducted."[38]

FISA was established to "regulate the collection of 'foreign intelligence information' from foreign powers or agents of foreign powers in the United States."[39] In more specific detail, under FISA, "foreign intelligence information" is defined as information about (1) an actual or potential attack or other grave hostile acts of a foreign power; (2) sabotage or international terrorism by a foreign power or an agent of a foreign power; (3) clandestine intelligence activities by a foreign power or agent; or (4) other intelligence concerning a foreign country that is necessary to the national defense or the security of the United States or the conduct of the foreign affairs of the United States.[40] To receive an order, in addition to meeting the preceding requirements, the official had to prove that the "purpose of the surveillance is to obtain foreign intelligence information."[41] This last requirement was interpreted by lower courts to mean that the "primary purpose" of the surveillance had to be for foreign intelligence and not criminal investigation. According to their argument, the "wall" dividing law enforcement from intelligence activities was thus built.[42]

---

[35] James Bamford, *The Puzzle Palace: A Report on America's Most Secret Agency* (New York: Penguin, 1983), 463.

[36] Interview with a senior CIA official, November 10, 2011.

[37] Breglio, "Leaving FISA Behind," 188.

[38] Cited in Baldwin and Shaw, "Down to the Wire," 454. Title III Omnibus (1968). 2511 (2)(f).

[39] Lee S. Strickland, "Civil Liberties vs. Intelligence Collection: the Secret Foreign Intelligence Surveillance Act Court Speaks in Public," *Government Information Quarterly* 20 (2003): 2.

[40] Quoted in Strickland, "Civil Liberties vs. Intelligence Collection," fn 8.

[41] 50 U.S.C. § 1804(a)(7)(B)(1980).

[42] Richard Seamon and William Gardner, "Does (Should) the PATRIOT ACT Raze (or Raise) "the Wall" between Foreign Intelligence and Criminal Law Enforcement" (August 22, 2004), available at SSRN, 2.

FISA created a framework for the use of pen registers and trap and trace devices – for use in federal investigations to obtain foreign intelligence.[43] It was expanded in 1994 to permit covert physical intrusions by providing for "sneak and peek" orders.[44] FISA's framework thus provides a judicial check on executive decisions in terms of gathering foreign intelligence, but the restrictions themselves incorporate quite a range of flexibility in operation. As mentioned previously, originally FISA allowed surveillance to be directed at a U.S. person if there was probable cause that the target was an agent of a foreign power and that the surveillance was directed at the facilities being used by this agent or foreign power.[45] FISA marks a compromise decision in terms of the judicial role in intelligence activities. As one author points out: "In return for subjecting the executive branch to regulation of its electronic surveillance activities, FISA does not provide the traditional protection against government abuse of its electronic surveillance in enforcing criminal laws. FISA put in place a much more government-friendly process."[46] Part of this "government-friendliness" lies in the structure and procedures of the Foreign Intelligence Surveillance Court (FISC).

The FISC was originally composed of seven judges, but since 9/11, it seats eleven district court judges. The judges are appointed by the chief justice and assume their roles in a staggered fashion, with a new one taking up his or her post every year. The tenure of the position is seven years. The court is tasked with reviewing applications for electronic surveillance, physical searches, and other demands, such as for access to targets' business documents.[47] The process of applying for a FISA court order is onerous and requires the involvement and approval of numerous senior executive branch authorities, including the secretary of defense – in the case of an NSA application – and the attorney general. The cases are presented *ex parte* and *in camera*. This means that

[43] Title IV of FISA, 50 U.S.C. §1841.

[44] Bedan, "Echelon's Effect," 429. The catalyst for this expansion was physical search of spy Aldrich Ames' home in October 1993. Physical searches were included under the FISC purview under the Intelligence Authorization Act of 1995.

[45] David Cole and Martin S. Lederman, "The National Security Agency's Domestic Spying Program: Framing the Debate," *Indiana Law Journal* 81 (2006):1356. See 50 U.S.C. 1801(b).

[46] William C. Banks, "The Death of FISA," *Minnesota Law Review* 91 (2007): 1231.

[47] Seamon and Gardner, "Does (Should) the PATRIOT ACT Raze (or Raise)," 2.

the information gathered is strictly limited to one side of the issue, in contrast to normal judicial proceedings, where the adversarial process leads to a broader range of potentially conflicting material. Department of Justice attorneys from the Office of Intelligence Policy and Review present the cases, the records of which are then sealed and secret. If an order request is denied, the matter can be appealed to the Foreign Intelligence Surveillance Court of Review, a three-judge panel. The relationship between the FISC and the Court of Review has conventionally been seen as somewhat irrelevant to the maintenance of judicial oversight of surveillance, as very few orders have ever been denied.

FISA was designed to provide a trade-off to the fundamental security issue – between civil liberties and security – affording protection to those being investigated, while also providing flexibility, speed, and secrecy so that the requirements of the executive could be met in terms of these sensitive issues.[48] It created a divide between the expected treatment of U.S. persons and foreigners and also codified a legal framework for foreign intelligence surveillance that was distinct and separate from the legal constraints concerning law enforcement operations.[49] Its intention was to provide a framework that would allow monitoring of surveillance activities while not binding intelligence gathering to the same constraints as the Fourth Amendment's standard of probable cause. As described by the FISC itself:

> In order to preserve both the appearance and the fact that FISA surveillances and searches were not being used *sub rosa* for criminal investigations, the [FISC] routinely approved the use of information screening "walls" proposed by the government in its applications. Under the normal "wall" procedures, where there were separate intelligence and criminal *investigations*, or a single counter-espionage investigation with overlapping intelligence and criminal *interests*, FBI criminal investigators and [DoJ] prosecutors were not allowed to review all of the raw FISA intercepts or seized materials lest they become de facto partners in the FISA surveillances and searches. Instead, a screening mechanism, or person, usually the chief legal

---

[48] Breglio, "Leaving FISA Behind," 187.
[49] David S. Jonas, "The Foreign Intelligence Surveillance Act through the Lens of the 9/11 Commission Report: The Wisdom of the PATRIOT ACT Amendments and the Decision of the Foreign Intelligence Surveillance Court of Review," *North Carolina Central Law Journal* 27 (2004–5): 96.

counsel in an FBI field office, or an assistant U.S. attorney not involved in the overlapping criminal investigation, would review all of the raw intercepts and seized materials and pass on only that information which might be relevant evidence. In unusual cases such as where attorney–client intercepts occurred, [DoJ] lawyers in [the Office of Intelligence Policy Review] acted as the "wall." In significant cases ... where criminal investigations of FISA targets were being conducted concurrently, and prosecution was likely, [the FISC] became the "wall" so that FISA information could not be disseminated to criminal prosecutors without the Court's approval.[50]

In a further move to create a divide between foreign intelligence and criminal cases, minimization procedures required that foreign intelligence information gathered from non-FISA criminal surveillance could not be provided to intelligence authorities without a court order.[51] The attorney general was required to supply to the United States Supreme Court and to Congress the total number of applications granted, modified, and denied under FISA. The duration of FISA orders and extensions was limited to ninety days.[52]

The original intention of FISA was to develop a pathway for the judiciary to grapple with intelligence collection and surveillance, given that the courts were entirely unaccustomed with the process and substance of these intelligence activities. In the words of a 1978 report distributed by the then-recently created House Permanent Select Committee on Intelligence, the view of judicial involvement in decision making regarding intelligence was damning:

> [T]he development of the law regulating electronic surveillance for national security purposes has been uneven and inconclusive. This is to be expected where the development is left to the judicial branch in an area where cases do not regularly come before it. [T]he development of standards and restrictions by the judiciary ... [threatens both civil liberties and national security, because it] occurs generally in ignorance of the fact, circumstances and

---

[50] *In re* All Matters Submitted to the Foreign Intelligence Surveillance Court, 218 F. Supp. 2d 611, 620 (Foreign Int. Surv. Ct. 2002). quoted in David Hardin, "The Fuss over Two Small Words: The Unconstitutionality of the USA PATRIOT Act Amendments to FISA under the Fourth Amendment," *George Washington Law Review* 71, no. 2 (2003): 313.

[51] Hardin, "The Fuss over Two Small Words," 313.

[52] Hardin, "The Fuss over Two Small Words," 313.

techniques of foreign intelligence electronic surveillance not present in the particular case before the court.

… the tiny window to this area which a particular case affords provides inadequate light by which judges may be relied upon to develop case law which adequately balances the rights of privacy and national security.[53]

Understanding the depth of change that FISA introduced is an important key to gauging the subsequent increased strength of the judicial oversight mechanism. Further, FISA proved pivotal in later arguments when the executive tried strenuously to abrogate judicial supervision, particularly under the George W. Bush administration.

The strengths and weaknesses of the FISC are the core of many polarizing arguments about executive authority over surveillance. Even when after the Snowden leaks the director of national intelligence (DNI) declassified a range of decisions, the body of law being established by the court can be difficult to understand and opaque. First, there is a great deal of margin within this construct for what constitutes a "foreign agent," and there is flexibility in terms of how the orders are used. While court approval must be sought, FISA allows surveillance to begin before approval as long as it is sought within seventy-two hours. Further, surveillance is permitted without approval for the first fifteen days of a war.[54] There is a further exception for surveillance that includes foreign powers, allowing a year of surveillance without a court order following certification from the attorney general to both the House Permanent Select Committee on Intelligence (HPSCI) and the Senate Select Committee on Intelligence (SSCI) that the target falls within the foreign power definition, that there is no substantial likelihood that U.S. persons will be involved in the surveillance, and that reasonable minimization procedures are followed.[55]

---

[53] H.R. Rep. No. 1283, 95th Congress, 2nd Session, pt. 1, at 21–22 (1978), quoted in Cinquegrana, "The Walls (and Wires) Have Ears," 808.

[54] David Cole and Martin S. Lederman. "The National Security Agency's Domestic Spying Program: Framing the Debate," *Indiana Law Journal* 81 (2006): 1356. See 50 U.S.C. 1801(b), 2.

[55] Robert M. Bloom and William J. Dunn, "The Constitutional Infirmity of Warrantless NSA Surveillance: The Abuse of Presidential Power and the Injury to the Fourth Amendment," *William and Mary Bill of Rights Journal* 15 (2006): 165.

The other side of the argument became part of the rationale for the Terrorist Surveillance Program (TSP): that the reason very few order requests are rejected is that the process of preparation for the application is lengthy, detailed, and onerous, requiring the involvement of a range of senior officials. The burden of presentation of process in order to obtain a FISA order could be seen as having a chilling effect on frivolous cases. Further, as has been mentioned by several attorneys in the intelligence community, an iterative process between the DoJ and the FISC allows for any deficits that could hinder the progress of the order request to be corrected prior to potential denial by the court. Thus, many argue that the process itself results in a system that would actually deny outright very few requests.[56] As former DNI Mike McConnell described it, applications for orders under FISA resemble "finished intelligence products," including "detailed facts describing the target of the surveillance, the target's activities, the terrorist network ... and investigative results or intelligence information that would be relevant to the Court's findings."[57]

The issue of surveillance and oversight is politically polarized, meaning that the inherent absence of data from the internal processes is compounded by opinion and bias from external commentators. Some argue that the FISA process is too cumbersome for modern warfare, in which targets move quickly and use a range of communications devices that cross the boundaries between domestic and foreign, challenging the divisions inherent to FISA. They argue that the process of asking for the order, involving extensive paperwork, requires too much time and needless effort. Others argue that the court still provides a bulwark against uncontrolled spying on both foreign and domestic targets. The Terrorist Surveillance Program during the Bush administration pressed upon this tension, exposing the holes in both sides of the argument and also very much bringing to the fore the question of what is an appropriate trade-off in terms of civil liberties in favor of security, *and* who is empowered to make this trade-off.

FISA opened a narrow aperture to enable a secret court to see a small slice of a specific type of intelligence activity. Judicial oversight

---

[56] Interview with senior CIA official, November 10, 2011.

[57] Stephanie Cooper Blum, "What Really Is at Stake with the FISA Amendments Act of 2008 and the Future of Foreign Surveillance Reform," *Public Interest Law Journal* 18 (2009): 294.

of intelligence thus occupies a unique position within the range of tools intended to maintain external accountability because its range of responsibility is narrow and very technical. The court was established to provide orders authorizing this type of intelligence gathering because of the abuses that occurred using this technique without oversight, particularly from the 1950s through the 1970s. The judicial mechanism is limited by the information asymmetry discussed throughout this book, and the aspect of intelligence activities overseen by the judicial branch has been perceived of as very arcane – electronic foreign intelligence gathering conducted within the United States. Finally, the stream of applications that the court can handle is slim, as the process for review and approval is rigorous. This type of intelligence is particularly controversial because it touches upon American expectations of privacy within the borders of their country, and it challenges legal constraints on search and seizure under the Fourth Amendment.

The creation of the FISC by the FISA legislation was a major turning point in the development of the judicial role in intelligence oversight. If one considers the judiciary to be a balance with the other two branches of government, then one could suppose that the introduction of FISA reestablished a balance – although not one in equilibrium – in terms of foreign intelligence surveillance. In theory, in a series of steps, post–Church Committee legislation reintroduced both congressional and judicial control over what appeared to be an executive run amok. FISA marked a radical turning point in terms of structuring domestic intelligence and surveillance; however, in the wake of 9/11, almost any level of judicial control over electronic surveillance has been challenged. The earlier trends and expectations of executive privilege over national security issues have been pushed to extremes, partially as a function of established historical precedent, but especially as a function of the Bush administration's interest in increasing the power of the president and the Obama administration's general adherence to this same path.[58] It could be argued that under this onslaught, the ability of the judiciary

---

[58] See Gordon Silverstein, *Imbalance of Powers: Constitutional Interpretation and the Making of American Foreign Policy* (Oxford: Oxford University Press, 1997), for a discussion of the trend of executive primacy over issues of foreign policy and national security. For a particularly disturbing popular account of the plan behind the Bush administration's focus on increasing power, see Barton Gellman, *Angler: The Cheney Vice Presidency* (New York: Penguin Press, 2008).

to supervise intelligence activities has crumbled. Others argue that the judicial review function of intelligence activities has simply adapted to the exigencies of an emergent and dynamic threat environment.

In terms of the criteria supporting the analytical framework for accountability that drives this book, one can conclude that the FISC is weak. In fact, in many ways judicial oversight of intelligence through the court is controversial because the characteristics of the composition and practice of the court collide with expectations of what constitutes an independent judiciary and a strong mechanism for the assurance of accountability. While the application process for an order allows the judges to require further information if they believe it necessary, the baseline of which targets should be focused on and why resides wholly in the executive branch. This was demonstrated when it was disclosed that the FBI had provided the court with fraudulent or incomplete information in several of its order requests. Also, the membership of the court rotates, thus expertise on these matters varies. However, I believe that minimal expertise on the part of the FISC judges is actually *less* of a problem when compared to legislative oversight, as the orders are granted based on their merits; congressional overseers are expected to understand the nuance of intelligence operations in greater depth.

Autonomy – independence from the executive branch and the agencies working for it, in this case – is the category that is most controversial when it comes to the FISC. One reason for this controversy is linked to the absence of the final category: transparency of the court. The proceedings are secret – even some of the instructions to the court are classified. Although the court has a process by which it reviews order requests, this process is secret and the files drawn from it are sealed. With no requirement to provide external documentation regarding decisions about orders, it is impossible to know how and why decisions are being made. In terms of the secret, *ex parte* nature of the court's proceedings, these procedures and the materials gathered therein have withstood FOIA requests based on the national security exception.[59] The

---

[59] Alison A. Bradley, "Extremism in the Defense of Liberty? The Foreign Intelligence Surveillance Act and the Significance of the USA PATRIOT ACT," *Tulane Law Review* 77 (2002–3): 480.

only external reporting required from the court is a yearly report to Congress on the number of orders granted or denied.[60] Thus the court raises interesting questions of what constitutes "autonomy." Is it linked to a chain of accountability, or is it remote from governance? Is it independent in its decisions, or is it locked in a subordinate role with the executive branch? As mentioned previously, some have argued that it is purely a "rubber stamp" of approval for executive activities. This argument has been made because the number of orders turned down is very small. One could argue that the court is deeply united with the executive in terms of creating a secrecy system to guard intelligence from transparency and accountability – there is virtually no leakage of information from the court, the court itself is barely acknowledged and almost never in the public spotlight, and its decisions until recently have been secret.

On the other side of this debate, as mentioned earlier, the argument is made that the internal process is so rigorous and judges' expectations and demands for information are so high that order requests are revised until they are acceptable. But a solid response to this concern will never be forthcoming due to the almost opaque nature of the court. Another aspect of independence that remains weak is the process of recourse in changing the behavior of the overseen. A court order from the FISA court is granted prior to the conduct of the intelligence activity or, in the case of emergency, immediately after the start of the activity. The court may stipulate requirements prior to the event, but has very little capacity to change the activity once it has begun. In terms of temporality of oversight, the court does have the capacity to prevent action until its stipulations regarding the parameters of the activity are met. Once again, however, very few order requests are ever permanently denied. Finally, in terms of overall accountability of the intelligence community to the judiciary, the FISC is responsible for supervising a small set of intelligence activities: electronic surveillance used to gather foreign intelligence within the United States. Thus, although there are still ambiguities with how independent the court actually is, the larger questions are why the purview of judicial oversight of intelligence is so narrow, and, normatively, whether it should be more comprehensive.

[60] 50 U.S.C. § 1807 (1994).

One further feature of the judicial oversight mechanism is the FISC Review Court. Appeals of decisions made by the FISC can be referred to the review court for its adjudication by three judges. The review court also has an ambiguous role – mainly because FISC decisions are rarely referred to it. The FISC Review Court has issued one decision since its creation in 1978. This decision will be discussed in depth later in this chapter. It has been argued that this decision – siding with the administration against the FISC – was definitive in demonstrating the passive dependence of the review court. I argue that while it was striking that the review court published its one decision siding with the executive, an N of 1 in this particular, very opaque environment establishes nothing definitive. The FISC Review Court does bring up another penetrating issue for this project: ostensibly it was established to provide an additional level of accountability to the procedure of applying for orders under FISA. What does it mean that it has made only one decision? Further, in the case that an FISC Review Court decision is contested, the final decider is the Supreme Court. No order has ever advanced to the Supreme Court.

Notable themes so far are, again, the information asymmetry between the executive and judiciary regarding intelligence activities, including lack of independent judicial access to intelligence information and the dependence on the executive both for scoping and planning intelligence activities and for providing appropriate and complete information about these plans for the court's review. Two other key issues involve the narrow scope of judicial oversight and controversies over the question of to what degree the executive still does and should maintain exclusive authority over foreign intelligence activities. This last issue has begun to be settled, in light of the Bush administration agreeing to place the Terrorist Surveillance Program under the supervision of the FISA court and also in response to the Snowden revelations, when the authority of the court has been reinforced in terms of having authorized the NSA programs that were leaked to the public.

USA PATRIOT ACT: EMERGENCY LEGISLATION AND THE EXPANSION OF FISA

The USA PATRIOT Act of 2001, signed into law on October 26, 2001, expanded the authority of federal agencies to operate domestically;

broke down the "wall" constructed from the Church Committee recommendations; expanded the limit on how information gathered under
FISA could be used; and redefined what constitutes "domestic terrorism."[61] Catalyzed by the 9/11 attacks, the PATRIOT Act was drafted,
passed, and signed remarkably quickly. In comparison, it took two years
of debate and compromise among the administration, the agencies,
and Congress to enact FISA.[62] Of course, the debates around FISA
occurred in a calmer threat environment; however, the post-9/11 environment notwithstanding, six weeks to pass legislation that had a great
deal of impact on the balance between security and civil liberties was
considered hasty, in some cases extreme, and potentially ideologically
driven rather than responsive to the actual demands of the threat. Even
close to the trauma of 9/11, there were concerns that the act was a huge
and perhaps unnecessary step that expanded federal powers at the cost
of civil liberties without even being aimed at detecting terrorists.[63]

The act marked once again a polarizing moment in executive
authority and foreign intelligence gathering. One set of arguments
asserts that outdated legislation, such as FISA and the "wall" that had
developed through custom, hindered counterterrorism efforts that
were needed as the country turned to a new type of war. On the other
hand, passage of the PATRIOT Act could be ascribed to widespread
panic at the time, increased public support for more stringent security
measures, and the need for perceived political action to assuage public anxieties. It must be remembered that President George W. Bush's
approval rating stood above 80 percent at that time, and it also must
be remembered that there *was* actually a time when terrorism was a
widely underexplored topic, among elites as well as the public. Policy
options were cruder at that time.

The act expanded the use of four main surveillance tools: wiretaps, search orders, pen-trap orders, and subpoenas.[64] Wiretaps were
expanded to include "roving" surveillance – that is, surveillance was

---

[61] Natsu Taylor Saito, "Whose Liberty? Whose Security? The USA PATRIOT Act in the
Context of COINTELPRO and the Unlawful Repression of Political Dissent," *Oregon
Law Review* 81 (2002): 1059.

[62] Bradley, "Extremism in the Defense of Liberty?" 473.

[63] Bradley, "Extremism in the Defense of Liberty?" 473.

[64] USA PATRIOT ACT §201–201, 206–207, 209–220, cited in Bradley, "Extremism in the
Defense of Liberty?" 485.

no longer tied to a particular location, but rather could be tied to the suspect and whatever means of communication he or she was using, which freed up investigation in a time of cell phones and other personal electronic devices. In a congressional press release at the time of the passage of the act, a member praised its modernization in the face of technological advance:

> The PATRIOT Act modernizes wiretapping laws to keep up with changing technologies such as cell phones, voice mail and e-mail. Current wiretapping laws are outdated. In today's technologically advanced society, people communicate through a variety of means.... By allowing "roving surveillance" of suspected terrorists, law enforcement officials will be able to more effectively monitor their communications and intercept terrorist activity.[65]

Roving, or multipoint, wiretaps are not new. They are, in fact, used in criminal investigations, but the use of them for intelligence activities, permitted based on much lower standards of proof, expands the scope of their use greatly, while also expanding the possibility of target errors; in this case, non-target individuals who may be caught up in surveillance activities by accident.[66] Pen register, and trap and trace surveillance were extended under the PATRIOT Act, allowing the government to forego the specific requirement that the line or communications device be used in communication with someone targeted by FISA, that is, someone involved in international terrorism or intelligence activities who could be violating U.S. law, or a foreign power or its agent whose communications are believed to concern terrorism or intelligence activities that violate U.S. law. Instead, the government – under the act – need only certify that the information gathered by these methods is "relevant to an ongoing criminal investigation."[67]

The PATRIOT Act allowed for the purpose of surveillance to be redefined, greatly loosening the restrictions fundamental to the original passage of FISA. Specifically, the language of FISA was changed from requiring that the *purpose* of surveillance be to gather foreign

---

[65] Press release of Representative Saxby Chambliss (R-GA), October 12, 2001, quoted in Bradley, "Extremism in the Defense of Liberty?" 485.

[66] Bradley, "Extremism in the Defense of Liberty?" 487.

[67] USA PATRIOT ACT §214a(1)(amending 50 USC §1842(c)(2), cited in Bradley, "Extremism in the Defense of Liberty?"488.

intelligence information to the significantly looser *significant purpose*.[68] This means that the scope of FISA is broader, but also that the division between law enforcement and intelligence use of information gathered under FISA was greatly diluted. Because court orders under FISC required a much lower burden of proof, there was a significant problem if the evidence gathered under the FISA order was used in a criminal case.[69] The "wall," however, also became symbolic as partly responsible for the intelligence failure on 9/11. As has been reported in great detail, the failure to share information between the FBI and CIA, the culture of turf protection, and "need to know" (the compartmentalization of information) all contributed to a failure to recognize the signs leading up to 9/11.[70]

Breaking down the divide was considered a partial solution to the operational problem of sharing information.[71] Arguably, one of the more challenging changes to FISA advanced by the PATRIOT Act was the section that allows intelligence information drawn from grand jury proceedings and wiretaps to be shared with "any federal law enforcement, protective, intelligence, immigration, and national defense or security personnel, provided that recipients of the information may only use such information in connection with their official duties and subject to the disclosure limitations in existing law."[72] This may seem an innocuous addition within the context of the other, more clearly invasive measures, but in practice it breaks down long-revered boundaries between the use of information by law enforcement as opposed to intelligence officers. The "wall" kept information gathered under the looser standards of proof separated from criminal investigations, which required information to be gathered based on the Fourth Amendment's standard of probable cause. At this point, under the

---

[68] Elizabeth Rindskopf Parker and Brian Pate, "Judicial Oversight of Intelligence," in *Reforming Intelligence: Obstacles to Democratic Control and Effectiveness*, eds. Thomas C. Bruneau and Steven C. Boraz (Austin: University of Texas Press, 2007), 51–72, at 64.

[69] Bradley, "Extremism in the Defense of Liberty? 484.

[70] See National Commission on Terrorist Attacks upon the United States (Philip Zelikow, Executive Director; Bonnie D. Jenkins, Counsel; Ernest R. May, Senior Advisor), *The 9/11 Commission Report* (New York: W.W. Norton, 2004).

[71] The criticism that the intelligence community (IC) did not share information among agencies was a crucial component of the *9/11 Commission Report*.

[72] Bradley, "Extremism in the Defense of Liberty? 492; §203 PATRIOT ACT.

PATRIOT Act, orders provided by the FISC can be used in criminal prosecutions, given that this is not the sole purpose of the original
investigation, and prosecutors and intelligence officers may consult
over the FISA order and application.[73]

Not only was this new language interpreted as allowing greater and
more flexible usage of domestic surveillance for law enforcement, but
it also catalyzed a debate leading to a new standard for FISA orders
that was challenged by the FISC itself.[74] Procedural concerns drove
the FISC, while ostensibly accepting the new language, to reject the
new measures outlined in the PATRIOT Act. The FISC, which modified specific stipulations and thereby challenged the administration,
appealed to the FISC Court of Review (FISCR), an unprecedented
move. This decision, *In re Sealed*, struck down the primary purpose
test, removing the "wall" between intelligence and law enforcement
and allowing material gathered by electronic surveillance to be used in
a criminal prosecution.[75] In the explanation of the FISCR:

> [The primary purpose] analysis, in our view, rested on a false pre-
> mise and the line the court sought to draw was inherently unstable,
> unrealistic, and confusing. The false premise was the assertion that
> once the government moves to criminal prosecution, its "foreign
> policy concerns" recede.... [T]hat is simply not true as it relates to
> counterintelligence. In that field the government's primary purpose
> is to halt the espionage or terrorism efforts, and criminal prosecu-
> tions can be, and usually are, interrelated with other techniques
> used to frustrate a foreign power's efforts.[76]

What does the PATRIOT Act signify for the court, as well as for
civil liberties? There are two sides to the expansion of FISA. On the
one hand, with loosened constraints and the breakdown of the strict
division between surveillance for foreign intelligence gathering and

---

[73] USA PATRIOT ACT. §218 (50 U.S.C. § 180(a)(7)(B), quoted in Breglio, "Leaving FISA
Behind," 180.

[74] Breglio, "Leaving FISA Behind," 65.

[75] J. Christopher Champion, "The Revamped FISA: Striking a Better Balance between the
Government's Need to Protect Itself and the 4th Amendment," *Vanderbilt Law Review* 58
(2005): 1672.

[76] *In re Sealed* Case, 310 F.3d 717, 743 (FISA Ct. 2002), quoted in Cooper Blum, "What
Really Is at Stake with the FISA Amendments Act of 2008," 282.

criminal investigation, the court could actually be seen as having more power than when its jurisdiction was strictly limited to foreign intelligence gathering within the United States. On the other hand, this loosening of the rules arguably comes at a cost, potentially to the public, with challenges to their civil liberties and constitutional protection under the Fourth Amendment against unreasonable search and seizure. The act allows law enforcement officers greater access to surveillance gathered under FISA. Proponents of the act argue that the "wall" was never written in statute and came about only through custom and bureaucratic practice. They state that the wall artificially hampered the smooth integration of investigations and information sharing between services. This, of course, was the major point of the 9/11 Commission in its statements regarding the intelligence community's inability "to connect the dots." The contention was that the components of the intelligence community were artificially divided from one another through culture, regulation, and parochial approaches to turf and information ownership.[77] The move thus appears to be a weakening of the external autonomy of the judicial mechanism in favor of loosened constraints on intelligence projects and administration objectives.

The decision of the FISCR supports this assertion. According to one scholar, the Court of Review's decision returned responsibility for balancing national security and privacy rights to where it should be: the executive and Congress.[78] This argument points to this balance as a political issue rather than one that can be settled in a secret court. The counterargument is, of course, that the Fourth Amendment clearly gives the judiciary the responsibility for ensuring the privacy rights of citizens.[79] *Transparency* is the missing ingredient tying the contention together. Stationing deliberations over the balance between national security and civil liberties in the legislative branch makes sense; legislators are proxies for the public and thus this is one way of making sure that the decisions made regarding this relationship are restrained by the chain of accountability. On the other

---

[77] See 9/11 Commission's critique of the "wall," in *9/11 Commission Report*, 78–9.

[78] Craig S. Lerner, quoted in Champion, "The Revamped FISA," 1691.

[79] Champion, "The Revamped FISA," 1692.

hand, this approach to national security would remove any responsibility for review of national security issues from the judiciary.

While the PATRIOT Act was seminal in terms of a relatively radical broadening of FISA, which had been in place for over twenty years at that point, the real contention within the context of the analytical framework was the attempted exclusion of judicial oversight by the Bush administration. The next section of this chapter discusses the program that found a way around the judicial oversight mechanism and concludes with an analysis of whether the evasion mattered in terms of the continued development of judicial oversight over intelligence activities.

FISA, THE NATIONAL SECURITY AGENCY, AND THE TERRORIST SURVEILLANCE PROGRAM

FISA was developed to strike a balance between foreign intelligence gathering requirements and protection of the civil liberties of U.S. citizens. It has been argued that there has been much attrition via statute to this framework in the post-9/11 environment, but the program of orderless surveillance that was undertaken by the National Security Agency under orders of the Bush administration is the most telling in terms of judicial subordination. The timing of the Terrorist Surveillance Program (TSP) overlaps with the developments under the PATRIOT Act, although the specific timing of its authorization remains unclear. I have listed these two events sequentially to clarify the analytical points that are key to the framework.

The Terrorist Surveillance Program, authorized by the Bush administration in 2001, allowed the NSA to intercept communications between individuals in the United States and individuals abroad without FISC order, the objective being to discover evidence of terrorist activity.[80] The focus of this surveillance was on the communications of those suspected of having links with al-Qaeda or other terrorist organizations.[81] The discussion here of TSP, a program conducted outside

---

[80] Wong, Recent Developments, "The NSA Terrorist Surveillance Program", in *Harvard Journal on Legislation* 43(2006), 517–34.

[81] Banks, "The Death of FISA," 1254.

of the bounds of the judicial oversight mechanism, is intended to demonstrate how arguments against the necessity of judicial oversight have been offered and whether or how they have been successful.

The program, in operation for three years at the time of its disclosure, was announced to the public in a front-page story in the *New York Times* on December 16, 2005.[82] By the time of its publication, the *Times* had held the story for a year due to national security concerns and the appeal from the administration not to "out" the program. The story described how the program was conducted outside of the auspices of the FISA statute and FISC and thus had not been subject to any external judicial review. Based on normal statutory interpretation, the program was illegal. The FISC was created to be the sole authorizer of electronic surveillance. The main thrust of the argument for the legality of the program relies upon its basis in the president's commander-in-chief authority, which includes authorization to collect intelligence information in a time of war.[83]

The perceived need that drove the development of TSP, designed to circumvent FISA, highlights several issues regarding how FISA was perceived to be inadequate to meet the task of post-9/11, twenty-first-century electronic surveillance. FISA focused the location of the target – that is, it was assumed when an order was requested that the government knew where the target was and what type of communications devices he or she was using.[84] FISA did not apply to surveillance gathered outside the United States or to communications strictly between foreigners within the United States. FISA was very specific, targeted to known cases and focused on gathering material from specific targets of interest. Whether one accepts the government's argument for the legality of the program, there is unanimous agreement that the challenges of the non-state threat coupled with technological advancement made changes in the supervisory legal framework necessary. The Internet alone challenges traditional interpretations

---

[82] Eric Lichtblau and James Risen, "Bush Lets US Spy on Callers without Courts," *New York Times*, December 16, 2005.

[83] John Yoo, "The Terrorist Surveillance Program and the Constitution," *George Mason Law Review* 14 (2007): 566.

[84] William C. Banks, "Response to the Ten Questions," *William Mitchell Law Review* 35, no. 5 (2009): 5008.

of communication and location by breaking information into digital packets that reach their destination through the most efficient pathway, in some cases passing through the United States to reach a foreign destination; in others, packets cross through foreign territory to reach a domestic destination.

Further, the current approach to locating potential terrorists is quite different from the close, focused practice required under FISA. While General Michael Hayden argued strenuously that TSP did not constitute a "dragnet," the approach to acquiring targets of interest is much different from that used when FISA was developed, although the operational details remain vague.[85] It has been asserted that the NSA gathered large quantities of information at switching stations, with the assistance of telecommunications companies. The data were then searched for patterns and relationships through data-mining methods. Potential targets of interest were drawn out of these patterns, and finally the targets chosen were referred to the FBI for further investigation.[86] There is a multitude of concerns buried in this rather technocratic explanation for the alleged change in targeting process.

Aside from the issues of the legality of TSP, one of the striking aspects of the program is the change in focus on the part of the NSA's targets. As I noted previously, the NSA under General Hayden was very careful about overstepping its bounds regarding the scope of its surveillance. Mirroring the overall trend of intelligence collection in the post-9/11 security environment, TSP marked a rapid shift from a few carefully chosen targets based on specific personal details, such as employment history and connections to others, to a wider range of targets chosen to represent nodes in larger networks or inputs into patterns of behavior.[87] Data mining, social network analysis, and other computer-based pattern-finding tools are all in use by the NSA and most of the other analytic components of the intelligence community.

[85] Remarks by General Michael V. Hayden, "Address to the National Press Club: What American Intelligence and Especially the NSA Have Been Doing to Defend the Nation", National Press Club, Washington DC, January 23, 2006.

[86] See Banks, "Response to the Ten Questions," 5010, as a caveat to *all* descriptions of TSP. The former NSA officials with whom I discussed this program were very defensive about any perceived indiscriminate data gathering.

[87] Recent Developments, "The NSA Terrorist Surveillance Program," 518.

The objective of all of these tools is to increase concurrently the breadth of field while narrowing the specificity of the target.

TSP introduced new techniques that virtually could not avoid including a wide range of non-target individuals within the broad nets intended for pursuit of terrorism suspects and also changed how the targets themselves were chosen. Under FISA, as described previously, a distinct process was in place for describing the nature of the individual chosen to be investigated as well as the methods chosen to pursue this investigation. With the advent of TSP, the targets were chosen along a more functional, bureaucratic level – by the NSA's "operational work-force" and then approved by a shift supervisor.[88] The idea that a "shift supervisor" would decide targeting for the program caused a good deal of controversy. As explained by Hayden, the "shift supervisor" is drawn from a number of very senior executive officers. In his words, "In military terms, a senior colonel or general officer equivalent; and in professional terms, the people who know more about this than anyone else."[89] I quote this comment here to point out the continued reference to the professionalism argument that was commonly used to support TSP. It is inarguably true that the NSA officers responsible for con-ducting surveillance under this program know most about the specific programs conducted by the NSA. However, any concerned observer would find it striking that this professionalism argument is being used to persuade audiences that their concerns about accountability can be dealt with adequately in-house.

Within the context of the accountability framework outlined in this book, the audacity of the legal arguments surrounding TSP is striking. As Bush administration attorney general Alberto Gonzales testified before Congress: "The President's constitutional powers include the authority to conduct warrantless surveillance aimed at detecting and preventing armed attacks on the United States."[90] The argument about

---

[88] Recent Developments, "The NSA Terrorist Surveillance Program," 519.

[89] Remarks by General Michael V. Hayden, "Address to the National Press Club: What American Intelligence and Especially the NSA Have Been Doing to Defend the Nation," National Press Club, Washington, DC, January 23, 2006.

[90] Attorney General Alberto Gonzales, quoted in Daniel J. Solove, *Nothing to Hide: The False Tradeoff between Privacy and Security* (New Haven, CT: Yale University Press, 2011), 82.

TSP also obliquely highlights the central focus of this book – to understand how oversight has developed and to explain why its effectiveness is constrained – by returning to the core argument asserted by the Bush administration. This argument is, of course, that the president is the "sole organ for the nation in foreign affairs," and thus was not overreaching in conducting orderless surveillance.[91]

In more concrete terms, the administration argued that Congress vested in the president the authority to prevent future attacks against the United States in the Authorization for Use of Military Force (AUMF), passed shortly after the attacks on September 11. In the words of FISA: "A person is guilty of an offense if he intentionally engages in electronic surveillance under color of law except as authorized by statute."[92] The administration argued that AUMF provides this statutory authorization in its "all necessary and appropriate force" clause. The argument thus was that surveillance of the enemy is an appropriate use of force.[93] The administration's argument states that the program was legal and, further, that it facilitated the gathering of useful intelligence information on the adversary.[94] Another argument advanced by the administration asserted that the program was lawful under the Fourth Amendment, because surveillance for the purposes of national security qualifies as a "special needs" search.[95] In such cases, it is argued, the government may undertake searches, even when there may be no individualized suspicion, in such instances where "special needs, beyond the normal need for law enforcement," are present; where the expectation of privacy is diminished, or intrusion is minimal; and/or where there is an increased need to act expeditiously.[96]

One line of the Bush administration's reasoning about the program progressed as follows: the constitutionality of the program was

---

[91] *US v. Curtiss-Wright Export Corp* (1936), quoted in Yoo, "The Terrorist Surveillance Program," 567.

[92] Quoted in Michael C. Miller, "Standing in the Wake of the Terrorist Surveillance Program: A Modified Standard for Challenges to Secret Government Surveillance," *Rutgers Law Review* 60, no. 4 (2008): 1053.

[93] Miller, "Standing in the Wake."

[94] Yoo, "The Terrorist Surveillance Program," 565.

[95] Adam Burton, "Fixing FISA for Long War: Regulating Warrantless Surveillance in the Age of Terrorism," *Pierce Law Review* 4, no. 2 (2005–6): 392.

[96] Burton, "Fixing FISA for Long War," 397.

assessed by breaking it down into two further subconsiderations. First, with regard to the metadata issue, the Supreme Court decided in *Smith v. Maryland* that there is no Fourth Amendment issue with the gathering of metadata. The second aspect of this analysis focused on data content. The presidential order was interpreted as requiring a probable cause finding, thus complying with Fourth Amendment requirements. As mentioned in the brief discussion of the *Keith* case at the beginning of this chapter, it is still unresolved whether this requirement holds when it comes to *foreign* – in contrast to domestic – intelligence. Second, in terms of FISA, the interpretation was that FISA allowed the president to act without FISA orders in an emergency, as otherwise FISA is unconstitutional in preventing the president from carrying out his constitutional commander-in-chief duties.[97]

Another contention was made by General Hayden, among others, who asserted that FISA was outdated because of the telecommunications revolution that had occurred since it was passed.[98] Linking the first to the last argument, the NSA argued that the president's inherent constitutional powers granted him the authority to conduct this surveillance outside of the supervision of the FISA court, while the increased number of targets post-9/11 challenged the court's ability to process the number of orders required. It has been argued that the reason for going around the FISA court was the sheer number of order requests, not any failing on the part of those requests to achieve the court's standards of appropriateness.[99]

Finally, it has been argued that TSP was legal due to the fact that it was reviewed by Department of Justice attorneys and approved by the attorney general, who reviewed and reauthorized it every forty-five days.[100] In General Hayden's words, "The trigger is quicker and a bit softer than it is for a FISA warrant, but the intrusion into privacy is also limited: only international calls and only those we have a reasonable basis to believe involve al Qaeda or one of its affiliates."[101] He also

[97] Personal communication, former senior intelligence executive with knowledge of the legal analysis, November 26, 2014.
[98] Hayden, "Address to the National Press Club."
[99] Interview with a senior CIA official, November 10, 2011.
[100] Hayden, "Address to the National Press Club."
[101] Hayden, "Address to the National Press Club."

describes the internal oversight framework devised for the program, mentioning that it is "the most intense oversight regime in the history of the National Security Agency," requiring the program to be thoroughly reviewed by the NSA's general counsel and inspector general, in addition requiring DoJ approval, as mentioned previously.[102]

In terms of legal analysis, real friction arose over whether TSP superseded FISA or vice versa. Critics argued that FISA dealt directly with the issue of surveillance during war by allowing the president a fifteen-day exception before application for court order was required.[103] Further, the original text of FISA was very explicit that it would be the sole means of authorizing electronic surveillance. Finally, as legal scholars Fletcher N. Baldwin, Jr., and Robert B. Shaw argue, AUMF does not compare to FISA in terms of specificity. FISA explicitly focuses on clarifying processes for dealing with wartime domestic surveillance, whereas AUMF broadly grants an authorization to wage war. AUMF does not address in any explicit language the exigencies of intelligence gathering.[104] Rather, the use of AUMF to support TSP was built upon inference. The precedence of specificity over generality in the rules of statute generation was articulated by the court decision in *ACLU v NSA*, which stated that the specific commands of FISA overruled the general authorization of AUMF.[105]

General Hayden often argued that he was *morally* bound to go to the edge of the constraints of the law in order to protect the country from its adversaries.[106] In terms of TSP, John Yoo and others argued that even critics did not doubt that the program yielded important information useful to the prevention of al-Qaeda plans directed at the United States.[107] In Yoo's words: "The main criticism has not been that the program is ineffective, but that it violates the Constitution and cannot be undertaken, no matter how successful or necessary to protect the public."[108] Attorney General Gonzales argued the "professional"

---

[102] Hayden, "Address to the National Press Club."
[103] Miller, "Standing in the Wake," 1053.
[104] Baldwin and Shaw, "Down to the Wire," 454.
[105] Provisions of *ACLU v NSA*, discussed in Baldwin and Shaw, "Down to the Wire," 471.
[106] Interview with General Michael Hayden, April 7, 2010.
[107] Yoo, "The Terrorist Surveillance Program," 572.
[108] Yoo, "The Terrorist Surveillance Program," 572.

case – that the intelligence professionals should make the decisions about appropriateness in intelligence gathering. This argument in itself is an outgrowth of the age-old contention regarding the superior efficacy and efficiency of the executive branch in terms of emergency decision making:

> The optimal way to achieve the speed and agility necessary to this military intelligence program during the present armed conflict with al Qaeda is to leave the decisions about particular intercepts to the judgment of professional intelligence officers, based on the best available intelligence information. These officers are best situated to make decisions quickly and accurately. If, however, those same intelligence officers had to navigate through the FISA process for each of these intercepts, that would necessarily introduce a significant factor of delay, and there would be critical holes in our early warning system.[109]

At issue here, of course, is the fact that the executive claimed the legality of this program based on (1) congressional support for the war on terrorism and, more interestingly, (2) the executive discretion of the president as commander-in-chief to undertake whatever he or she deems necessary to support national security requirements. Leaving aside the merits of these two assertions, it does seem immediately apparent that if the executive is claiming purview over electronic surveillance that should by the requirements of FISA be supervised by the FISC, any judicial supervisory traction over the conduct of domestic intelligence operations is significantly weakened. It seems odd to claim absolute executive privilege regarding foreign intelligence – particularly in terms of the fact that the FISC had worked fairly consistently in support of executive demands, and the president had even invoked FISA in his description of the administration's activities. In President Bush's words: "… Any time you hear the United States government talking about wiretap, it requires … a court order. Nothing has changed. When we're talking about chasing down terrorists, we're talking about getting a court order before we do so."[110] The president's

---

[109] Former attorney general Alberto Gonzales' congressional testimony, quoted in Solove, *Nothing to Hide*, 83.

[110] President George W. Bush's remarks in a discussion on the PATRIOT ACT in Buffalo, NY, April 20, 2004, quoted in Banks, "Response to the Ten Questions," 1255.

assertion was clearly not accurate. The political response to the program was intense, with House and Senate Democrats and Republicans demanding hearings, and in a surprising move for a member of the secret court, an FISC judge resigned.[111]

Ultimately, the Bush administration, under pressure, placed TSP under the supervision of the FISC in 2007 and did not reauthorize it. This decision was in response to an FISC ruling that an aspect of the program was illegal. The result of the ruling was a series of immediate attempts to amend the FISA legislation.[112] In addition to pointing to the complexities of judicial oversight, the details of the debate about TSP are illustrative of the complexities of the relationship among executive power, surveillance, and public opinion. For example, when the program was described in the *New York Times* in 2005, it was met with a wave of negative reaction at the political level, but the general public remained remarkably unmoved by the revelations. In Judge Richard Posner's words (writing in 2008): "It is remarkable how tepid the public reaction to the Terrorist Surveillance Program has been."[113] This rather feeble reaction to what could be perceived of as a gross infringement of civil liberties contrasts not only with the angry reactions to the intelligence abuses uncovered in the 1970s, but also with congressional response to the program, at least immediately after it was disclosed. The dynamics of public response to intelligence activities are not easy to measure, and most public reaction polling yields meager data. In this case, I would argue that the absence of heated response to what could have been a major public scandal was due to several factors. By 2005, the American public was very familiar with increased stages of security precautions that were very public, including the color-coded threat index issued by the Department of Homeland Security; invasive levels of security at airports; and increased security in virtually all public places in major cities.

[111] Baldwin and Shaw, "Down to the Wire," 432. There is no concrete clarification for the reason for the resignation of the FISC judge. It does remain a signal move, however, regardless of how it is interpreted. Most argue that it was in protest of the TSP, and from the hostile reactions I have received from Bush administration officials when asked about the resignation, I believe this to be the case.

[112] Carol D. Leonnig and Ellen Nakashima, "Ruling Limited Spying Efforts: Move to Amend FISA Sparked by Judge's Decision," *Washington Post*, August 3, 2007.

[113] Richard Posner, "Privacy, Surveillance, and the Law," 75 *University of Chicago Law Review* 245 (2008): 245–60, at 259.

This "crisis fatigue" was compounded with a sense of distance from the NSA program in two ways. First, the NSA is virtually unknown among the public, and access to even a limited awareness of its activities is extremely difficult. This distance from a federal agency, no tangible proof of personal invasion of privacy, and the program's focus on terrorism and specifically individuals drawn from al-Qaeda compounded this distancing effect. Further, by 2005, the public had decades to understand the nature of the security and intelligence agencies in the United States. Concerted efforts – such as publicity campaigns on the part of the CIA and FBI, or exposure to movies, television shows, and museums, such as the International Spy Museum in Washington, D.C. – have familiarized the public with the activities of the intelligence community. This was not the case in the 1970s, when, in a far different political context, the revelations of domestic intelligence activities conducted by the CIA, FBI, and NSA were first made public.

Finally, as a senior CIA official mentioned to me, there is a vast difference in the political environment between the mid-1970s – when the first crises regarding intelligence appeared – and the current era. Then, the United States was struggling with the final throes of the Vietnam conflict and the resignation of President Nixon.[114] There was very little institutional legitimacy left to cover the egregious abuses propagated by the intelligence services. Finally, the threat environment was less personal in the 1970s. Vast numbers of young men were drafted and sent to Vietnam during that period, leaving families to deal with absence, injury, and death, but there was not a sense that the "homeland," as it were, could come under attack – that ordinary employees showing up to work could be killed simply by showing up on time. This sense of vulnerability on the part of those most likely to be exposed to news of TSP created a public response evocative of Goldsmith's pendulum approach to intelligence and intelligence oversight. News of TSP was also buried under the unending flow of information about security issues that was a function of the increased attention to security and terrorism after-9/11, but also to the unending news cycle. This is a very different dynamic from the network news body counts of the

[114] Interview with a senior CIA official, November 10, 2011.

Vietnam era that were the public's main exposure to the war at that time.

While TSP was in place for a brief and still ambiguous interlude, the legality of which continues to be argued about strenuously on both sides of the political spectrum, it marks a unique moment in the institutional development of the intelligence oversight mechanisms I discuss throughout this book. FISC did not cease to exist during the period of the TSP – beginning and end dates are still unknown – but the administration chose to argue that the prior executive authority over foreign intelligence surveillance took precedence over the constraints of the FISA-created mechanism. I have described how the sequence of decisions regarding foreign intelligence surveillance developed prior to FISA, each decision leaving an exception for the purposes of national security. As one senior CIA official commented, TSP simply went back to the executive authority era, turning a full circle back from all of the developments that had created FISA and FISC.[115] A break this drastic would prove to be untenable within legislative oversight structures, and thus the conflict around TSP introduced real questions regarding whether judicial oversight of intelligence is actually perceived of as legitimate, constituting an independent check on intelligence, or whether it is, in fact, so subordinate that it has difficulty balancing the asymmetrical relationship at all.

THE PROTECT AMERICA ACT AND THE FISA AMENDMENTS (2008)

The legislative implications of both the political and technological complexities were realized in a two-step revision of FISA, undertaken in 2007 and 2008. This act amended FISA to allow orderless surveillance of foreign-to-foreign communications routed through the United States; allowed orderless surveillance of U.S. citizens communicating with individuals overseas, as long as the target of surveillance was reasonably believed to be located outside of the United States; and "[gave] the attorney general and the director of national intelligence (DNI)

---

[115] Interview with a senior CIA official, November 10, 2011.

the power to approve the international surveillance," thus removing the FISA court from this supervisory role.[116] According to the Protect America Act, the FISA court's only role was "to review and approve the procedures used by the government in the surveillance *after* it had been conducted [emphasis in the original text]."[117] The Protect America Act is, thus, interesting in that it legitimized TSP *after* the fact through legislation. In fact, it absorbed TSP, with the main difference between them being that TSP allowed surveillance of targets within the United States with the criterion for collection being the target's alleged relationship with Al-Qaeda, while the Protect America Act allowed surveillance based on the location of the target.[118]

The argument regarding whether TSP was constitutional is so politically polarized that doubtlessly no firm decision will ever be reached on this point. Even if Bush administration officials refuse to cede violating FISA as law breaking, it is undeniable the administration broke a *rule*. I differentiate *rule* from *law* here because the FISC was intended to be the source of supervision regarding electronic surveillance; this was established by norm, custom, and legal regime. When the administration chose to bypass this regime by appealing to another legal authority, it certainly bypassed a regime of rules that governed behavior on these matters. When required to bring the program back under the auspices of the FISC, the administration did so, but demanded a change to statute, including providing *retroactive immunity* to the private telecommunications companies that provided the information to the NSA's arguably illegal program.

One could argue that one factor in the change and development of judicial oversight is executive challenge to existing law through operational practice. Another way of putting this is that executive rule breaking in this context led to expansion of legal constraints, in contrast to the 1970s, when executive *law* breaking led to the creation of oversight mechanisms and the strengthening of constraints on the intelligence community. Development of the judicial mechanism of intelligence oversight is driven by the requirements of a changing

---

[116] Cooper Blum, "What Really Is at Stake with the FISA Amendments Act of 2008," 296.

[117] Protect America Act of 2007, Pub. L. No. 110–55 Stat. 552, quoted in Cooper Blum, "What Really Is at Stake with the FISA Amendments Act of 2008," 296.

[118] Banks, "Response to the Ten Questions," 5013.

threat environment and developing technology, both of which have
driven the statutory changes governing the court's makeup, role, and
the scope of its purview. There are arguments to be made that the
reason the changes were absorbed into the new regime was that there
was merit to the administration's objections to oversight controls at
that time. I am not passing value judgments on the merits of these
changes according to the law. I am simply underscoring the importance of assessing rule breaking as a pathway to intelligence oversight
regime change.[119]

The Patriot America Act expired in February 2008 because of disagreement between the Bush administration and Congress concerning retroactive immunity for the telecommunications companies that
had participated in TSP.[120] It was followed by a second wave of FISA
revisions, the FISA Amendments Act of 2008, which diluted FISA
significantly but reintroduced significant procedural mechanisms.
For example, added were such requirements that the order application be presented to the FISA court *prior* to the proposed surveillance;
that the targeting be limited and focused on individuals believed to
be located outside of the United States, intended, of course, to limit
the purposeful acquisition of domestic information; that minimization
procedures must be in place; and that the attorney general and DNI
must certify that a "significant purpose" of the surveillance is to obtain
"foreign intelligence information."[121] While certain FISA constraints
were hardened, further revisions to FISA completed in 2008 definitely
served in the executive's purposes. These included an increased range
of acceptable surveillance activities by no longer requiring the FISC
to consider individual surveillance operations, but rather requiring
only that the court monitor whether the general procedural requirements of FISA were being followed. The amendments also granted
retroactive immunity to the telecommunications firms that assisted the
NSA in conducting the orderless surveillance of American citizens.

---

[119] See Cooper Blum, "What Really Is at Stake with the FISA Amendments Act of 2008,"
296, for the argument stating the merits of the Bush administration's challenges to the
FISA regime at that time. Several of my intelligence community interlocutors made the
same argument.

[120] Cooper Blum, "What Really Is at Stake with the FISA Amendments Act of 2008," 296.

[121] 50 U.S.C. 1881.

The amendments also expanded FISA to address the surveillance of Americans living overseas – thus actually protecting Americans from invasion of their personal privacy while living overseas.[122] In the words of Senator Dianne Feinstein (D-CA), "This bill does more than Congress has ever done before to protect Americans' privacy regardless of where they are, anywhere in the world."[123] One part of the FISA amendments that has come under scrutiny in the wake of the Snowden revelations is section 702, which allows for the collection on non-U.S. persons suspected of being outside of the United States.

I do not wish to overstate the impact of Snowden's leaks on the trajectory of intelligence oversight. The revelations themselves struck deep chords among the public – particularly a public fatigued by years of war and a growing sense that the security state has led to a mismatch between threat and reality. I mention section 702 here because it did draw attention to FISA, forcing a public discussion of what it means, how it works, what its limits are, and who is determining the extent of its applicability.

In the political and public levels, the post-9/11 context caused those charged with oversight of intelligence to be pressured strenuously to acquiesce to executive expectations when it came to limiting these operations. This is also linked to the enormous pressure for governments to deliver on their promises of safety and security.[124] This political pressure was alluded to by an FISC judge speaking on a conference panel, when he commented that no FISC judge wants another attack to happen "on his watch."[125] While the intensity of this feeling may have waned as years have passed since 9/11, political tension and potential blame in the public eye have infiltrated even this most secret of courts.

[122] S. 2248, 110th Congress, discussed in Jonathan D. Forgang, "'The Right of the People': The NSA, the FISA Amendments Act of 2008, and the Foreign Intelligence Surveillance of Americans Overseas," *Fordham Law Review* 78, no. 217 (2009–10): 237–9.

[123] 154 Cong Rec. S6097, S6119 (June 25, 2008), quoted in Cooper Blum, "What Really Is at Stake with the FISA Amendments Act," 300.

[124] Peter Gill, "Democratic and Parliamentary Accountability of Intelligence Services after September 11," paper prepared for the Workshop on Democratic and Parliamentary Oversight of Intelligence Services, Geneva, October 3–5, 2002, 305, 312.

[125] Comment by FISC judge, Los Angeles Terrorism Early Warning Group/RAND Corporation Conference, "Terrorism and Global Security." May 9, 2008.

CONCLUSIONS

Concerning accountability, the trends in judicial oversight of intelligence activities are much more troubling than the post-9/11 changes that have been made, for example, to congressional oversight during the same era. Congress has been slow to enact reform in its oversight procedures, even though slipshod oversight was blamed, in part, for the intelligence failure that led to the success of the attacks, although it has been quick to draft legislation loosening the constraints on federal law enforcement. An argument could be made that the strong response in terms of legislation could be the byproduct of public reaction to the attacks, whereas strenuous congressional oversight has always been the victim of the range of countervailing impulses discussed at length in Chapter 2 of this book.

FISA was originally installed because of evidence of vast domestic intelligence abuses conducted during the Cold War. While there were some zealots in the intelligence agencies during that period, many intelligence officers felt that they were responding appropriately to a penetrating domestic threat to the country. In the current threat environment, strides to weaken judicial oversight have been supported by arguments asserting that the nature of a non-state threat and the advancement of technology require that the oversight regime be diluted. When the regime has been perceived to be slow or unwieldy, it was bypassed with impunity, as with the NSA's TSP. In the words of one senior CIA official: "judicial oversight now is pretty thin gruel."[126]

The themes that emerge from the debates over the appropriateness of the FISC to meet the challenges of the post-9/11 threat environment highlight very clearly the importance of the accountability categories of the analytical framework. The external autonomy of the court is still a question – not just for this analysis, but also in practice. The question of whether the judiciary even *has* a role in supervising intelligence activities has reappeared multiple times in the more than two decades that a judicial mechanism has existed and highlights the asymmetry in the relationship between the executive and the judiciary regarding intelligence information. The questionable external independence

---

[126] Interview with a senior CIA official, November 8, 2010.

of the mechanism comes to the fore particularly when one looks at the politics of the changed FISA statutes. On the one hand, normal political processes operated to change the statute to absorb the emergent exigencies of the threat environment.[127] On the other, change was driven by executive rule breaking and prerogative. Further, the issues of knowledge and scope – access to intelligence information and the question of how wide the purview of the mechanism should be – have both been crucial in analysis of the changing nature of the FISC. Dual problems have been caused by faulty provision of information on the part of the executive and technical complexities involved in the process on the part of the judiciary. Organizational complexity is not overly problematic, as the judiciary deals with only a small slice of the intelligence enterprise, and the procedures, when they are followed, are clear-cut.

Temporality receives more of an emphasis within the context of judicial oversight than with the other types of oversight discussed in this book. The issue of temporality was core to the arguments regarding the Terrorist Surveillance Program. Those arguing for the necessity of the program stated that the increased flow of order requests in the post-9/11 pursuit of terrorist suspects would overwhelm the judicial oversight process – which involves, incidentally, officials from both the executive and judicial branches to act in concert – and that this flow would hinder the effective and timely processing of the orders. Beyond TSP, the "wall," discussed throughout this book, did limit the timely transmission of information between sides of the investigation. Thus the issue that the wall raises is not purely one of privacy protections and Fourth Amendment protections, but also one of the oversight mechanism being changed to facilitate more efficient transmission of intelligence information. The process of FISA would not only hinder the efficiency of gaining an order to monitor a suspect, but, according to this argument, the process could curtail surveillance if the means or location changed during the course of monitoring.

The final category in the analytical framework of accountability – transparency – is a crucial point here. Rather than eliciting yet another

---

[127] "Normal" is relative here. There was an extreme level of anxiety about national security in the political environment during the period immediately following 9/11.

statement that the court is not transparent, this opacity raises the question of whether variations within the overall category of transparency would be useful to measure and how this measurement would be operationalized. This is similar to requiring a breakdown of the category of "internal autonomy" of the CIA into constitutive variables with regard to the executive. As expected, the emphasis within the framework is different depending on the branch of government responsible for the accountability of the intelligence community. This opacity also raises the normative question of how transparent the court *should* be. Is there a moment in the process when it would be acceptable to divulge some details of an operation? Prior to the Snowden revelations, virtually nothing was known about how decisions by the court were made. Now, with the declassification of some decisions, there is a broader awareness of the basis for decisions and the criteria. Having said that, with heavy redaction, the internal operations of the court are by no means transparent at all and most likely never will be.

6 CONCLUSIONS AND ADAPTING OVERSIGHT MECHANISMS FOR THE FUTURE

The analytical framework of accountability has driven this book, providing core criteria to be used across the branches of government in the assessment of intelligence and accountability. The categories used illuminate the strengths and weaknesses of the mechanisms in all three branches of government. The core of intelligence and accountability is the problem of asymmetric information. Information is key to the process of intelligence programs, and thus it is highly guarded within the executive branch. This careful marshaling of intelligence information through these mechanisms has also led to the creation of a system of secrecy that hinders the expansion of transparency of these types of activities. This was clearly highlighted by the December 2014 release of the executive summary of the Senate Committee's Study of the Central Intelligence Agency's Detention and Interrogation Program. The details contained within the four hundred-page executive summary have shocked many because of the torture methods described as well as what seems to be clear misrepresentation of their effectiveness on the part of the CIA. Beyond this, the problem of asymmetry has been intensified by what has been described as incomplete information on the programs by senior CIA officials provided to external oversight mechanisms in Congress and the Department of Justice, as well as challenges to internal mechanisms, for example, to the inspector general within the CIA. Issues with the redaction and release of the report also led to extreme political stress between the Senate oversight committee and the CIA, as well as between Congress and the White House. These issues concerned how to redact enough of the information in the report to protect the identities of CIA officers who had taken part in the program and how to avoid divulging too many details, such as locations and foreign involvement, of the programs themselves.

The current situation brings up a range of questions, including what accountability means in the American democracy and, particularly, how much do Americans think transparency is core to this concept. For the most part, since the 1960s Americans have grown to expect that good citizenship requires one to be informed, and thus citizens should have access to government materials. This concept falters when dealing with national security, particularly in regard to intelligence activities, with their perceived uncertain borders, ambiguous limits, and what appears to be a limitless mandate. The United States has a pendulum-like relationship with security and intelligence matters. Following the Cold War, it seemed that there would be no future need for intensive – and expensive – intelligence operations abroad. The shock of 9/11 challenged that assumption, and now more than a decade after the attacks, Americans again try to come to terms with what security means, what appropriate secrecy should look like, and where the limits of intelligence activities both at home and abroad should be placed. The usual defense of these programs is that they were designed and conducted in a period of extreme national anxiety regarding security. National security officials were very concerned that an additional attack or attacks were in the immediate offing and thus extreme measures were deemed appropriate. Now is the time for public officials to redetermine where boundaries on protective measures should be placed; the public, for its part, should, in theory, have an understanding of what is going on its name. Accountability is a chain of relationships that ultimately leads to the public, as it has delegated its power to its representatives and thus to the agencies that support them. But how much can the public know about secret intelligence operations and what could the public do if it, in fact, disagrees with the direction intelligence activities are taking?

The exposition of this book has shown that there is indeed a system to manage secrecy that has developed over the years through the interactions of the branches of government and the matrix of oversight mechanisms. The introductory phases of this developmental trajectory were rather haphazard; later developments were comparatively intentional. The breakthrough events that led to the creation of oversight mechanisms – usually public, blatant, and political – have led many to believe that an integral part and value of these mechanisms are transparency and openness to the public. In practice, however, once the mechanisms settle from raw movement to core institution, they tend to support the regime in place with regard to managing secrets. Within this context, this means that the norms of secrecy derived from the security services penetrate those who are charged with supervising them. This is an entirely rational approach to the enormous charge of dealing with national security secrets. There are procedures in place to gain and maintain security clearances; there are locations where it is acceptable to read classified documents; and there are individuals with whom one may discuss these matters, while leaving the vast majority outside of this select realm. The technical core of the CIA is information, and through this matrix of mechanisms, this information is protected by the system.

Interestingly, while an increase in access to intelligence information could improve accountability, both the legislative and judicial branches have not generally pressed for greater mandates during both the Bush administration and more recently under the Obama administration. This lack of political will to expand external oversight mechanisms has many causes. First, the post-9/11 security environment became highly politicized due initially to a sense of penetrating national anxiety about terrorism and later to the political polarization of the second term of the Bush administration. The politicization subdued criticism of the national security apparatus in the early period after the attacks and even later during the Bush administration, as Democrats did not want to appear weak on national security – a usual taunt thrown at them. By the second term, political polarization in the intelligence committees deadlocked expansion or change in the process of intelligence oversight. Small structural changes, such as the end of term limits in the Senate Select Committee on Intelligence (SSCI) or the creation of subcommittees, were the norm in Congress. These changes bear mentioning within the context of the development of mechanisms discussed throughout this project, but they pale in comparison with the wide-ranging reorganization of the intelligence community after 9/11.

The absence of change among congressional oversight mechanisms during the immediate post-9/11 period provides an interesting contrast to the post–Church Committee era, when progress in expansion and specification of the oversight process did occur. The pendulum swing during the earlier era, in response to political scandal, was headed toward increasing intervention and bringing the security services in out of the dark. The Iran-Contra scandal highlighted the weaknesses of the oversight system in yet another scandal, but movement toward greater transparency was halted in response to the attacks on 9/11. It is not surprising that there was a general upsurge in patriotic rhetoric and support for the hallmarks of patriotism: the military, law enforcement, and national security agencies. What is interesting in this context is that in a time of drastic organizational change within the intelligence community and throughout the United States, as resources were poured into law enforcement and counterterrorism efforts, the congressional oversight committees changed so minimally to address these challenges.

In many ways, overseers took a step back from intelligence activities during this period. The tools used by the intelligence community expanded during this period, under the order of the administration. The Snowden revelations highlighted this expansion fiercely in terms of domestic intelligence and surveillance. Issues of covert action and espionage are an expected aspect of intelligence activities; however, the use of torture by the CIA outlined in the Senate torture report has shocked consciences and tested the relationship between the Agency and the oversight committee. The complications and ethical issues here are legion. Questions will always remain, in terms of what is appropriate behavior for an intelligence agency; to what extent an agency should be permitted to expand its tools in pursuit of intelligence information; and what trade-offs should be made, not just between civil liberties and security, but between *human rights* and *American* security. It is not surprising that legislators would be loath to engage when the benefits of criticism ending up looking like obfuscation – such as Speaker Nancy Pelosi's unwillingness to admit she had been briefed on enhanced interrogation techniques.

As the immediate experience of 9/11 fades, other more complex criteria will govern the focus – or lack of focus – on intelligence oversight. This complexity will not just guide homeland security decision making, but will also change over time how the public views the requirements of security and intelligence. This change will be driven by the combination of specific intelligence activities and the vicissitudes inherent to both the prestige of security and the dynamic political environment. Early examples of this could be the gradual shift of attention away from intense scrutiny of domestic intelligence and homeland security issues and toward a foreign intelligence and integrated military presence as the focus of American activities. Next steps in oversight development will also require that a realistic assessment be made of the state of the intelligence community. By this, I mean the proliferation of intelligence entities in the post-9/11 security environment; the increased use of contractors, muddying the divide between what constitutes public in contrast to private use of information; and the increased integration of the military into national intelligence activities. All of these must be considered challenges to conventional conceptions of the division of labor among the intelligence agencies. This, then, challenges the current framework of mechanisms, which either focus on such a narrow slice of activity, such as the FISC, or are spread far too thin to conduct effective oversight, such as Congress.

Beyond the structural components of the intelligence community and the mechanisms that have been discussed at some length here, further conceptual complexities of accountability exist that I have introduced through the accountability framework. By separating and analyzing the component parts of accountability, I have attempted to provide a basis for a more nuanced set of policy recommendations regarding where intelligence oversight should go from here. What has the framework indicated in terms of the weaknesses in maintaining the accountability of intelligence agencies? First, the information asymmetry is still extraordinarily oriented to benefit the executive branch. I say "extraordinarily" here because this analysis demonstrates that even after decades of development, oversight is still heavily dependent on executive acquiescence in the sharing of information about intelligence. While reporting requirements have certainly improved over the years, the fact is there is little recourse should the intelligence community choose not to be forthcoming about its activities. The limits in terms of reporting audience have proven difficult across the board in terms of external oversight mechanisms. In the judiciary, the secret court has been overwhelmed with order requests – this deluge being one of the rationales for the TSP's creation. In Congress, limitations on reporting audiences, such as the Gang of Eight, mean that the information is not even distributed to the wider committees, let alone to the full Congress. These limitations require that eight individuals be charged with maintaining the accountability of the intelligence programs considered the most difficult and sensitive. The burden is simply unfair and the process unsustainable if *effective* oversight is the objective.

In terms of recommendations to strengthen the mechanisms, they come down to the requirements of good governance. The existing external mechanisms are barely transparent and the internal mechanisms not transparent at all. While security is the paramount concern when it comes to intelligence, the mechanisms *must*, in some way, provide a greater degree of openness to the activities of the intelligence community. I make this assertion understanding how difficult such a recommendation would be to carry out, as well as how naïve the statement would sound to an intelligence officer. Further, I realize that a fundamental question here is: who decides? Who decides how transparent the intelligence services or the mechanisms that supervise them should be: legislators, the judiciary, the executive, or interest groups? As has been demonstrated throughout this book, the first two of these have vested interests in *not* making this type of judgment call; the third wants to keep this world as opaque as possible; and the fourth has no access to any information, nor does it possess very much traction on policy making.

To facilitate improved active oversight and mechanism engagement, the processes by which the external mechanisms function must be updated and made more efficient. It is easy to blame a supine congressional oversight process, but it is much more difficult to find a solution to the task of supervising seventeen agencies engaged in highly technical work, with minimal staff – or, in some cases, none – and sometimes limited expertise. The expertise issue should shift as the term limits on Senate committee members have been lifted, but the task is still huge, onerous, and thankless. I suggest that strengthening the link between the oversight mechanisms and the boundary spanners to facilitate a more efficient flow of intelligence information. This proposal could be vociferously opposed in the intelligence community, but perhaps this presumed opposition might indicates that the internal oversight mechanisms could provide legitimate supervision and disseminate information to the external world far more effectively than the current format of congressional committees can accomplish given the committees' limited breadth and technical skill. For this process to function, however, the normative expectations of the boundary crossers – in the case of the CIA, the statutory inspector general (IG) – must change and the position must be legitimized. The issue of legitimacy is not so problematic for Congress, but rather for the Agency itself, which has fought against what it perceived to be invasive practices.

Linking the strong attributes of both internal and external accountability mechanisms could tighten recourse and smooth the transmission of information – two of the main sticking points of intelligence oversight. Further, in a very optimistic vein, the problems of temporality could be ameliorated with a tighter and more trusting information-sharing relationship between the Agency and Congress. I do not suggest that such an approach would solve all problems or would even be practicable or possible, but it is necessary to move beyond exhortations that Congress stiffen up and get more focused on intelligence. The complexities of the task are simply too great to be dealt with effectively via this particular external mechanism, and the political motivation for the legislative overseers is clearly lacking. Another avenue or type of structure may be able to aid the rather feeble congressional attempts at appropriate intelligence supervision.

The issues inherent to the dysfunction of the legislative branch in terms of intelligence oversight extend in a slightly modified fashion to the judiciary and its process of oversight as well. In the case of the judiciary, the process of application for orders must be simplified. This is not to suggest that the standards should be lowered, but rather that the onerous bureaucratic burden be lightened a little to enable a greater volume of requests to pass through the FISC. The application process for a FISA order requires the engagement of a number of individuals up to the attorney general. While this careful system of checking and double-checking the merits of a particular applications should assuage anxieties of a surveillance organ gone rogue, the process limits effectiveness of the mechanism by slowing it and not allowing it the nimbleness it needs to deal with a dynamic threat that has blended the boundaries between foreign and domestic operation. Further, some level of transparency of the court is important in order to reestablish broken or weakened ties between the branches and the public when it comes to issues of surveillance. This is particularly the case because the boundaries of what constitutes appropriateness in terms of electronic surveillance became rather muddied in the post-9/11 years, as programs such as the Terrorist Surveillance Program evaded the constraints provided by FISA and the FISC. Openness need not be total; this would obviously be impossible given the temporal point of this mechanism's responsibilities. Some transparency is, however, key so that the other branches and the public may understand both the limitations and the extent of judicial control of these matters.

In terms of internal mechanisms, one approach, as mentioned previously, is to strengthen their role in the overall project of intelligence and accountability, allowing the internal mechanism to integrate more thoroughly with the external. I believe this would be an ideal approach to solving some of the manifold problems described and explained throughout this book. More realistically, however, internal mechanisms remain the most stable and opaque of all throughout the trajectory of oversight development. This is the case partly because their responsibilities are protected by the needs of the executive branch, but also because their activities are off-limits to the public and, generally, the other branches of government. They are considered *control* tools rather than those that enrich and maintain accountability through traditional democratic modes of transparency.

The post-9/11 era has seen its share of extreme behavior on the part of the intelligence community. While the more extreme activities, such as torture, have not generally been directed toward American citizens, some of it, such as orderless wiretapping, has been. Activities that don't immediately affect Americans tend not to get a public reaction. The idea that the CIA could be using techniques on detainees that might be considered torture is distasteful to most, but not something considered worthy of active public agitation.

Finally, transparency comes down to a public role in deciding what the United States stands for in terms of human rights, rule of law, and acceptable international citizenship. The link between the public and the intelligence community can be tightened, but the relationship hinges on the active involvement of the mechanisms, particularly congressional oversight, to provide an aperture. Whether they can engage remains an open question, but it is important that they claim their rightful role, regardless of procedural constraints or the demands of political expediency.

BIBLIOGRAPHY

Aberbach, Joel D. "The Congressional Committee Intelligence System: Information, Oversight and Change." *Congress and the Presidency* 14 (1987): 51–76.

Aberbach, Joel D. *Keeping a Watchful Eye: The Politics of Congressional Oversight.* Washington, DC: Brookings Institution Press, 1990.

Adams, Gordon and Cindy Williams. *Buying National Security: How America Plans and Pays for its Global Role and Safety at Home.* London: Routledge, 2009.

Aldrich, Howard, and Diane Herker. "Boundary Spanning Roles and Organization Structure." *Academy of Management Review* 2 (1977): 217–30.

Allen, Michael. *Blinking Red: Crisis and Compromise in American Intelligence after 9/11.* Dulles, VA: Potomac, 2013.

Andrew, Christopher. *For the President's Eyes Only: Secret Intelligence and the American Presidency from Washington to Bush.* New York: Harper Collins, 1995.

Baker, James E. *In the Common Defense: National Security Law for Perilous Times.* Cambridge: Cambridge University Press, 2007.

Baldwin, Jr., Fletcher N., and Robert B. Shaw. "Down to the Wire: Assessing the Constitutionality of the National Security Agency's Warrantless Wiretapping Program: Exit the Rule of Law." *University of Florida Journal of Law and Public Policy* 17 (2006): 429–72.

Bamford, James. *The Puzzle Palace: A Report on America's Most Secret Agency.* New York: Penguin, 1983.

Banks, William C. "The Death of FISA." *Minnesota Law Review* 91 (2007): 1209–1301.

Banks, William C. "Response to the Ten Questions." *William Mitchell Law Review* 35 (2009): 5007–17.

Barrett, David M. *The CIA and Congress: The Untold Story from Truman to Kennedy.* Lawrence: University Press of Kansas, 2005.

Barry, James A. "Managing Covert Political Action: Guideposts from Just War Theory." *Studies in Intelligence* 36, no. 5 (1992): 19–31.

Bean, Hamilton. "Organizational Culture and US Intelligence Affairs." *Intelligence and National Security* 24, no. 4 (2009): 479–98.

Bearden, Milton and James Risen. *The Main Enemy: The Inside Story of the CIA's Final Showdown with the KGB.* New York: Random House, 2004.

Bedan, Matt. "Echelon's Effect: The Obsolescence of the U.S. Foreign Intelligence Legal Regime." *Federal Communications Law Journal* 59, no. 2 (2007): 426–44.

Best, Jr., Richard A. *Intelligence Authorization Legislation: Status and Challenges.* CRS Report R40240, January 27, 2010.

Betts, Richard K. "Analysis, War, and Decision: Why Intelligence Failures Are Inevitable." *World Politics* 31 (1978): 61–89.

Betts, Richard K. *Enemies of Intelligence: Knowledge and Power in American National Security.* New York: Columbia University Press, 2007.

Bloom, Robert M., and William J. Dunn, "The Constitutional Infirmity of Warrantless NSA Surveillance: The Abuse of Presidential Power and the Injury to the Fourth Amendment." *William and Mary Bill of Rights Journal* 15 (2006): 147–202.

Boren, David L. "The Winds of Change at the CIA." *Yale Law Journal* 101, no. 4 (1992): 853–65.

Bovens, Mark. "Analysing and Assessing Accountability: A Conceptual Framework." *European Law Journal* 13 (2007): 447–68.

Bradley, Alison A. "Extremism in the Defense of Liberty? The Foreign Intelligence Surveillance Act and the Significance of the USA PATRIOT ACT." *Tulane Law Review* 77 (2002–3): 465–93.

Breglio, Nola K. "Leaving FISA Behind: The Need to Return to Warrantless Foreign Intelligence Surveillance." *Yale Law Journal* 113 (2003): 179–217.

Brooks, David G. Presentation at International Spy Museum, Washington, DC, February 7, 2011.

Burton, Adam. "Fixing FISA for Long War: Regulating Warrantless Surveillance in the Age of Terrorism." *Pierce Law Review* 4 (2005–6): 381–404.

Cain, Bruce E., Patrick Egan, and Sergio Fabbrini. "Towards More Open Democracies: The Expansion of Freedom of Information Laws." In

Democracy Transformed? Expanding Political Opportunities in Advanced Industrial Democracies, edited by Bruce E. Cain, Russell J. Dalton, and Susan E. Scarrow, 115–39. Oxford: Oxford University Press, 2003.

Calvert, Randall L., Mark J. Moran, and Barry R. Weingast, "Congressional Influence over Policymaking: the Case of the FTC." In *Congress: Structure and Policy*, edited by Mathew D. McCubbins and Terry Sullivan, 493–522. Cambridge: Cambridge University Press, 1987.

Campbell, Colton C., Nicol C. Rae, and John F. Stack, Jr. *Congress and the Politics of Foreign Policy*. Upper Saddle River, NJ: Prentice Hall, 2003.

Central Intelligence Agency, Inspector General. *OIG Report on CIA Accountability with Respect to the 9/11 Attacks: Executive Summary*, June 2005, publicly released April 2007. Available online at https://www.cia.gov/library/reports/Executive%20Summary_OIG%20Report.pdf (downloaded March 18, 2009).

Central Intelligence Agency, Inspector General. *Key Unclassified Conclusions from CIA Inspector General Report: "(U)Procedures Used in Narcotics Airbridge Denial Program in Peru, 1995–2001,"* August 25, 2008. Available online at http://hoekstra.house.gov/UploadedFiles/Peru_Release_Key_Unclassified_Conclusions_from_CIA_Inspector_General_Report.pdf (downloaded March 6, 2009).

Central Intelligence Agency. *Family Jewels* 00418 (1973). Available online at http://www.foia.cia.gov.

Champion, J. Christopher. "The Revamped FISA: Striking a Better Balance between the Government's Need to Protect Itself and the 4th Amendment." *Vanderbilt Law Review* 58 (2005): 1671–1704.

Check, Ryan M., and A. John Radsan. "One Lantern in the Darkest Night – the CIA's Inspector General." William Mitchell College of Law Legal Studies Research Paper Series, paper no. 119, July 28, 2009: 1–50

Cinquegrana, Americo R. "Dancing in the Dark: Accepting the Invitation to Struggle in the Context of 'Covert Action,' the Iran-Contra Affair and the Intelligence Oversight Process." *Houston Journal of International Law* 11 (1988–9): 177–209.

Cinquegrana, Americo R. "The Walls (and Wires) Have Ears: The Background and First Ten Years of the Foreign Intelligence Surveillance Act of 1978." *University of Pennsylvania Law Review* 137 (1989): 793–828.

Colby, William. *Honorable Men: My Life in the CIA*. New York: Simon and Schuster, 1978.

Cole, David. "Reviving the Nixon Doctrine: NSA Spying, the Commander-in-Chief and Executive Power in the War on Terror."

Washington and Lee Journal of Civil Rights and Social Justice 13 (2006): 17–40.

Cole, David, and Martin S. Lederman. "The National Security Agency's Domestic Spying Program: Framing the Debate." *Indiana Law Journal* 81 (2006): 1355–1425.

Conner, William E. "Reforming Oversight of Covert Actions after the Iran-Contra Affair: A Legislative History of the Intelligence Authorization Act for FY 1991." *Virginia Journal of International Law* 32, no. 4 (1991–2): 871–928.

Cooper Blum, Stephanie. "What Really Is at Stake with the FISA Amendments Act of 2008 and Ideas for Future Surveillance Reform." *Public Interest Law Journal* 18, no. 2 (2009): 269–314.

Cumming, Alfred. *"Gang of Four" Congressional Intelligence Notifications.* CRS Report R40698, January 29, 2010.

Cumming, Alfred. *Sensitive Covert Action Notification: Oversight Options for Congress.* CRS Report R40691, January 29, 2010.

Daugherty, William J. *Executive Secrets: Covert Action and the Presidency.* Lexington: University of Kentucky Press, 2008.

Davidson, Roger H. "Congressional Committees as Moving Targets." *Legislative Studies Quarterly* 11 (1986): 19–33.

Davies, Philip H. J. "Intelligence Culture and Intelligence Failure in Britain and the United States." *Cambridge Review of International Affairs* 17 (2004): 495–520.

Diamond, John. *The CIA and the Culture of Failure: US Intelligence from the End of the Cold War to the Invasion of Iraq.* Stanford, CA: Stanford University Press, 2008.

Dowdle, Michael W. "Public Accountability: Conceptual, Historical, and Epistemic Mappings." In *Public Accountability: Designs, Dilemmas and Experiences*, edited by Michael W. Dowdle, 1–29. Cambridge: Cambridge University Press, 2006.

Drumheller, Tyler. *On the Brink: An Insider's Account of How the White House Compromised American Intelligence.* New York: Carroll and Graf, 2006.

Evans, Diana. "Congressional Oversight and the Diversity of Members' Goals." *Political Science Quarterly* 109 (1994): 669–87.

Faddis, Charles S. *The Decline and Fall of the CIA.* Guildford CT: Lyons Press, 2010.

Fenno, Jr., Richard F. *Congressmen in Committees.* Boston: Little, Brown, 1973.

Ferejohn, John. "Accountability and Authority: Toward a Theory of Political Accountability." In *Democracy, Accountability and Representation,* edited by Adam Przeworski, Susan Carol Stokes, and Bernard Manin, 131–53. Cambridge: Cambridge University Press, 1999.

Final Report of the National Commission on the Attacks on the United States. New York: W. W. Norton, 2004.

Fisher, Louis. "How Tightly Can Congress Draw the Purse Strings?" *American Journal of International Law* 83, no. 4 (1989) 758–66.

Forgang, Jonathan D. "'The Right of the People': The NSA, the FISA Amendments Act of 2008, and the Foreign Intelligence Surveillance of Americans Overseas." *Fordham Law Review* 78 (2009–10): 237–9.

Gannon, John C. "Managing Analysis in the Information Age." In *Analyzing Intelligence: Origins, Obstacles, and Innovations,* edited by Roger Z. George and James B. Bruce. Washington, DC: Georgetown University Press, 2008.

Gates, Margaret J., and Marjorie Fine Knowles. "The Inspector General Act in the Federal Government: A New Approach to Accountability." *Alabama Law Review* 36 (1985): 473–514.

Gates, Robert M. "American Intelligence and Congressional Oversight." Presentation to World Affairs Council of Boston, January 15, 1993.

Gates, Robert M. *From the Shadows: The Ultimate Insider's Story of Five Presidents and How They Won the Cold War.* New York: Simon and Schuster, 1996.

Gellman, Barton. *Angler: The Cheney Vice Presidency.* New York: Penguin Press, 2008.

Gerber, Burton. "The Ethical Aspects of Intelligence Work: The Cold War and Beyond." Presentation at DePauw University, March 22, 2001.

Gill, Peter. "Democratic and Parliamentary Accountability of Intelligence Services after September 11." Paper presented at Workshop on Democratic and Parliamentary Oversight of Intelligence Services, Geneva, October 2–5, 2002.

Gill, Peter. "The Politicization of Intelligence: Lessons from the Invasion of Iraq." In *Who's Watching the Spies,* edited by Hans Born, Loch K. Johnson, and Ian Leigh, 12–33. Washington, DC: Potomac, 2005.

Goldsmith, Jack. *The Terror Presidency: Law and Judgment Inside the Bush Administration.* New York: W. W. Norton, 2007.

Goldsmith, Michael. "The Supreme Court and Title III: Rewriting the Law of Electronic Surveillance." *Journal of Criminal Law and Criminology* 74 (1983): 1–171.

Grant, Ruth W., and Robert O. Keohane. "Accountability and Abuses of Power in World Politics." *American Political Science Review* 99, no. 1 (2005): 29–43.

Grossman, Andrew. *Neither Dead nor Red: Civil Defense and American Political Development in the Early Cold War*. New York: Routledge, 2001.

Gumina, Paul. "Title VI of the Intelligence Authorization Act, Fiscal Year 1991: Effective Covert Action Reform or 'Business as Usual'." *Hastings Constitutional Law Quarterly* 20 (1992–3): 149–205.

Hardin, David. "The Fuss over Two Small Words: The Unconstitutionality of the USA PATRIOT Act Amendments to FISA under the Fourth Amendment." *George Washington Law Review* 71 (2003): 291–346.

Hayden, Michael V. "Address to the National Press Club: What American Intelligence and Especially the NSA Have Been Doing to Defend the Nation." National Press Club, Washington, DC, January 23, 2006.

Hersh, Seymour. "Huge CIA Operation in US against Antiwar Forces, Other Dissidents in Nixon Years." *New York Times*, December 22, 1974.

Hinrichs, Christine E. "Flying under the Radar or an Unnecessary Intelligence Watchdog: A Review of the President's Foreign Intelligence Advisory Board." *William Mitchell Law Review* 35, no. 5 (2009): 5109–18.

Hitz, Frederick P. *Why Spy? Espionage in an Age of Uncertainty*. New York: Thomas Dunne, 2008.

Howard, Michael, and Peter Paret, trans. *On War (Carl von Clausewitz)*. Princeton, NJ: Princeton University Press, 1976.

Hulnick, Arthur S. "Openness: Being Public About Secret Intelligence." *International Journal of Intelligence and Counterintelligence* 12 (1999): 463–83.

Jehl, Douglas. "Report Warned CIA on Tactics in Interrogation." *New York Times*, November 9, 2005.

Jeffreys-Jones, Rhodri. *The CIA and American Democracy*, 3rd edition. New Haven, CT: Yale University Press, 2003.

Jervis, Robert. "Intelligence, Civil-intelligence Relations, and Democracy," in *Reforming Intelligence: Obstacles to Democratic Control and Effectiveness*, edited by Thomas C. Bruneau and Steven C. Boraz, vii–xx. Austin, TX: University of Texas Press, 2007.

Jervis, Robert. "Intelligence, Counterintelligence, Perception, and Deception." In *Vaults, Mirrors, and Masks*, edited by Jennifer E. Sims and Burton Gerber, 69–80. Washington, DC: Georgetown University Press, 2009.

Jervis, Robert. *Why Intelligence Fails: Lessons from the Iranian Revolution and the Iraq War*. Ithaca, NY: Cornell University Press, 2010.

Johnson, Loch K. "The U.S. Congress and the CIA: Monitoring the Dark Side of Government." *Legislative Studies Quarterly* 5 (1980): 477–99.

Johnson, Loch K. *A Season of Inquiry*. Chicago: Dorsey Press, 1988.

Johnson, Loch K. *America's Secret Power: The CIA in a Democratic Society*. Oxford: Oxford University Press, 1989.

Johnson, Loch K. "Covert Action and Accountability: Decision-Making for America's Secret Foreign Policy." *International Studies Quarterly* 33 (1989): 81–109.

Johnson, Loch K. *Bombs, Bugs, Drugs and Thugs: Intelligence and America's Quest for Security*. New York: New York University Press, 2002.

Johnson, Loch K. "Bricks and Mortar for a Theory of Intelligence." *Comparative Strategy* 22 (2003): 1–28.

Johnson, Loch K. "Governing in the Absence of Angels." In *Who's Watching the Spies?* Edited by Hans Born, Loch K. Johnson, and Ian Leigh, 57–78. Washington, DC: Potomac, 2005.

Johnson, Loch K. "A Framework for Strengthening U.S. Intelligence." *Yale Journal of International Affairs* 1 (2006): 116–131.

Johnson, Loch K. "The Church Committee Investigation of 1975 and the Evolution of Modern Intelligence Accountability." *Intelligence and National Security* 23 (2008): 198–225.

Johnson, Loch K. "A Shock Theory of Congressional Accountability for Intelligence." In *Handbook of Intelligence Studies*, edited by Loch K. Johnson, 343–60. London: Routledge, 2009.

Johnston, David, and Scott Shane. "CIA Fires Senior Officer over Leaks." *New York Times*, April 22, 2006.

Jonas, David S. "The Foreign Intelligence Surveillance Act through the Lens of the 9/11 Commission Report: The Wisdom of the PATRIOT ACT Amendments and the Decision of the Foreign Intelligence Surveillance Court of Review." *North Carolina Central Law Journal* 27 (2004–5):

Jones, Ishmael. *The Human Factor: Inside the CIA's Dysfunctional Intelligence Culture*. New York: Encounter, 2008.

Kahn, David. "An Historical Theory of Intelligence." *Intelligence and National Security* 16 (2001): 79–92.

Kaiser, Frederick M. "Statutory Offices of Inspector General: Past and Present." CRS Report for Congress, updated September 25, 2008.

Kaiser, Frederick M. *Congressional Oversight of Intelligence: Current Structure and Alternatives*. Washington, DC: Congressional Research Service, 2011.

Kessler, Ronald. *The CIA at War: Inside the Secret Campaign against Terror.* New York: St Martin's Griffin, 2003.

Kingdon, John. *Agendas, Alternatives, and Public Policies,* 2nd edition. Boston: Addison-Wesley, 1995.

Kitts, Kenneth. "Commission Politics and National Security: Gerald Ford's Response to the CIA Controversy of 1975." *Presidential Studies Quarterly* 26, no. 4 (1996): 1081–98.

Koh, Harold Hongju. *The National Security Constitution: Sharing Power after the Iran-Contra Affair.* New Haven, CT: Yale University Press, 1990.

Legislative Oversight of Intelligence Activities: The US Experience. Report prepared by the Select Committee on Intelligence, United States Senate, October 1994.

Leonnig, Carol D., and Ellen Nakashima, "Ruling Limited Spying Efforts: Move to Amend FISA Sparked by Judge's Decision." *Washington Post,* August 3, 2007.

Lester, Genevieve. "Societal Acceptability of Domestic Intelligence." In *The Challenge of Domestic Intelligence in a Free Society: A Multi-disciplinary Look at the Creation of U.S. Domestic Counterterrorism Intelligence Agency,* edited by Brian A. Jackson, 79–104. Santa Monica, CA: RAND, 2009.

Lichtblau, Eric, and James Risen, "Bush Lets US Spy on Callers without Courts." *New York Times,* December 16, 2005.

Lowenthal, Mark M. *Intelligence: From Secrets to Policy,* 4th edition. Washington, DC: CQ Press, 2009.

Lundberg, Kirsten. *Congressional Oversight and Presidential Prerogative.* Harvard Case Study C14-01-1605.0, (2001).

Lupia, Arthur, and Mathew D. McCubbins, "Designing Bureaucratic Accountability." *Law and Contemporary Problems* 57 (1994): 91–126.

MacGaffin, John. "Clandestine Human Intelligence." In *Transforming U.S. Intelligence,* edited by Jennifer E. Sims and Burton Gerber, 79–95. Washington, DC: Georgetown University Press, 2005.

Manget, Frederic F. "Another System of Oversight: Intelligence and the Rise of Judicial Intervention." In *Strategic Intelligence: Windows into a Secret World,* edited by Loch K. Johnson and James J. Wirtz, 407–13. Los Angeles: Roxbury, 2005.

Manget, Frederic F. "Intelligence and the Rise of Judicial Intervention." In *Handbook of Intelligence Studies,* edited by Loch K. Johnson, 329–42. London: Routledge, 2009.

Mansfield, Mark. "A Discussion on Service with Former CIA Director Michael Hayden." *Studies in Intelligence* 54, no. 2 (2010): 1–7.

Marchetti, Victor, and John D. Marks. *The CIA and the Cult of Intelligence.* New York: Borzoi, 1974.

Mayer, Jane. "The Secret Sharer: Is Thomas Drake an Enemy of the State?" *New Yorker,* May 23, 2011.

Mayer, Jane. "The Black Sites: A Rare Look inside the CIA's Secret Interrogation Program." *New Yorker,* August 13, 2007.

Mazzetti, Mark. "CIA Chief Defends Review on Agency's Inspector General." *New York Times,* October 23, 2007.

Mazzetti, Mark. "CIA Tells of Changes for Its Internal Inquiries." *New York Times,* February 2, 2008.

Mazzetti, Mark, and Scott Shane. "Watchdog of CIA Is Subject of CIA Inquiry." *New York Times,* October 11, 2007.

McCubbins, Matthew D., and Thomas Schwartz, "Congressional Oversight Overlooked: Police Patrols versus Fire Alarms." *American Journal of Political Science* 28 (1984): 165–79.

McDonald, Catherine. "Government, Funded Nonprofits and Accountability." *Nonprofit Management and Leadership* I8 (1997): 51–64.

Medina, Carmen A. "What to Do When Traditional Models Fail." *Studies in Intelligence* 46 (2002): 23–8.

Meyer, John W., and Brian Rowan, "Institutionalized Organizations: Formal Structure as Myth and Ceremony," in *The New Institutionalism in Organizational Analysis,* edited by Walter W. Powell and Paul J. Dimaggio, 41–62. Chicago: University of Chicago Press, 1991.

Miller, Greg. "Departing CIA Chief Hayden Defends Interrogations." *Los Angeles Times,* January 16, 2009.

Miller, Michael C. "Standing in the Wake of the Terrorist Surveillance Program: A Modified Standard for Challenges to Secret Government Surveillance." *Rutgers Law Review* 60, no. 4 (2008): 1039–72.

Mulgan, Richard. "'Accountability': An Ever-Expanding Concept?" *Public Administration* 78, no. 3 (2000): 555–73.

Mulgan, Richard. *Holding Power to Account: Accountability in Modern Democracies.* New York: Palgrave, 2003.

Naftali, Timothy. *Blind Spot: The Secret History of American Counterterrorism.* New York: Basic Books, 2005.

Nakashima, Ellen, and Jerry Markon, "NSA Leak Trial Exposes Dilemma for Justice Department." *Washington Post,* June 10, 2011.

Odom, William E. *Fixing Intelligence for a More Secure America,* 2nd edition. New Haven, CT: Yale University Press, 2003.

Ogul, Morris S. *Congress Oversees the Bureaucracy: Studies in Legislative Supervision.* Pittsburgh: University of Pittsburgh Press, 1976.

Ogul, Morris S., and Bert A. Rockman. "Overseeing Oversight: New Departures and Old Problems." *Legislative Studies Quarterly* 15 (1990): 5–24.

Orton, James Douglas. "Enactment, Sensemaking and Decisionmaking: Redesign Processes in the 1976 Reorganization of US Intelligence." *Journal of Management Studies* 37 (March 2000): 213–34.

Oseth, John M. *Regulating U.S. Intelligence Operations: A Study in the Definition of the National Interest.* Lexington: University of Kentucky, 1985.

Pallitto, Robert M., and William G. Weaver. *Presidential Secrecy and the Law.* Baltimore: Johns Hopkins University Press, 2007.

Pillar, Paul R. "Intelligence, Policy and the War in Iraq." *Foreign Affairs* (March/April 2006).

Pillar, Paul R. *Intelligence and U.S. Foreign Policy: Iraq, 9/11, and Misguided Reform.* New York: Columbia University Press, 2011.

Pincus, Walter. "Lawmakers Criticize CIA Director's Review Order." *Washington Post,* October 13, 2007.

Pines, Daniel L. "The Central Intelligence Agency's 'Family Jewels': Legal Then? Legal Now?" *Indiana Law Journal* 84 (2009): 637–88.

POGO Report, *Inspectors General: Accountability Is a Balancing Act.* Washington, DC: POGO, 2008.

Posner, Richard A. "Torture, Terrorism, and Interrogation." In *Torture: A Collection,* edited by Sanford Levinson, 291–8. Oxford: Oxford University Press, 2004.

Posner, Richard A. *Preventing Surprise Attacks: Intelligence Reform in the Wake of 9/11.* Stanford, CA: Hoover Institution Press, 2005.

Prados, John. *The Family Jewels: The CIA, Secrecy, and Presidential Power.* Austin, TX: University of Texas Press, 2013.

Prados, John. *President's Secret Wars: CIA and Pentagon Covert Operations since World War II.* Morrow: New York, 1986.

Prados, John. *Safe for Democracy: The Secret Wars of the CIA.* Chicago: Ivan R. Dee, 2006.

Priest, Dana, and William M. Arkin, *Top Secret America: The Rise of the New American Security State.* New York: Little Brown, 2011.

Radsan, A. John. "*Sed Quis Custodiet Ispos Custodes:* The CIA's Office of General Counsel?" *Journal of National Security Law and Policy* 2, no. 201 (2006–8): 201–55.

Reisman, W. Michael, and James E. Baker. *Regulating Covert Action: Practices, Contexts, and Policies of Covert Coercion Abroad in International and American Law.* New Haven, CT: Yale University Press, 1992.

Report to the President by the Commission on CIA Activities within the United States (Rockefeller Commission Report), June 1975.

Richelson, Jeffrey T. *The US Intelligence Community*, 5th edition. Boulder, CO: Westview Press, 2008.

Rizzo, John. *Company Man: Thirty Years of Controversy and Crisis in the CIA*. New York: Scribner, 2014.

Roberts, Alasdair. *Blacked Out: Government Secrecy in the Information Age*. Cambridge: Cambridge University Press, 2006.

Rockman, Bert A. "Legislative-Executive Relations and Legislative Oversight." *Legislative Studies Quarterly* 9 (1984): 387–440.

Rodriguez, Jr., Jose, and Bill Harlow. *Hard Measures: How Aggressive American Actions after 9/11 Saved American Lives*. New York: Threshold, 2012.

Romzek, Barbara S., and Melvin J. Dubnick. "Accountability in the Public Sector: Lessons from the Challenger Tragedy." *Public Administration Review* 47 (1987): 227–38.

Rosen, Bernard. *Holding Government Bureaucracies Accountable*, 3rd edition. Westport, CT: Praeger, 1998.

Rudgers, David F. "The Origins of Covert Action." *Journal of Contemporary History* 35 (2000): 249–62.

Sample, Timothy R. "A Federal Approach to Domestic Intelligence." In *Vaults, Mirrors and Masks: Rediscovering U.S. Counterintelligence*, edited by Jennifer E. Sims and Burton Gerber, 241–60. Washington, DC: Georgetown University Press, 2009.

Sappington, David E. M. "Incentives in Principal–Agent Relationships." *Journal of Economic Perspectives* 5 (1991): 45–66.

Savage, Charlie. "President Weakens Espionage Oversight: Board Created by Ford Loses Most of Its Power." *Boston Globe*, March 14, 2008.

Schwarz, Jr., Frederick A. O., and Aziz Z. Huq, *Unchecked and Unbalanced: Presidential Power in a Time of Terror*. New York: New Press, 2007.

Schoenfeld, Gabriel. *Necessary Secrets: National Security, the Media, and the Rule of Law*. New York: W. W. Norton, 2010.

Sciaroni, Bretton G. "The Theory and Practice of Executive Branch Oversight." *Harvard Journal of Law and Public Policy* 12 (1989): 397–432.

Scott, W. Richard. *Organizations: Rational, Natural, and Open Systems*, 5th edition. New Jersey: Prentice Hall, 2003.

Seamon, Richard, and William Gardner. "Does (Should) the PATRIOT ACT Raze (or Raise) 'the Wall' Between Foreign Intelligence and Criminal Law Enforcement?" (2004) Available at SSRN: 1–116.

Shenon, Philip. *The Commission: The Uncensored History of the 9/11 Investigation*. New York: Twelve, 2008.

Shulsky, Abram N., and Gary J. Schmitt. *Silent Warfare: Understanding the World of Intelligence*, 3rd edition. Washington, DC: Potomac, 2002.

Silverstein, Gordon. *Imbalance of Powers: Constitutional Interpretation and the Making of American Foreign Policy.* Oxford: Oxford University Press, 1997.

Simon, Herbert A. *Administrative Behavior,* 4th edition. New York: Free Press, 1997.

Sims, Jennifer E. "Twenty-first-Century Counterintelligence: The Theoretical Basis for Reform." In *Vaults, Mirrors and Masks: Rediscovering U.S. Counterintelligence,* edited by Jennifer E. Sims and Burton Gerber, 19–50. Washington, DC: Georgetown University Press, 2009.

Sinclair, Amanda. "The Chameleon of Accountability: Forms and Discourses." *Accounting, Organizations and Society* 20, no. 2/3 (1995): 219–37.

Smist, Jr., Frank J. *Congress Oversees the United States Intelligence Community: 1947–1994,* 2nd edition. Knoxville: University of Tennessee Press, 1994.

Snider, L. Britt. "Creating a Statutory Inspector General at the CIA." *Studies in Intelligence* 44, (2001): 15–21.

Snider, L. Britt. *The Agency and the Hill: CIA's Relationship with Congress, 1946–2004.* Washington, DC: Center for the Study of Intelligence, 2008.

Solove, Daniel J. *Nothing to Hide: The False Tradeoff between Privacy and Security.* New Haven, CT: Yale University Press, 2011.

Spaulding, Suzanne E. "Power Play: Did Bush Roll Past the Legal Stop Signs?" *Washington Post,* December 25, 2005.

Stolz, Barbara Ann. "The Foreign Intelligence Surveillance Act of 1978: The Role of Symbolic Politics." *Law and Policy* 24 (2002): 269–98.

Strickland, Lee S. "Civil Liberties vs. Intelligence Collection: the Secret Foreign Intelligence Surveillance Act Court Speaks in Public." *Government Information Quarterly* 20 (2003): 1–12.

Taylor Saito, Naitsu. "Whose Liberty? Whose Security? The USA PATRIOT Act in the Context of COINTELPRO and the Unlawful Repression of Political Dissent." *Oregon Law Review* 81 (2002): 1051–132.

Tenet, George, and Bill Harlow. *At the Center of the Storm: My Years at the CIA.* New York: HarperCollins, 2007.

Thelen, Kathleen. "How Institutions Evolve: Insights from Comparative Historical Analysis." In *Comparative Historical Analysis in the Social Sciences,* edited by James Mahoney and Dietrich Rueschemeyer, 208–40. Cambridge: Cambridge University Press, 2003.

Theoharis, Athan. *Spying on Americans: Political Surveillance from Hoover to the Huston Plan.* Philadelphia: Temple University Press, 1978.

Thompson, James D. *Organizations in Action: Social Science Bases of Administrative Theory*, 4th printing. New Jersey: Transaction, 2006.

Treverton, Gregory F. *Covert Action: The Limits of Intervention in the Postwar World*. Basic Books: New York, 1987.

Treverton, Gregory F. "Intelligence: Welcome to the American Government." In *A Question of Balance: The President, the Congress, Foreign Policy*, edited by Thomas E. Mann, pp. 70–108. Washington, DC: Brookings Institution, 1990.

Treverton, Gregory F. *Reshaping National Intelligence for an Age of Information*. Cambridge: Cambridge University Press, 2001.

Treverton, Gregory F. *Intelligence for an Age of Terror*. Cambridge: Cambridge University Press, 2009.

Turner, Michael A. "A Distinctive U.S. Intelligence Identity." *International Journal of Intelligence and CounterIntelligence* 17, no. 1 (2004) 42–61.

Turner, Stansfield. *Burn before Reading: Presidents, CIA Directors, and Secret Intelligence*. New York: Hyperion, 2005.

Vaughan, Diane. *The Challenger Launch Decision: Risky Technology, Culture, and Deviance at NASA*. Chicago: University of Chicago Press, 1996.

Waldron, Jeremy. "Security and Liberty: The Image of Balance." *Journal of Political Philosophy* 11 (2003): 191–210

Waller, Douglas. *Wild Bill Donovan: The Spymaster Who Created the OSS and Modern American Espionage*. New York: Free Press, 2011.

Weiner, Tim. *Legacy of Ashes: The History of the CIA*. New York: Doubleday, 2007.

Wetzling, Thorsten. "Intelligence Accountability in Germany and the United Kingdom: Same Myth, Different Celebration?" Ph.D. diss., University of Geneva, 2010.

Willis, Henry, Genevieve Lester, and Gregory F. Treverton, "Information Sharing for Infrastructure Risk Management: Barriers and Solutions." *Intelligence and National Security* 24 (2009): 339–65.

Wilson, James Q. *Bureaucracy*. New York: Basic Books, 1989.

Wohlstetter, Roberta. *Pearl Harbor: Warning and Decision*. Stanford, CA: Stanford University Press, 1962.

Wong, Katherine. Recent Developments, "The NSA Terrorist Surveillance Program." *Harvard Journal on Legislation* 43 (2006): 517–34.

Yoo, John. "The Terrorist Surveillance Program and the Constitution." *George Mason Law Review* 14 (2007): 565–604.

Zegart, Amy B. *Flawed by Design: The Evolution of the CIA, JSC, and NSC*. Stanford, CA: Stanford University Press, 1999.

Zegart, Amy B. *Spying Blind: The CIA, the FBI, and the Origins of 9/11.* Princeton, NJ: Princeton University Press, 2007.

Zegart, Amy B. *Eyes on Spies: Congress and the United States Intelligence Community.* Stanford, CA: Hoover Institution Press, 2011.

Zegart, Amy B. "The Domestic Politics of Irrational Intelligence Oversight." *Political Science Quarterly* 126 (2011): 1–25.

Zelizer, Julian E. Arsenal of Democracy: The Politics of National Security – from World War II to the War on Terrorism. New York: Basic Books, 2010.

INDEX

Note to index: An *n* following a page number denotes a note on that page.